Australian Bush to
Tiananmen Square

Australian Bush to Tiananmen Square

Ross Terrill

HAMILTON BOOKS
Lanham • Boulder • New York • London

Published by Hamilton Books
An imprint of The Rowman & Littlefield Publishing Group, Inc.
4501 Forbes Boulevard, Suite 200, Lanham, Maryland 20706
Hamilton Books Acquisitions Department (301) 459-3366

6 Tinworth Street, London SE11 5AL, United Kingdom

British Library Cataloguing in Publication Information Available

Library of Congress Cataloging-in-Publication Data Available

ISBN: 978-0-7618-7196-5 (pbk: alk. paper)
ISBN: 978-0-7618-7197-2 (electronic)

∞™ The paper used in this publication meets the minimum requirements of
American National Standard for Information Sciences—Permanence of Paper
for Printed Library Materials, ANSI/NISO Z39.48-1992.

IN MEMORY of
杨炳章
Yang Bingzhang
1945–2020

Contents

List of Figures

Prologue

Premier Zhou Enlai asked me with a smile, "Where did you study Chinese?"

"In America," I replied, a little surprised the world-famous premier had even understood my poor Chinese, with its Australian accent, let alone showed an interest in my studies.

Zhou Enlai said with spirit: "That is a fine thing, for you, an Australian, to learn Chinese in America!"

It was 1971. I had been introduced to Zhou Enlai by Ma Yuzhen, later Chinese ambassador to England. I was accompanying Australian Labor Party leader Gough Whitlam at an evening session with Zhou in the Great Hall of the People.

Australia, China, and the USA were to be the three countries shaping my life. In the pages ahead, recounting China's recent story, a child from the Australian Bush becomes a Harvard professor linked, in ways personal and professional, with China in an era of globalization. A rural boy discovers in China's cities a laboratory of the human condition. An Australian who grew up in a society fearful of China, because of the Korean War, finds inspiration to be a writer in interaction with the Chinese.

The international scene in 1964 when I first saw China was not propitious. A tense Cold War gripped Europe and Asia alike. Asia was known not for economic progress but for the Korean War and the Vietnam War. In Beijing, Mao Zedong ruled and life was regimented. The changes in China post- Mao are amazing, with the economy growing like a vine in the tropics. Where will they lead next?

A decade after that first visit to China, in 1974, when I was a faculty member at Harvard, I was given the task of shepherding the prime minister of Singapore, Lee Kuan Yew, around campus. I supervised a swim for him at Harvard's indoor pool. Then I left Lee free for an hour. Over dinner, he told me he went to Yenching Library to read some issues of Chinese-language People's Daily. "As I read the propaganda," he said of Beijing's Communist Party newspaper (which Lee did not then permit in Singapore), "I suddenly wondered how on earth Americans, peering through a peephole, could ever understand a society like [China]."

"We Westerners don't really understand China," I said to the Singapore prime minister. "We invent Chinese Communist society according to our wish." Still, these days we gain rich experience of China realities. Thus armed, we periodically revise the image we have created.

The year 2008 brought me two experiences that reflected a changed world for these three countries of Australia, China, and the United States. Prime Minister Kevin Rudd invited me to lunch at the Australian Embassy in Washington to chat about China. During the 1980s, Rudd lived in Beijing as a diplomat. He speaks good Chinese. I have known many Australian prime ministers since Gough Whitlam and none, until Rudd, spoke Chinese. Rudd talked expansively of hopes for Australia-China relations, as China was snapping up Australian resources and Chinese students were flocking to Australian campuses. He praised President Bush's handling of U.S relations with Beijing. About to leave Washington for China, he asked my views on Tibet.

Four months later, in July 2008, also in Washington, former secretary of state Henry Kissinger and the Chinese foreign minister, Yang Jiechi, were at the Woodrow Wilson Center to inaugurate the Kissinger Institute on China and the United States. The event reflected progress in US research on China.

During the celebratory lunch, Kissinger, my former professor, greeted me warmly: "Oh, I read your writings on China often!" he said. At eighty-five years of age, he was cheerful and mellow. He looked splendid, though moving slowly.

Kissinger said, "I've believed in the importance of United States-China relations for nearly forty years, without wavering." That is true, although Kissinger's reasons for valuing the relationship have varied from decade to decade. As Chinese Foreign Minister Yang remarked at the table, "Kissinger himself is an institution."

By 2008, the tentative ties of the early 1970s among Australia, China, and the U.S. had involved into fruitful structures. "China and America no longer have a common enemy," Kissinger said, "but a common opportunity."

All my adult lifetime, United States-China relations, or lack of relations, have shaped Asia-Pacific. World War Two saw Japan attack China, Japan and the United States declare war against each other, and Japan bomb northern Australia; China, the United States, and Australia became tight allies.

Five years after the end of World War 2, the Korean War, which would not have occurred without Sino-American hostility, solidified the Russia-China bloc, crystallizing the Cold War. Stunningly, the Richard Nixon-Mao hand-shake of 1972 ended the danger of war between China and the United States. It turned a bipolar world into a triangle and ushered in an age of economics in East Asia; the American market was catalyst and the Chinese economy was beneficiary.

Into the 21st century, China and the United States are interlocked. Like lovers, they kiss and quarrel by turns. Australia, now friends with both giants of Asia–Pacific, breathes more easily in its region. Conflicting interests, of course, occur in all three relationships. Yet, I believe the United States-China relationship will continue to make or break us.

Chapter One

An Australian Door to China

Bruthen sits in a green valley 200 miles east from Melbourne, Australia. The sounds of a Bruthen night return as if I had just woken up there. The mellow chime of bellbirds. A sighing wind in the eucalyptus trees. My father was the head schoolteacher in this township of 600 people in the state of Victoria. My mother was an assistant teacher.

National events seldom touched us. Even Melbourne was far distant to a small boy. Our universe was nature, and a ragbag of local characters assembled by chance within its harsh but beautiful realm. In Bruthen, children came barefoot to school. My elder brother and I wore shoes only on Sunday for church. This was not because of poverty, but closeness to nature. Climate was benign. Paths of soft earth and green grass were gentle on our sun burnt toes. We learned to watch out for the occasional snake.

One day during family breakfast in 1941 the radio brought news that two Japanese submarines were in Sydney harbor. A worried look crossed my father's face. What were "the Japs" doing so far south from Tokyo? A child of four does not understand war, but everyone in Bruthen believed the Japanese were dangerous. Soon, in 1942, Japan bombed our northern city of Darwin.

World War II gave the Australian Bush a new consciousness of Asia-Pacific. As a toddler, I was tossed candies, wrapped in foil of brilliant colors, by American GIs who arrived to resist Japan and defend Australia. We heard tales of the USA's wealth and energy. We also knew that China was on our side in the war. My mother's father heard a lot about Japan's attack on China in 1937 from his Chinese friends.

Yes, in Melbourne of the 1940s, where my relatives lived, grandfather knew Chinese folk. He had taught English to merchants and workers in the evenings in the city's China Town. In these narrow, aromatic streets, descendants of Chinese who had come to seek gold a century earlier ran shops, restaurants, and civic organizations serving new arrivals from China. For many ordinary Melbourne folk "China" meant mainly the Chinese cooks and laundrymen in China Town.

On the walls of grandfather's living room in the Melbourne suburb of Murrumbeena were two beautiful cork-carved "paintings" depicting south China scenes. Their camphor-wood frames of a rich golden color hung by a thin wire at a forward-tilted angle. Grateful Chinese from grandfather's evening classes gave them to him as a memento of his volunteer teaching. I often gazed at these pictures of lakes, pavilions, and hills, the cork landscapes set against a background of pale blue cloth. The smell was fragrant and old, quite unlike the plastic, modern smells of my grandparent's home. I tried to imagine this land to Australia's north. My elders told me only that China was old and big and in chaos.

It must be strange for Chinese people to read these thoughts on China from an isolated son of the Australian Bush in mid-20th century. That is how life proceeds. We come out of a particular environment; we learn of life in wider spheres; we try to make a unity from our background and our successive encounters.

Chinese people and Australia met each other because of gold. In the early 1850s as the Taiping Rebellion erupted and the Qing Dynasty fumbled the problem of an intruding Britain, Chinese sailed to Australia in search of fortune on gold fields. Earlier they had done so in San Francisco. Hundreds of thousands came. Soon 20% of the population at the gold fields of Victoria was Chinese. In one decade, thanks in part to the Chinese, the population of Australia trebled, passing one million.

Cooktown, a village in the far north, became the second busiest port in Australia, after Sydney, as boats came south from Canton (Guangzhou). Full of Chinese hoping for wealth from gold, the vessels passed by Singapore and reached Cooktown as the first port of call in Australia.

Today Cooktown (named after British explorer James Cook) is not much bigger than Bruthen. However, it has three large cemeteries from gold rush days. One for blacks (the original Aboriginal inhabitants of the continent of Australia), one for "Europeans," as white people were called in Australia in the 19th century, and one for Chinese. When I visited the cemeteries in 1987, on assignment to write a story for the *National Geographic*, the largest of the three still was the Chinese.

Like everyone else who came to Australia, the Chinese arrived in boats. Tens of thousands of years ago, the Aborigines island-hopped eastward from western Asia and reached Australia. Later arrivals also got to Australia by sea, mostly through a roll of the legal, climatic, economic, or political

Figure 1.1. Author with his Chinese girlfriend, c.1949, Bruthen, Australia. Author's sister photo.

dice. In part because European boats, by the 17th century, were superior to Asian boats—unlike in the 15th century, when China had fine ships but no desire to found colonies—the long isolation of the Aborigines was ended by white arrivals rather than by non-white. The Chinese turned out to be latecomers.

A legacy in Bruthen of the gold rushes of the mid-19th century was Violet, a dark-haired, demure girl who attracted me. Violet's father, the local pharmacist, was the township's only Chinese by the 1940s. As a primary school boy, I did not know that my first girlfriend was half-Chinese.

Children are not much aware of race. In later years, traveling in Sichuan Province, on another assignment for *National Geographic*, I would learn that Han (Chinese) and Tibetan village children did not care whether their playmates were of the same race as themselves. However, I wonder, today, what Violet thought of the notices, a common boast of quality and mark of Australian defensiveness in the 1940s that were branded in purple paint on Australian furniture: MANUFACTURED BY EUROPEAN LABOR ONLY.

My parents moved from the Bush to Melbourne in 1950, a few months after the Communist Party headed by Mao Zedong came to power in Beijing and just before the Korean War burst out. The reason was for my sister, brother, and me to go to a fancy Methodist school. I forced my feet into leather shoes. I wore a cap and tie in the school colors of purple and yellow. Guessing at my future, I kept away from science and chose history and politics.

My teachers at Wesley College urged attention to China and the rest of neighboring Asia. They pushed the principle of economic equality and a social-gospel version of Christianity. These teachers gave me the idea that the anti-colonial movements of the 1950s in Asia and Africa had more to gain from Marxism than from capitalism.

Of course, as a boy of thirteen or fourteen, I was unaware of political standpoints. I knew only a few simple things. Japan bombed northern Australia. Britain was the traditional friend of Australia. The U.S. rescued us in World War 2. China stood huge astride Asia-Pacific.

The war in Korea made us fear Mao's communism may percolate south, through Malaya, to dominate Australia (just as Japs, as my father called them, had planned to take us over for our natural resources). Some political groups drew maps of the region, with large red arrows superimposed over the various countries, pointing downward from China, area by area, Hong Kong to Singapore, and Malaya to Indonesia, with the final target being the wide-open spaces of Australia.

At Melbourne University, where I began as a freshman in 1957, my teachers were left wing. They were very interested in China, but certainly not Maoists. They did believe, however, that Communists could be negotiated with successfully, that Washington was inclined to throw its weight around, and that the UN and other international organizations were the hope of the world.

Similar in their views of Asia, my teachers nevertheless had diverse backgrounds. Professor McMahon Ball had been the representative of the British

Commonwealth on the Allied Council for Japan after 1945. While based in Tokyo, he dealt with domineering Douglas McArthur, which made him wary of brash Americans. Ball felt the famous American general took him for granted as a mere Australian. Still, he judged the post-World War 2 occupation of Japan a remarkable success.

From Tokyo, Ball looked out upon an Asia, which, he told us in class, was juggling nationalism and communism. He saw the new China founded in 1949 as a tremendous challenge to the West, because it was a Communist regime that enjoyed patriotic legitimacy. In his *Nationalism and Communism in Southeast Asia*, Ball drew the conclusion that the direction of many Asian countries would be determined by whether this Chinese blending of nationalism with communism was successful. He urged the Western countries, including Australia: "Don't push Southeast Asia into Beijing's arms by resisting its nationalism." Years before Lee Kuan Yew and others began to stress "Asian Values," Ball believed that varieties of nationalism in the region, notably Indonesia's, reflected values that Australia should respect.

Still, this was early days for Asian studies in Australia. Ball, who was head of the political science department at Melbourne University, did not know any Chinese, Japanese, or other Asian language.

My teacher of modern Chinese history was typical of his time and place. Dr. John Gregory had studied in England and his approach to the Qing Dynasty was to view it in terms of the British Empire's reach into East Asia. He wrote a book on the Taiping Rebellion, *Great Britain and the Taiping's,* still read in Western universities. The title was revealing of how "Oriental History," as Gregory's course was called, was taught in Australia (and much of the West) in the late 1950s. China was studied as the object of the West's expansion, a recipient of Western impact, a "responder" to the masterful world of Europe and North America.

For Dr. Gregory's class I wrote my research essay on the Treaty of Nanking of 1842. This gave me a vivid sense of the passions aroused in Guangdong Province by the Opium War. The Qing court and London misunderstood each other thoroughly. Beyond that, the power inequality between a China in crisis and a Britain on the upswing was crucial to the outcome of the encounter.

My teacher of Chinese politics, Arthur Huck, had yet another background. He was a product of a recent strategic step to teach the Chinese language in preparation for military and political challenges in Australia's foreign relations. At Point Cook, the Australian military had established a language center and there Huck learned Chinese. He took a cautious but sympathetic approach to the early years of the PRC. He insisted we read Mao's writings and speeches. We became familiar with volume one and two of Mao's *Selected Works*. We hungry students snapped up other books, too, at left-wing bookstores in downtown Melbourne, from the Foreign Languages Press in Beijing. How eagerly I devoured "On Practice" and "On Contradiction" from volume one of Mao's works. With what fascination I studied "Combat Liberalism" from the second volume!

Data on the PRC during the 1950s was limited. There existed New China News Agency bulletins. "China has friends all over the world," these cried. Steel output leaps ahead. . . . Africans in their thousands have arrived in Beijing to "pay their respects to Chairman Mao." Fearful rumors also flew down to Australia from Hong Kong. Some were exaggerated stories of tribulations in China from angry and relieved refugees reaching the West. Ideological special pleading also existed among Maoists in Melbourne and Sydney; and among angry anti-Communists, including Western ex-missionaries who saw Christianity threatened by communism.

The Australian Catholic Church became especially anti-PRC after the Korean War. Indeed, leading members of the left-of-center Labor Party who were Catholics came under pressure from Bishops to form a separate, anti-Communist party. They did this, and the Democratic Labor Party split the Labor vote and enabled conservatives to govern Australia throughout the 1950s and well into the 1960s. This was one reason why Australia did not recognize the PRC diplomatically.

Communism as a doctrine was not radioactive for us; in class, we sat next to Communists and survived. The Australians who supported the PRC were mostly Communists or members of "Friendship" groups with numerous Communist members. The Communist Party of Australia was a fact of life around us. My teacher of Soviet Union politics at the University of Melbourne, Lloyd Churchward, was a Party member. It was a usual assignment for students in his class to apply Lenin's theory of imperialism to this or that event of 19th or 20th century history. I can still see the array of Stalin's writings on the shelves behind Churchward's chair. I still smell the glue from the binding of my own navy blue copies of the Moscow-published *Selected Works of V. I. Lenin.*

However, a Communist presence does not make everyone a Communist. Christian influence immunized me against Marxist faith. I had my religion already. In the student ranks of the Labor Party, to which I belonged, we knew the difference between (our) social democracy and (their) Marxism. Nikita Khrushchev's secret speech attacking Stalin in 1956 caused Mao great consternation. We watched our Communist acquaintances squirm, protest, or leave "the Party."

As an undergraduate, I read not only works of Marx and Engels, but also Milovan Djilas's *The New Class* and other criticisms of Stalinism. We were social democrats who kept our distance from communism. We were not impressed when Australian Communists, after the Sino-Soviet dispute flared in the early 1960s, trying to keep up with the wider world, split into two Communist parties, one pro-Beijing and one pro-Moscow.

Later in the 1960s, during the Cultural Revolution when a "new man" in Beijing appealed to some of my classmates in graduate school at Harvard, this quasi-religious belief in Maoism had scant appeal to me. I remained an Australian nativist in some ways. I never felt seriously alienated from mainstream Western values centered on individual freedom.

Australia, living close to volatile nature, was not a self-conscious country. It seldom deigned a glance at small New Zealand and the islands of its South Pacific backyard. Melbourne and Sydney hardly paid attention even to the empty western and northern half of Australia's own continent. Australia cast a longing eye on the faster lane in Europe and America. It worried about Asia, wondering if Australia would ever be truly part of it. Especially, it was ambivalent about China. Huge, but poor. An old civilization yet wracked with the struggles of becoming modern. In addition, China offered a starkly different social and cultural alternative to the Western world from which Australia had sprung. Would we succumb to its influence?

In the 1950s and 1960s, Australia did not diplomatically recognize the PRC. Its recognition of the Republic of China (ROC) headed by Chiang Kai-shek, continued after the Communist Liberation of 1949, though all through the 1950s Australia did not actually set up an embassy in Taipei, nor receive an ROC embassy in Canberra. As an undergraduate, I helped form a "Recognize China" group advocating a switch of recognition from Taipei to Beijing. Along with some of my classmates, I saw China as the heart of Asia, yet Australia seemed to be hiding its head in the sand from China. "It is difficult to conceive a satisfactory future for the policy of non-recognition," I wrote in one of my first published articles. "Facts may be fought; they cannot be denied."[1]

In a paper for the "Recognize China" group at Melbourne University, I wrote, "Moral disapprobation [of the PRC] is no valid ground for obstructing international intercourse and creating misunderstanding." In criticizing the American policy that Australia was following, I wrote, "The Soviet Union went unrecognized by the USA until 1933, and this did no one much good. Co-existence should be pursued, neither as conciliation to world communism nor as condescension from a position of supposed moral and physical superiority, but as a policy rational and moral in itself."

In my eyes, the issue of China conjoined with Australia's anti-Asia immigration policy and its poor treatment of Australia's Aborigines. Having ceased to be a British colony, our country, I believed, must come to terms with the non-white region in which our vast continent was located.

We Melbourne students struggled to end the "White Australia policy," which made it almost impossible for Asians to migrate to Australia and for full civil rights for Aborigines, who then lacked the right to vote, cross state borders without permission, or buy alcoholic drinks. Linking these two issues with the demand to recognize China, in our organization Student Action, may have been excessively moralistic, but we young social democrats did it out of idealism.

In Bruthen, the family next door to us ran a shop in the village center that sold beer, wine, and other alcoholic drinks. Each year the family's husband or wife traveled to Melbourne to renew the shop's license to sell alcoholic drinks. The liquor licensing authority would ask them, "What would you do if an Aboriginal came into the shop and asked to buy a bottle of whisky or beer?" My neighbors said they would refuse the request. Their drinks license was renewed. "I knew the rules," the wife told me, looking back on those years.

One day in 1961, I got a surprise at the front gate of my family's house in Murrumbeena. Fetching the newspaper and bottles of milk, as I did each morning, I found writing in large white-paint letters with arrows pointing from the words into our gateway. "TRAITOR," it said. "ROSS TERRILL IS A NATIONAL PERIL." My throat tightened. I realized what had happened. I was active in a student group against racism and had written a letter in the *Age* newspaper a few days before. My letter began: "It is a source of satisfaction that the attitude of superiority towards non-white races is losing ground in Australia." The white-painted insults were my reward. "TERRILL WANTS BLACKS TO STAB WHITES IN THE BACKS," the message on the pavement continued, probably using "black" as a general term to cover all non-whites.

At that time, Europeans could get their fares paid to immigrate to Australia, but Asians or Africans could not. Asian students on our campuses had to promise not to have a child while completing their studies in Australia. We campaigned against both major political parties, since the Labor Party, based on the trade unions, was even guiltier of white supremacy than were the right-wingers.

In the latter part of the gold rushes, gold diggers in New South Wales formed a Miners' Protective League. "We invite men of all nations," began the prospectus, "except Chinamen, to enroll themselves." (The miners went on to embrace the principles of the French Revolution, and call for "Fair Play for All"). In 1901, when the Commonwealth of Australia was born, one purpose was to reduce the danger of "Asiatic" invasion. "Australian" and "white man" were inseparable terms. The early Minister for Home Affairs declared at a public meeting, "The policy of the country is that the Chinese population shall gradually become extinct."

Figure 1.2. Protesting "White Australia" immigration policy, Melbourne 1962. Author's photo.

It was trade unions, not employers, which kept Chinese out of Australia in the 19th century after the gold rushes were over. Unions wrote the term "White Australia" into their policy statements. Victoria (then a direct colony of Britain) passed legislation excluding Chinese immigration as undesirable. Curiously, around the same time, California, also reacting to a post-gold situation, passed similar legislation excluding Australians as undesirable!

For a long time after the gold rushes, to be anti-Chinese was as Australian as the eucalyptus tree. Rumors ran that opium was fed to Australian children. Were the Chinese chefs not cooking lovely Australian pet cats for their dumplings? One of the Labor Party's leading figures, William Hughes, an early prime minister of Australia, declared of his party: "Our chief plank, of course, is a White Australia. There is no compromise about that! The hard-working colored brother has to go—and remain away." The state of Queensland clinched the race connection by passing legislation that specifically denied Asians the right to employ Aborigines.[2] Hughes' sentiment about Chinese was simply racist, different and far worse than the anti-communism of Australian Catholics.

The Australian institution of a "birthday ballot" brought me into the Australian army. The Lord Mayor of Melbourne stood before a barrel containing 365 marbles and drew one out at a time until the army had enough recruits for immediate needs. My birth date came out early. I found myself dressed in khakis and shooting an outmoded 303-rifle. I had to obey strict orders for the first time in my life. Instead of rising toward noon, which was my habit, a bugle summoned me in pajamas to a parade ground at 6 am.

In the Melbourne University Regiment, my unit, I heard our officers, who had fought in the Korean War, talk about Asian armies. I realized that both North Korea and the PRC were aggressive when it came to using force to protect their interests. My officers also made racist remarks (blunter by far than racist remarks heard in the US in 2019) about their Korean War experiences. I did not like these remarks, but I doubt they influenced me.

The year I began at Melbourne University, *The Bulletin*, a leading weekly published in Sydney, still carried on its masthead the motto: "AUSTRALIA FOR THE WHITE MAN." The Labor Party, to which I belonged, made me choose between my membership in its ranks and my agitation against White Australia. I received a letter giving me thirty days to make the choice.

As students, we simply made a fresh start in our opinions on Asia. We had not witnessed Japanese atrocities in World War II, and in our midst were thousands of students, many of Chinese race, from Singapore, Malaysia, Indonesia and Hong Kong. We were the first Australian student generation to sit in class with a scattering of non-whites. From the Asian students I learned to find diversity not threatening but exciting.

The influence of Professor Ball and other teachers took me to India in 1960. For these university men (no women), "the Bandung spirit" was important. India, Indonesia, Egypt, Burma and others had pioneered a non-alignment movement at a meeting in Bandung, Indonesia in 1955. Shining especially brightly in Bandung, and among Melbourne academics, were Jawaharlal Nehru and Krishna Menon of India; this pair, like some of my teachers, had studied in London and devoured the British left-wing weekly *New Statesman*.

I traveled to Bombay, Delhi and other cities as the first Australian participant in the Experiment in International Living. This admirable organization, its headquarters in Vermont, USA, specialized in giving youth all over the world a first-hand experience of cultures other than their own. I wrote in answers to the questions asked me by the Indian organizers, "I am 21 years of age and 6' 1. I am a student of history and politics at Melbourne University. My leisure activities are dramatic art and playing the piano. During the holidays, I take temporary jobs in factories and shops. I really want to seize this opportunity of going to India. As to my future, I am not yet certain of my calling. . ."

China and India were much on my mind as the dominant two countries in Asia. In Melbourne, my teachers proffered China and India as alternative paths for the Afro-Asian world. India was trying to build democracy while upholding the Bandung spirit. China was part of the Soviet bloc while also claiming allegiance to the Bandung spirit. However, in Delhi I heard stories of the border clashes of 1959 that made me realize an element of China-India rivalry was inevitable. While I was in India, Zhou Enlai visited Delhi and his talks with Nehru, seeking to ease tensions, electrified the Indian households that hosted me.

Huge, proud, old, poor China seemed to invite comparison with huge, proud, old, poor India. They both felt the center-piece of a region, China of east Asia and India of south Asia. Both were slow to understand the wounds and irritations of neighbors. Both enjoyed a cultural influence in the world, and an aspiration to be a great power.

China's long tradition of a strong state marked it off from India, where the coming of British institutions resulted in a sharp divide between state and society; essentially Hindu society.

After seeing India, I concluded that Hindu moralism was a mixed blessing. It brought depth to Indian culture. However, it assumed a noble view of human nature that may have been incorrect. By comparison with China's land reform, the "Land Gift Movement" of Vinoba Bhave seemed a mere band-aid. I also considered India disorganized. "The universities, especially in the north," I wrote in my trip report to the National Union of Australian University Students, "are on the verge of chaos, with the teachers in despair and the students in revolt."

Asked by the Union of Students to make suggestions for future Experimenters, I wrote, "Clothes must be simple. If you're dressed for a cricket match, you'll pass in India." I said of eating habits: "You will not normally be served meat, fish, eggs or cooked vegetables. Birds and beasts are significant religiously, as I discovered one evening in a Bombay restaurant, when a sparrow flew in, unmolested by the waiters, to share my meal."

I could see that India as well as China was going to be important in Australia's future. "Which other country," I wrote in my report, "has had visits from Khrushchev, Zhou Enlai, Eisenhower and Macmillan in one year, as India has in 1960?" Yet, when my teachers lionized India as the democratic path, I wondered if China's authoritarian path might be more effective. This was the seed of my interest in seeing China. I bounced off India to land in China.

NOTES

1. Ross Terrill, "Recognize China," *Fact*, Melbourne, June, 1962, 64.
2. On this story of race, see the author's *The Australians*, New York, Simon and Schuster, 1987, 78–84.

Chapter Two

Beijing in 1964

Few Westerners set foot in the PRC then. Australians needed permission from their own government to go there. Some got a green light, but Beijing guarded visas for people from non-Communist countries like precious jewels. Australia, in step with the U.S.A., still had not recognized Mao's government, which made getting a Beijing visa tougher.

During the summer of 1964, while hitchhiking through Europe, I knocked hopefully on the tall carved wooden doors of Beijing's embassies in East Europe (few existed in West Europe), saying I would like to see New China. I had previously obtained permission from the Australian government to travel to China.

In Prague, Budapest, and Belgrade, I was told to wait a couple of weeks for an answer. Alas, I had to take the train on to the next capital, to protect my dwindling funds, before a reply came at the Chinese embassy of the previous one. I felt I was in a revolving door, with a Chinese visa always just out of my grasp.

Warsaw was my last stop in East Europe. At the PRC embassy on Bonifraterska Street, feeling I now had nothing to lose, I boldly asked to see the ambassador to debate whether it was a good thing for the world to understand China. A senior diplomat emerged from an inner room, smiling slightly. Two cups of tea appeared before us; I made my case, offering the dubious opinion that the youth of Australia's opinion of New China hinged upon my visit.

Next day I was phoned at the Bristol Hotel and told my Chinese visa could be picked up that morning at Bonifraterska Street.

Visiting Moscow on a stopover to China, I wrote a wide-eyed letter to my parents: "You can imagine how excited I am to be having my first sight of the USSR. It is a long-standing dream come true." I was impressed to see women and men working together on road repair and other work, chatting and taking lunch together. I admired the gleaming Metro train system, the unrivalled Bolshoi Ballet, the stress on sport to bring glory to the nation, the ornate Kremlin and other grand public edifices. The Palace of Congresses was so beautiful, a Russian friend told me, that people came just to look at the building and the décor: "Many people gape at the beautiful design, go up and down the escalators, buy chocolates in the foyer, and then just leave." The 400th anniversary of the birth of William Shakespeare was being widely celebrated across Moscow, as also in Prague.

I wrote in my diary, "There exists a sense of social purpose that lacks in Australia. There is little rationality for the individual in the Soviet Union, but a great deal collectively." I had never before seen such strong women, or been served cold fish and vodka for breakfast. Much was gigantic, including a department store that extended for one whole block.

At a collective farm, a large sign hung over the stage of the school auditorium: "The Present Generation of Soviet People Will Live under Communism." I said to a teacher at the school that in Australia our rural schools were smaller than in the USSR because we had no collective farms. "But you will have them in the future," she cried with a huge smile. I was naïve about collectivism, for I wrote in my diary, "The farm seems to be a community. The isolation, the personal loneliness of rural life in many countries is not found here. These people play together, share facilities, and love together—all that is probably good."

I was taken to the Palace of Pioneers. It looked like an exhibition of photos of Lenin. I wrote with irritation in my diary, "Lenin all over the bloody place. This kind of thing is not how leaders are produced. A real Lenin could never emerge from a Pioneers group."

I took a tour of the Lenin State Library with its 21 million volumes, conducted by a blond female librarian who said, when told I was heading for China: "Remember, the present government of China is just a dictatorship of one man, the chauvinist Mao Zedong. It is not a government of the people—and it is bent upon war." The Soviet librarian's words were a blunt introduction to the burgeoning Russia-China split. I tried to suggest the USSR and China were at different stages of development and it was inevitable that outlooks would vary. The librarian cut me off. How could a kid from a capitalist country understand the finer points of Marxism!

Whether in connection with our conversation or not, a "Statement of the Soviet Government" was delivered to my room at the Ostankino Hotel next day. It was a 20,000-word refutation of the Chinese government's statement opposing the treaty of 1963 banning nuclear tests in the atmosphere.

Walking the streets of Moscow, I wondered why a butcher shop had photos of meat in the window, why there were huge, colorful stamps for foreigners but small plain stamps for Russians, and why drivers of the tough little Russian cars carried the ends of the windscreen wipers from the vehicle with them when they left. I wrote in a letter to my mother in Melbourne, "One good thing about being in the USSR is there's no frustration about not having time or money to shop, since to an Australian there's really nothing worth buying."

From Moscow, I took a worn Aeroflot turboprop to Omsk. About half the passengers were Chinese. Two Hungarians struggled aboard with melons in string bags. A Finnish woman, on her sixth trip to China, wanted to buy textiles at a trade fair in Shanghai. Albanian commerce officials were on their way to North Korea for a vacation. Omsk looked like a town in Alaska or the far north of Japan. In a terminal that was full of sleeping Russians, we sipped sweet-scented Siberian lemonade.

Another stop at Tomsk, and then after a night flight we reached Irkutsk. A Siberian Intourist guide led me to a breakfast of buns, apricots and mineral water. As we ate, the Chinese (CCAC) airliner that was to take me to Beijing rolled up outside the window. I sensed the enormousness of the cohabitation of the Soviet Union and China, the pair leaning upon each other for 4300 miles, bodies together like reclining dinosaurs, minds far apart, one in Europe and the other in Asia.

Changing to CCAC, we began a four-hour flight to Beijing. During many months in Europe, this was my first flight with no Americans. The cultural transition to China was agreeable. The cabin smelled of bamboo fans and fragrant tea. Hostesses brought chewing gum, cigarettes, and plastic envelopes for the protection of fountain pens. We flew over Lake Baikal and the ginger waste of the Gobi Desert, and later over North China's yellow streams and green velvety hills.

At Beijing airport, a customs officer sealed up my rolls of film exposed in East Europe, so that I would be able to take them out of China, and made me undertake to have any film used during my stay developed within China. A guide from the China International Travel Service awaited me. Even a wandering Australian student could not arrive in Mao's China unmet. He needed an escort to ensure an appropriate experience of New China.

A stubborn idealist, I wanted to see for myself the new China that had turned off the lights of Treaty Port China and excluded the West, throwing out the last American and Australian diplomats in 1950 and treating each succeeding American president as the world's devil of the moment. The revolution that Mao clinched in 1949 was still a shimmering abstraction for most people around the world, the way the Russian Revolution was for Europeans through the 1920s and 1930s. I was too young to buy an abstraction, and energetic enough to hunt down a few realities.

My first vista of Beijing was a huge crowd in white shirts and blue pants assembled in Tiananmen Square. It was a rally of 800,000 Chinese protesting President Johnson's attack on North Vietnamese vessels in the Gulf of Tonkin, just a few score miles from Chinese territory. Nearby, Chang An Avenue, the spine of Beijing, swarmed with bicycles. Amidst them, occasional busses, like carp among minnows, made a sedate progress. Hooked together in pairs with a folding canvas connection, giving a caterpillar effect, the busses ploughed forward packed to capacity. My taxi dashed at fifty miles an hour for half a mile, then coasted at fifteen miles an hour for a few hundred yards a maddening way to drive, which I thought at the time meant engine trouble, but learned later was to save gasoline.

The only major new buildings in Beijing were Soviet-style government monoliths: The history museum, the Great Hall of the People, the central train station, all put up in the fevered years of the Great Leap Forward (1958–59). They did not look Chinese. A waiter at the Beijing Hotel said the train station went up from the moment of its design to the last coat of paint in ten months. I wrote in my diary, "The Chinese acknowledge no limitations, whether on the speed of putting up a building, set about with trees that arrive fully grown in boxes, or on controlling the historically uncontrollable waters of their great rivers." No highrise or international chain hotels existed, nor did any foreign airline other than Aeroflot fly to China.

Drivers of the few cars, imports from Russia and Poland, with an occasional battered Morris or Chevrolet from "imperialist" days, made constant use of the horn, sending little boys scurrying and old men hauling wagons lurching to one side with seconds to spare. I wrote in my diary, "My guide said in the future there will be many more cars in China. If there are one tenth the cars in Beijing that there are in Melbourne, people will be deaf within a day from the noise of the tooting."

As Chinese as many things were, from the curved tiles of the Forbidden City's palaces in the hue of a goldfish's skin, to the nasal cries of the hawkers and stone-grinders, and the smell of Chinese noodles and sauces and vegetables, Beijing nevertheless bespoke the Communist bloc. I stayed in the Russian-style Xin Qiao Hotel, a rectangular cement block that nestled against a remnant of the city wall in the old Legation Quarter.

Most of the pre-1949 city walls had been pulled down. I wondered in what way this destruction was intrinsic to a Communist revolution. Did aesthetics not count at all, and were the citizens of Peking really better off without the walls; or would the Communists just feel purer in their anti-feudal zeal by demolishing them?

Mao often said, "Destroy the old, create the new," but this was not a simple task. An old culture could not be removed like a rotten branch from a tree, and a new culture would not blossom from a single, separate source, any more than a rose could unfold from its bud on a branch severed from the rose bush.

My room at the Xin Qiao had no shades and sun streamed in upon the bed at 4.30 AM, as outside my window cicadas sang as if in millions. In the hotel courtyard, the bushes, although lush, exuded heat. Beside them, old Chinese men and women did rhythmic, snakelike *tai ji quan* exercises.

The Xin Qiao Hotel had parties of Laotian dancers and Cambodian table tennis players. Many Africans were on visits of "Goodwill," for in 1964 one-third of China's forty-eight embassies were located in Africa. Except for three Western resident journalists, the main foreigners in the city were French visitors. They strode out into the terrible August heat in Parisian clothes, feeling proud that France, under Charles de Gaulle, had led the way among Western powers in establishing full diplomatic ties with the PRC. Some East European technical residents of Beijing became disgruntled as the Sino-Soviet quarrel made the atmosphere chilly. An engineer from Budapest carried in his wallet a piece of paper on which he crossed off one by one the days until his longed-for departure from China.

I had never seen a pedicab before. Patched all over, they were being phased out as the government saw them as an imperialist relic. I liked them because of the open-air ride, the absence of a tooting horn, and the leisured pace that permitted real sightseeing. The only drawback was the rather precarious seat and the feeling that it might be "unsocialist" to be pedaled by a Chinese worker.

To my room at the Xin Qiao each afternoon an attendant brought an English edition of a bulletin from the New China News Agency (*Xinhua*). The main theme of reports on world events was anti-colonialism. One morning during breakfast, four Africans with whom I had flown from Siberia to Beijing came into the restaurant. They approached my table and we shook hands and chatted. From the hotel staff came a murmur of oohs and ahs. After further experiences at the opera and in museums of greeting Asians or Africans and evoking a buzz from Chinese bystanders, I saw the point. To the Chinese, schooled in Marxist orthodoxy about imperialism and national liberation forces, human warmth across the chasm between a white person and Third World brothers seemed to come as a shock.

The end of colonialism was supposed almost automatically to solve the problems of the Afro-Asian World. My bulletin from the Chinese news agency spoke of "old forces" of the West being swept aside by a tide of "new forces" of Afro-Asian socialism. Many people, including to a degree myself, believed in this upward evolution of the oppressed. Of course, it would be a long process.

No longer an abstraction, here was China as steel plants, crying babies, 3000-year-old tombs, soldiers with fixed bayonets at the gates of unlabeled buildings, bookstores selling Albanian political pamphlets and the social realist works of Jack London, Mark Twain, and Charles Dickens, all in Chinese translation. Also a populace with a genius, born of necessity, for deriving pleasure from simple things.

The hotel dining room staff used bread as a magic tool to keep Westerners content. These cheerful young men and women were convinced no European could eat a meal that did not include slices of dense, dry bread. A culture needs pigeonholes for dealing with other cultures, and for these folk, bread was the key to our civilization (as, for many Westerners, rice was the essence of Eastern civilization). If I ordered a meal that did not include bread, the server would look at me as if to say, "Haven't you forgotten something?" flash a knowing smile, and write the Chinese characters for bread on her docket book.

When I took a taxi to the Summer Palace, the driver, dropping me at the gate, said I would need sunglasses against the glare and lent me his own pair. After lingering longer than planned in the hillside pavilions, I could not find the taxi or the driver. I took another taxi back to the Xin Qiao Hotel and tried to ensure that the sunglasses were returned and full payment made. I was not able to press upon the taxi cooperative the 60 yuan agreed upon originally for the round trip to the Summer Palace. They would accept only 40 yuan plus the return of the glasses. No tip, even if disguised as a rental fee for the sunglasses. "Let us shake hands instead!" said the staffer when I tried to tip. Tipping had been abolished as a relic of colonialism (twenty years later it would come back as a prized badge of competitiveness).

Everything belongs to everyone in China, I was told, so tipping would be absurd. Still, it felt like state-enforced honesty. The postage stamps were colorful and enormous. There was a joke at the Xin Qiao: "What part of the stamp do I put the postcard on?" Stamps were cheap, but cables expensive, and no phone call to Australia was possible.

I knew little of China, nothing of its language, and my eyes were my only investigative tool. Still, I could see the CCP was keeping a tight rein on Buddhists and Christians. Religion seemed a test of China's new society. I asked to see a Protestant pastor, Zhao Fusan, head of the Beijing Research Institute of Theology, and he received me at Beijing's Rice Market Church. I knew of Zhao, since he had represented China at international Christian gatherings in the years before the Cold War put an end to Chinese participation in world Christian activities.

Zhao wanted to talk about socialist China, not about theology. He put everything in a framework of imperialism, which my education made me inclined to accept. "There is little light for us in Western theology," he

complained. However, I got little light from Zhao Fusan about Chinese theology. I asked him, "Which parts of the Bible do you turn to most often?"
Looking impassive, he replied, "All parts of the Bible have appeared in a new
light to us since 1949."[1]

I had a great time at the Beijing Library, which had six million books
and subscriptions to nine thousand periodicals. The head librarian, who had
learned some English and German in his spare time, led me through airy reading rooms and a rare book room. I asked him what sections of the library were
the most popular. "The one on Marxism-Leninism," he replied. "Next would
come the fiction sections, both Chinese and literature from all over the world."

I looked up the English name C. Wright Mills, whose sociology books I
read at Melbourne University, and found four of his works in English. Learn-
ing I had been in Moscow, the librarian inquired: "Is it also your impression
that the Soviets are plain revisionists, and that a bourgeois strain has appeared
in Soviet society?" I was startled when he answered my question about rules
for borrowing: "Generally speaking, only organizations may borrow books
not individuals."

The Chinese ultra-leftists, soon to jump to center stage, were quite right to
say that a lot of "the old crap" remained in China of the early 1960s. The traditional Tian Qiao folk entertainment area, south of Qian Men gate, attracted
happy crowds with its painted magicians, expressive storytellers, huge wres-
tlers, and doublejointed acrobats. It was not forbidden to consult the writings
of Confucius and the Taoist philosopher Lao Zi, to enjoy the symphonies of
Mozart and Beethoven, or to go dressed in a colorful skirt to a dance on Saturday night and prepare with a session at a hair salon. Not everyone yet realized
or could say that the new orthodoxy (much of it Soviet socialist realism) was
not necessarily better than the old.

Rightly or wrongly, I sensed a slightly oldfashioned world. My room at the
Xin Qiao was equipped with a chamber pot and a steelnibbed pen beside a
bottle of ink. In a nearby park, older Chinese men played tennis in long white
flannels, gravely inching their way through a baseline game. Silverhaired veterans staffed leading restaurants, hotels, and embassies, their elegant manners
learned from imperialist tutelage. The boutiques of Wang Fu Jing and the art
shops of Liu Li Chang offered lovely antiques from mansions recently turned
into schools or offices or dormitories. The occasional dilapidated 1940s Morris and Chevrolet seemed like remnants from a junk yard. When I bought an
ice cream, the seller took time to carefully unwrap it and put the paper in a
trash can before handing me the ice with a smile.

Packed up to leave Beijing, I reported to the CCAC air terminal office near
the Beijing Hotel at the corner of Wang Fu Jing. The little old colonial

building was deserted. "There is a storm over south China," an official said cheerfully. "No flight to Guangzhou until it's over. Try again in two hours."

In Canton (today, Guangzhou), a sign in Chinese, English, and French rose opposite my hotel: "Welcome to the Businessmen for the Chinese Export Commodities Fair." Even Australians came to the Canton Trade Fair, as foreigners called the event. Business folk were the only link with New China for many Western countries. Again, in the south, the issue of the Soviet Union came up. My guide said crisply, "In Russia a new bourgeoisie has appeared, of which Khrushchev is the political spokesman. They are playing a 'great power' game. The sort of game that made them put missiles into Cuba. It's national egoism, nothing to do with class struggle." She told me weirdly: "Albania is the only socialist country left in Europe."

The view of the Pearl River from the top of the Aiqun Hotel was wonderful. The yellow water was alive with boats of every shape and size. Some were sampans, with boxes of chickens affixed to the back, home for families who refused to live ashore, despite government efforts to remove them as a pre-Liberation relic. The only (live) cat I saw in China was on the deck of one of these sampans. On the roofs of buildings lower than the Aiqun Hotel, small restaurants, people asleep and little boys playing football. The clipclop of wooden sandals on the crowded pavements had almost given way, given some economic development, to the rustle of plastic shoes. "It makes Canton quieter than before Liberation," a shopkeeper told me.

At a bus station, the photos in a display sixty feet long were fiercely political. One showed a large crowd in Japan demonstrating against the United States. A grasping hand was superimposed over the crowd to represent Uncle Sam, and the chairman of the Japanese Communist Party was addressing the throng. I was shaken to see a photo exhibition called "Four Wicked Men." Truman, with a clenched fist, Eisenhower, looking moronic, Kennedy, old and bewildered, and Johnson, leering into microphones that resembled guns. I objected to an official. "These men are enemies of China," he declared with a shrug. "Consider their deeds. Their deeds are a caption to the pictures."

Flying home from Hong Kong to Melbourne, I wrote in my diary that China seemed to the left of the Soviet Union, just as Yugoslavia was to the right of the Soviet Union. China seemed more ideological than the Soviet Union, its citizens more swept up in public purposes. Fifteen years after Liberation, I found the snap and bustle of a confident new order. Yet, in Moscow, I discerned more prudence about nuclear weapons than in Beijing.

The quarrel with the Soviet Union seemed less an ideological dispute, than one arising from the different stages of the Soviet and Chinese revolutions. Beijing's focus, after only fifteen years of the new regime, had to be on feeding people, industrializing, and modernizing. Moscow's talk of "goulash communism" was dangerous for the Chinese, who could afford only rice. Therefore, the battle with the Soviet Union was not an abstract dispute, but a matter of life and death.

I was wrong in thinking the Russia-China split would likely have a negative impact on China's cultural evolution. "Communism in Rome and Paris and London, as well as in East Europe," I worried in my diary, "could be a bridge between the Chinese Marxists and Western culture. By 'going it alone' the Chinese are cutting themselves off from all manifestations of European culture." It did not turn out that way.

I saw China poised among Chinese tradition, Western culture, and the new Communist culture. These were similar to the three forces jostling in the May Fourth Movement of 1919, a prelude to China's later convulsions.

In Guangzhou, I mentioned in my diary an appealing side of Chinese society: "The alleyways are crowded and they are poor, yet no one is in rags, no one is sitting or lying around in hopeless-looking poverty familiar in some Asian cities. The clothing is standardized to an extreme degree, but it is neat and adequate. Everyone seems to have a task, and consequently no one comes running after you, ingratiatingly, to beg something, or even to sell something. In the midst of poverty there is order and a certain dignity."

Most of my teachers in Australia at the time saw the PRC as nationalistic, fairly successful in economic development, and bound for a large role in Asia. They did not yet see the full scope of the social engineering mistakes of the Great Leap Forward of 1958–59. The international comparison they made was always with the Soviet Union.

Disagreements between Moscow and Beijing were plain to Australian China Hands, but most thought they stopped well short of enmity. The older school of China Hands from the 1940s, including Professor C. P. Fitzgerald in Canberra, who had seen the Communists in Yanan as "agrarian democrats," felt any split between Beijing and Moscow just proved the CCP had never really been Communist in the first place. In general, Mao's communism was considered intriguing and probably more flexible than Moscow's.

My teachers on China never mentioned India, just as Indians knew little of China. However, I was interested in this comparison. India displayed pervasive religion, an accompanying fatalism, and British-flavored intellectuals. All were a contrast with China. The Chinese in their secularity seemed more rational, more modern than the Indians seemed, and imbued with a Promethean spirit. China was less influenced by the West than India was by Britain. China was more insular yet more intellectually challenging. I was spurred to serious study of China by an impression that, virtually unknown as the condition of the PRC was, China was Asia's center.

Figure 2.1. Anna and Rupert Murdoch with author at Rupert's farm in New South Wales, Australia. Author's photo.

Such bald thoughts went into a six-part series I wrote in Rupert Murdoch's *The Australian* after my China trip. Murdoch had just founded this newspaper (four decades later it is one of the world's best) and he was its editor. He pruned my articles with a blue pencil and wrote out the payment check with a fountain pen.

In one of my articles, I criticized the American policy of non-recognition of the PRC. "One can only be astonished at the continued American policy of isolating China—to the extent of refusing citizens, including the late Eleanor Roosevelt and Averell Harriman, permission to go to China and cut through the cobwebs of myth with a bit of human communication. Can ignorance benefit anyone? Can it benefit us in the West whose cause is bound up with the irreducible nature of freedom?"[2]

A tendency exists in some quarters, perhaps especially in Europe and the USA, to think international problems get steadily worse, but 1964 was a more troubled time than 2019 as I write these lines. All of East Asia was immensely poorer than it is four decades later. Tumult beset the politics of a truculent Soviet Union. China exploded its first atomic weapon in 1964, rejecting the Test Ban Treaty signed by the three nuclear powers in 1963. In Beijing and Guangzhou, photos of Chinese children cheering at the news of President Kennedy's assassination nine months before made me pessimistic about U.S.-China relations.

However, I knew many Chinese did not believe each word the party-state said. In Beijing, David Wilson, then a young British diplomat, later British Governor of Hong Kong, told me of a recent rally against the Vietnam War. "I happened to be minding a friend's Dalmatian dog," said Wilson, "and I arrived at the [British] office in my red Triumph Spitfire with the dog sitting beside me. The people assembled for the demonstration against us burst into fits of laughter. It opened the whole atmosphere up—they let me pass through the door." Wilson said, "A fascination with the West and its goods existed" even in the China of 1964, "but it was suppressed." I suppose a red Triumph Spitfire, a mountainous Dalmation, and a Briton in a Scottish kilt was a spectacle for the people of Beijing.

A novice at age twenty-five, I did not realize in 1964 that "Liberation" was a facade behind which lay a mixture of social change, political control, and cultural continuity. Mao, it turned out, had more doubts about the results of the Liberation than Westerners who saw China in the early 1960s detected. Nikita Khrushchev was more prescient about the excesses of the Great Leap Forward communes than China specialists in the West were. He told Senator Hubert Humphrey, later U.S. vice-president, as early as December 1958 that they would certainly not succeed.

My last article for *The Australian* ended: "All around the world, from Singapore to San Francisco, you see pockets of Chinese society. Yet, only in China can you behold the vast and formidable civilization in its power and its old and beautiful setting. Only in China do you realize what the Chinese as a race and a nation must increasingly mean in the pattern of future decades. Just as once in the past, long before the present barren era of clashing ideologies and wrenching divisions, China was the greatest power on earth, so in the future she may become so again."[3]

I felt that observing this huge slice of humankind had launched me on a path that might last many years.

NOTES

1. The conversation is written up by the author in *Christian Century*, January 13, 1965.

2. Ross Terrill, "China Face to Face," *Australian*, Canberra, March 22, 1965.
"Goodwill is Big Business," March 23, 1965.
"In the Temple of Perfect Tranquility," March 24, 1965.
"Chinese are So Honest," March 25, 1965.
"Canton's Still in Business," March 26, 1965.
"China Sows the Seeds of Hate, March 27, 1965.

3. Ross Terrill, "China Sows the Seeds of Hate," *Australian*, Canberra, March 27, 1965, final part of series of six.

Chapter Three

Harvard's China

Wanting to learn Chinese and study modern China, I made applications to universities in Europe and the USA. It would be hard to tear myself away from Melbourne, where I was a junior activist in the Labor Party, but I hungered for a wider world. The London School of Economics and Harvard University both offered a Ph. D fellowship in political science. Having read Professor John Fairbank's *Trade and Diplomacy on the China Coast* inclined me to choose Harvard, where he taught. I also had a hunch that life in the U.S. would suit me better than life in "Mother England," as my grandmother called Britain.

The prickly China issue in U.S. politics almost put a stop to my reaching Harvard. Getting admission to the USA was difficult because of my 1964 visit to "Red China." As I packed for Massachusetts in September 1965, American officials in Melbourne denied me a visa, on the ground that I opposed the Vietnam War and favored recognition of the Beijing government. "Your views are incompatible with the American national purpose," wrote Consul Lin Roork in rejecting my application, like a surgeon telling me I belonged to the wrong blood group.

Carrying the letter of denial, I took a tram to the U.S. Consulate-General, pondering possible meanings of "American national purpose." Ms. Roork asked if I had been to China, and I admitted to this offense, citing curiosity as my motive. She pushed a stapled sheaf of papers across the desk. "Is that your signature on a petition to the United States government protesting our testing of nuclear weapons?" Yes. "Do you see who signed the petition next after you?" I looked at the column of signatures and recognized the name of a well-known Melbourne Communist. Miss Roork was not impressed when I said that you never know who might come and sign a petition after you have signed it.

Life, alas, is less a debate than a struggle, and it was not counter argument but the intervention of the Labor Party that reversed the verdict. The Leader of the Opposition, Arthur Calwell, wrote to the American ambassador in Canberra saying that I was a social democrat with no Communist connections. Miss Roork backed down graciously, gave me a visa, and wished me well in the United States.

On a warm September day in 1965, I arrived in Boston, with just a few hours to register at Harvard and find accommodation. I saw a notice on a bulletin board. "Mr. J. Vincent" offered a room for rent. Unaware of what lay ahead, I spent my first night in Massachusetts under the roof of a celebrated victim of the American "Loss of China." "Mr. J. Vincent" was John Carter Vincent, formerly of the State Department and posts all over China, starting in Changsha in 1928. In retirement, after secretary of state John Foster Dulles removed him from the Foreign Service, this senior purged China Hand had chosen the liberal atmosphere of Cambridge.

A few weeks later, sitting in front of Professor Fairbank's desk, I proposed a Ph. D thesis on the 19th century political philosopher Kang Youwei. "How is your Classical Chinese?" Fairbank shot back. Having just begun modern Chinese language class, I realized I would have to wait years to read Kang in old Chinese. However, a shiver of delight ran down my spine at meeting the man who virtually founded the study of modern Chinese history in the U.S.

I was on the way to friendship with two of the most influential U.S. China Hands of the mid-twentieth century. Vincent, who had spent fourteen years in China and been Secretary of State Acheson's chief China officer; and Fairbank, a former U.S. government official in Chongqing in the 1940s, now doyen of China studies in the U.S. Could I in Cambridge study Chinese and the politics of China and begin to understand Mao's realm?

From my rented room in Vincent's house, I trudged through the snow to my classes on Chinese language from a Taiwan teacher, Chinese history from Fairbank, and political philosophy from leading scholars. I felt small and alone in this famous world of Harvard. For many months, I doubted I could succeed against fierce competition and sky-high standards. I also had to get used to the Taiwan-orientation of China studies at Harvard. In Australia, few took much notice of Taiwan, but Cambridge was different. I did not think Chiang Kai-shek's regime in Taiwan was China, but the U.S. government and many Americans did.

One morning in my second semester at Harvard, my class was a lecture by Benjamin Schwartz on current Chinese politics. Everything was "complex," he warned us, his expressive eyes bulging. One approach to the PRC was "totalitarianism," of which Schwartz was skeptical:

"It doesn't fit the Chinese case." Schwartz also said, "Modernization theory doesn't explain very much." Of Communist systems such as the PRC and the Soviet Union, the professor wondered, "Perhaps the future will bring more individual liberty, together with an elite at the top making all the big decisions. Indeed, some say the U.S. itself is moving in this direction."

Schwartz studied Mao's ideology closely; that was his strength as a scholar. However, ideology close to home discomforted him. Like many other liberal China Hands, he was tortured by the intrusion of the anti-Vietnam War movement into China discussion; and somewhat incoherent when it came to policy.

As an indirect result of being in Vincent's house as a tenant, I wrote an essay on his career in *Atlantic Monthly*, under the title "When America Lost China: The Case of John Carter Vincent."[1] The piece was a sensation in some political circles. It said tartly and with exaggeration, "Just as Mao Zedong conjured up the myth of Liu Shaoqi's apostasy to guard the image of his own leadership as correct and wise, so certain mandarins in Washington conjured up a myth of the China Hands' apostasy in order to guard their image of American leadership as Omni competent and innocent. It proved more satisfying to say America could have stopped Mao if the China Hands like Vincent had not betrayed their country, than to admit that the world was a very complicated place, diverse in culture, polycentric in power, in which prudence and tolerance might be worth as much as zeal."

I wrote in my diary the next month, "Dinner with the Vincent's. We look through letters they have received about my *Atlantic* essay. Former secretary of state Dean Acheson wrote warmly. So did Elizabeth and Arthur Schlesinger, the historian and advisor to President Kennedy. Also, a number of former colleagues from diplomatic posts in China, Morocco, and Switzerland wrote nice letters to John Carter and Betty."

One day Vincent showed me a letter he had written to his wife from Chongqing in 1942. "Had dinner with Madame Sun Yatsen. Dick Smith was the other foreigner present; the rest . . . were Chinese. Madame C[hiang Kai-shek] was also there. We played bad bridge afterwards until very late . . . Dick and I both like the Chinese and they recognize it. More than that: there is no conscious or subconscious feeling of superiority and they recognize it. There is no question of 'using' each other's company. We are simply enjoying each other's company. That is hardly normal in China. Even the missionaries 'love' with a purpose."

Betty Vincent was more rough-edged than her diplomat husband. She had strong opinions, especially about American right-wingers who had done in Vincent's career. She also sharply distinguished, after many years of living in East Asia, between Chinese and Japanese. "Lovely bones, the Chinese have lovely bones, so firm and clear," she said one evening. "The Japanese have no bones."

I later expanded the *Atlantic* essay on Vincent into a chapter in a book of essays, *China and Ourselves*, which I coedited.[2] Edgar Snow, the pioneer journalist in Mao's China and author of *Red Star over China*. wrote a warm preface to the book. He was enthusiastic about my chapter on Vincent. He called it "trenchant," and said it deserved "four cheers." On a trip to Europe, the Vincent's' stayed with Ed and Lois Snow in Switzerland. From Naples, Betty Vincent wrote, "We saw Edgar and Lois and great was our rejoicing. We spoke of your book, and the Snows said they had seen an early review that said your chapter on J.C. was brilliant."

I admired Snow's career and several of his books. He was, of course, a man of his era. His faith in the Chinese Communists was part of a hope in a better future for mankind. The era was less crowded, less cynical, more naive than our own. People were carried to great heights, and depths, by ideas; "revolution" was a term that exhilarated not only Marxists but many liberals.

Snow had "a romantic vision of independence both for himself and for others," as his biographer wrote.[3] His errors on China were those of an honest optimist who felt outside the establishment of his own country, who instinctively embraced hope as the necessary basis for a moral course.

I was more disturbed by Snow's bleak view of America than his fairly rosy—yet far from euphoric—view of China. Some of his deep-rooted personal frustrations were projected into shadows on his view of American institutions. While he was never cynical about China, he came to be so about mainstream America. Overly influenced by Spengler's *Decline of the West*, he failed to foresee the resilience of capitalism and the ongoing positive role for America in Asia.

Snow wanted Americans to judge the Chinese Communists by a moral yardstick—were they good for the Chinese people, did they match the values of brotherhood he learned in Missouri? It might have been better to weigh the case in terms of American interests—would a Communist China serve or undermine the American position in Asia? Some of his insights into Mao's revolution could have fitted well into the second optic.

In many ways, Snow, for complex reasons rejected America more than America rejected him—long before his years in Switzerland.

As I was one of the very few people at Harvard who had been in Mao's China, I was viewed as a kind of messenger from China. Churches in Boston invited me to speak on what I had seen. A department store in Connecticut asked me to enlighten its customers about "this Mao Zedong." The Harvard student guide to world travel, *Let's Go*, hearing about my presence on campus, commissioned an article on "Travel to Red China" for their next edition. It was the first time *Let's Go* had included the topic of travel to the PRC.[4] Even Fairbank asked me questions about my 1964 experience in China.

Fairbank was tall and benign, often in a bow tie, and quick to give a slight smile. A kindly and single-minded professor, he offered total attention to any person talking with him. He would stride across the Harvard campus with head down, mentally drafting a letter demanding a job for a graduate student, or seeking funds for China studies from the Ford Foundation. His dedication inspired much loyalty and gratitude.

When Fairbank went to Oxford University in 1929, the field of modern Chinese history hardly existed in the West. Living in Beijing from 1932, he learned Chinese and turned himself into a historian of China, a student of its language and society, and a pedagogue with an eye for the betterment of the world.

As a young Harvard professor, Fairbank arrived in Chongqing to work on cultural affairs at the U.S. in 1941. His fundamental concern was the accumulation of knowledge, and a social environment in which knowledge could lead to peace and happiness. He was neither very political nor worldly. He possessed an idealist's notion of progress as the child of enlightenment. Get the data, know other cultures first-hand, and understanding will result.

In wartime Chongqing, and later in Shanghai, Fairbank acquired materials on China for American educational institutions, set up exchanges between Chinese and American scholars, and befriended Chinese liberals who hovered uneasily between the Nationalists of Chiang Kai-shek and the Communist Party (CCP). He tried to bring the Chinese history he learned at Oxford in the late 1920s and in Beijing during the early 1930s into alignment with the churning society that he was observing first-hand.

From Chongqing, Fairbank wrote to Mary Wright, an historian friend at Yale that he felt "definitely unlike a scholar of the old school of liberal both-sides-objectivity. The world is full of many bastards and one's only duty is to work against them . . . the battle goes on everywhere and scholarship is either an effective part of it or meaningless."

Of Zhou Enlai's Communist group in Chongqing, he wrote to his mother, "Our impression of them generally is very favorable. . . [They] are more like one of the religious communities of a century ago than anything else I can think of."[5] He later said candidly of his personal mindset in Chongqing: "The CCP as the living embodiment of the cause became the parental figure in the life of the believer."[6] It was a damning admission.

In the second preface to his great book *Trade and Diplomacy on the China Coast* Fairbank said it was a kind of accident he got into the study of China. Yet I felt Fairbank and China were a match. I once asked him, "What is the secret of the unity you said you observed in China?" He replied, "The concern that comes out of the culture for rational, orderly procedures." Here was what he admired in China and here was a trait of Fairbank's own values and conduct. Perhaps it was more than an accident that Fairbank and China came together.

To say "China" in the U.S. in the mid-1960s and later-1960s was to conjure up two related unsettling images. One was of the Chinese masses as a bottomless pit of support for the Vietnamese Communists in their war to pull Saigon out of America's reach. The other image was of Mao's unique revolution, with its communes, class struggle ideology, hostility to the West, and Spartan ways, perhaps a sign of the rising power of the East.

During 1965, I wrote a four-part series on China in *The New Republic* magazine, which aroused debate about these images.[7] One fellow graduate student assailed me in a letter to the editor of *TNR* entitled "Road to Xanadu." He did not like my frequent mention of Mao. He complained that I lacked experience of China prior to 1949 (as he did too). He said I was deceived by "the exotica of a revolutionary mass society." He seemed to think an Australian shouldn't comment on China when Americans knew much more about it. We almost came to blows one afternoon.

I was also criticized from the left. "New Left" students saw a New Man in China and sought a similar miracle in America. I did not share this vision. Moreover, most Americans, being individualists, recoiled from collective political emotion, so the majority view of the Cultural Revolution, beyond the campuses, was negative. Of course, the U.S. being what it was, negatives sometimes went to extremes, as American enthusiasms could go to extremes. This was America's alternating love and hate for China.

An American's view of loyalty had to do with his ideals as an individual. The Chinese is no less loyal, but his nationality and family ties define his loyalties; to an American, he can seem to lack loyalty as an individual.

The New Left generation of China specialists attacked the idea of the PRC as America's enemy. The U.S. alienation from Beijing was our fault, these scholars in their twenties suggested; the PRC was a beacon of hope, not a threat. As American campuses sprouted anti-Vietnam War protests, left-wingers interpreted Mao's Great Leap Forward as an exciting rejection of old ways, both capitalist and Soviet-socialist.

At a leading book store I found all the China books in a section called "Revolutionary Studies." The Harvard Coop, the largest book store in the area, added to its sections of books on "Education," "Fiction," Politics," and so on a new section called "Dissent," and here one found pro-Maoist books, pro-Viet Cong books, pro-Castro books and so on. China as "area studies" was swallowed up by China as "revolutionary studies" or "voices of dissent."

Classes were disrupted, professors were shouted down, bombs were thrown at military ROTC buildings, and "strikes" against university authority were organized. East Asian studies at Harvard was gripped by daily debate over what Washington should do about Vietnam, China's relation to the war, and the impact of the crisis on Sinology.

After a Harvard East Asian studies student-faculty meeting on Vietnam I wrote in my diary, "What amazes me as an Australian is the boldness with which students talk to their teachers—and the way the teachers take it. One kid got up and said Reischauer [who had been President Kennedy's ambassador to Japan] was a coward not to speak up against the war. Reischauer listened gravely and said very little." James Peck, a fellow graduate student, told Fairbank to his face he was 'just an American imperialist, repressing Asian people.'" This same Fairbank was lambasted from the right during the Senator Joseph McCarthy period.

Vincent often pointed out to me that Fairbank and Reischauer did not know Southeast Asia, only China and Japan, respectively, so they were unprepared for Vietnam. In the 1930s and 1940s, Americans neglected the rest of Asia, Vincent explained, because it was in the "dirty colonial hands" of France, Britain and others.

However, even among senior China specialists, there was discontent with the East Asia policies of President Johnson, who had come to the White House in November 1963. Embargos on the PRC throughout the Eisenhower and Kennedy years were mostly still in place. Students could not go to the PRC; that disappointed the professors. Journalists were unable to report from China; that frustrated the newspaper editors. Clergy could not preach the Christian gospel from Shanghai pulpits; that saddened former missionaries.

Fairbank, facing a polarized atmosphere, as in Chongqing during World War 2, tried to steer a middle course that did not exist. This was not only because he had imbibed Confucian doctrines of moderation and balance; Fairbank always preferred pedagogy to prophecy. He simply wanted to protect a generation of graduate students from political conflagration, so they would go on to become scholars of China.

At the height of the Cultural Revolution, I published an article on China's "siege mentality" toward the world and I asked Fairbank when China's sense of grievance about the international order would end. He replied, "It is un-Confucian for the Chinese to attribute so much causation to forces outside China." Because it was un-Confucian to self-portray China as a victim beset on all sides, Fairbank thought (correctly) that Beijing would one day modify if not reject the "siege mentality."[8]

"Area specialists by definition try to stand between cultures," Fairbank told us in one of his seminars. This, however, can be an awkward place to stand, as Americans have often learned in the Middle East, and in China.

In September, 1972, Stuart Schram of the University of London, invited Fairbank, myself, and others to a conference on contemporary China at a Manor House in southern England. After his talk, in answer to a question about China-U.S. relations, Fairbank said: "Perhaps it would have been a good thing if one of the bombs America dropped on Japan in 1945 had blown up over the U.S.—maybe Chicago—because then Americans would have understood the bomb's power and perhaps behaved differently in the postwar world." This was a shocking remark, which probably Fairbank would not have uttered on American soil. Perhaps it showed a scholar's sincere attempt to stand between two cultures and see reality "from the other side's point of view."

China specialists have sometimes taken exaggerated positions for or against China. The illustrious diplomat George Keenan even said that, whereas those who studied the Soviet Union ended up hating the Soviet Union, those who studied China ended up hating themselves. The China specialist can lapse into using his own entrails to construct the world. "The sincerity of our beliefs does not ensure their worldwide triumph," Fairbank remarked sagely.

In a letter to a former Melbourne classmate, I wrote of the disjunction I felt between the smooth life of Cambridge and the trauma the U.S. was inflicting on Vietnam: "The weekend air is full of loudspeakers on elections to the local school committee. Frenzy about a bloody school committee, but hardly a thought for the carnage in Vietnam! It seems a symbol of Americans' lack of historical sense at their impact on the world."

I felt some Americans failed to understand China's re-entry into world history. In *Motive*, a left-of-center monthly magazine, I wrote in 1966, "Qing Dynasty China could be seen as exotic because we managed to force her into the Procrustean bed of our imperialist pattern. Mao's China has to be seen as a threat because she declines to cooperate with our efforts to fit her into that successor to European imperialism, the Pax Americana." Perhaps passion carried me too far about the U. S.'s faults. "The U. S., stronghold of a liberal idealism and optimism that Europe is too weary to retain," I wrote, "sallies forth, quivering with power, uttering liberal rhetoric, to bid up a fragmented Asia. That Pax Americana can replace European imperialism, however, is doubted in many parts of the world. China is potentially the greatest resisting force to a new co-prosperity sphere on Washington's terms."[9] I believed France and Britain could look more steadily at the PRC because "they have known in their bones" the setbacks during the later 20th century to the West's sense of entitlement.

Some of us at Harvard were afraid of a widened war. "The Americans can only 'win' by destroying Vietnam," I wrote in another letter to a Labor Party leader in Melbourne. They cannot win in the sense of winning Vietnam over, because they have no social faith to offer. And the obsession with China is so great here, even among otherwise calm and reasonable people, that it is quite likely the Americans will keep pounding away [at Vietnam] until they can also, with some shred of excuse, pound away at China too." In the *Motive* essay, I rashly declared, "It is not to express hostility to liberalism, but merely to observe history, to say Beijing's very existence today as a center of Asian Communist power constitutes a historical nightmare for those who make absolute the values of the liberal Christian West."

Soon after Henry Cabot Lodge came back from being U.S. ambassador in Saigon, I chatted with him in Cambridge about the Vietnam War. "My grand-children have been talking to me," he said over a glass of sherry at the Harvard

Figure 3.1. Before the years of conflict, Mao with Liu Shaoqi, Deng Xiaoping (far right). Zhou Enlai (far left) and Chen Yun (second left), discussing Vietnam. Charles L. and Lois Smith Collection on Contemporary China, Harvard-Yenching Library, Harvard University.

Faculty Club, explaining how his views had changed. "And my wife—she gets bothered by the scenes of Vietnam on TV. The war is a tragedy—we must get it over with."

One evening William Bundy, a leading foreign policy official in Washington for some years, came to speak at Harvard. Bundy seemed to blame the American public for not staying the course in Vietnam. At one point he remarked that Americans had "declined the gauntlet" in Vietnam. At dinner afterwards, Fairbank went out of his way to tell Bundy of my *Atlantic* piece on Vincent. "Oh yes, that was a terrible case," the East Coast mandarin said airily. I noted in my diary, "But Bundy didn't show any enthusiasm; even, I thought, some discomfort. And the question remains why even the slightest gesture was not made to Vincent by the Kennedy and Johnson Democratic administrations of the 1960s."

After a couple of drinks one night in November 1968, Vincent confided that when he was head of the Far East Division at the State Department, he said to Secretary of State Acheson that it would be a good idea to give responsibility, and promotion, to Dean Rusk, for he seemed a good and reasonable man. He also told me that in the previous week's presidential election he voted, not for the Democratic candidate for President, but for the Socialist.

I wrote in my diary after two years of knowing Vincent. "John Carter is a different breed from the other two ex-ambassadors around Harvard—John Kenneth Galbraith [Kennedy's ambassador to India] and Edwin Reischauer. He reminds me of an America at once refreshing and hard to credit. What brought this man down? Simply the perils of dealing with China? The system? McCarthy's one-man crusade? Beyond arises another question: Who runs this society, where does power really lie in the U.S.? I do not yet know. Perhaps Wright Mills was right to detect a hidden Power Elite. Perhaps it's just that American society is a headless monster, like so many other entities that at first appear to have a personality and a unity."

One night at the Vincent's' home, Betty, bidding me farewell, leaned down from the top of the stairs and said, "I can never thank you enough for what you've done for John Carter." Yet he had done more for me, a young arrival from Australia. He was a classy man, a sincere diplomat, and a real friend of China. I never knew Vincent to have an ulterior motive. He hated stupidity and injustice. He did not suffer fools gladly; nor was he impressed with people whose only good point was that they were trying to do good.

During that same visit, Vincent said to me, "For sheer sentimentality, I've been reading Ann Bridge's novel *Peking Picnic*. It was under the moonlit pines of that wonderful city that Mrs. V and I became betrothed." The pair of them loved Beijing (of course, it was the old Peking) until their dying days.

Others of the purged China diplomats came to visit Harvard. Fairbank organized a dinner at the Signet Society for John Paton Davies, hounded from the State Department after China fell to Mao. Davies was visiting the U.S. from Peru, where he earned his (post-diplomat) living carving furniture.

Davies was an engaging man with bright eyes and boyish wit. He was born in China of Protestant missionary parents. He served in many China posts and in the Soviet Union. During an important period, he was political advisor to the commander of the China-Burma-India Theater. Davies was awarded the Medal of Freedom for an amazing parachute jump into the Burma jungle during World War 2.

During our dinner, Davies, like Fairbank, dwelled on America's religious and social involvement with the Chinese people. It struck me that missionary and educational experiences had deeply influenced key American China Hands. After dinner Harold Isaacs of MIT, himself with long residence in China, asked Davies what he had really thought of the Chinese during his years in China and what had they thought of him. Davies confessed that in retrospect, although China had been his life, very few Chinese became his friends.[10] That puzzled and discouraged me. It was a remark I would store in mind until, with much happiness, I eventually became close friends during the 1980s with Chinese across the PRC.

John Stewart Service also visited Harvard at the invitation of Fairbank. Born in Chengdu, Service, too, was the son of Protestant missionaries. Lean and hardworking, he was known in China, from his first posting in Kunming in 1933, for acute observation of geography and physical detail, and later for his good Chinese. Service's sessions with Mao in the early 1940s provided influential guidance for the U.S. Government.

After leaving the Foreign Service, Service found employment at the University of California as a librarian. He was working on a memoir of his mother that later came out as *Golden Inches: The China Memoir of Grace Service*.[11]

Service was a good-natured man, though bitter about the attacks he had endured from Senator McCarthy. However, he told me he found the views of the anti-Vietnam War leftists "a bit apocalyptic." He remained the liberal diplomat, bewildered by extremes. I wrote in my diary, "Vincent, Service and Davies, all really knew China. They clashed with people who created a China out of their own psychological and political ideology."

Despite all, Elliott Richardson wrote Betty Vincent a nice letter, after Richard Nixon's election in 1968, from his new post as Under Secretary of State: "The recent granting of a security clearance to Mr. [John Paton] Davies was a welcome sign that the kind of thinking which forced your husband's resignation is no longer prevalent here."

Henry Kissinger was one of our professors of government. His seminar, "National Security Policy," was popular. To any registered graduate student of our department, all professors readily gave advice and contacts for a foreign trip. One day in early 1968, I walked into Kissinger's office in Divinity Avenue to seek help. He was in shirtsleeves and a dark blue tie. Would Prof. Kissinger please give some advice for a forthcoming trip to East Europe? I did not tell him I planned to attend a Peace Conference, knowing he would not approve of such left-wing idealism.

While I was in Kissinger's office, the phone rang and a secretary asked me to step outside. I learned Kissinger had been talking with Nelson Rockefeller, former Governor of New York and a candidate for the Republican nomination in the presidential election of 1968. Kissinger was his foreign policy advisor. At that time, Kissinger conveyed no particular interest in China. He was the opposite of an "area specialist." He knew enough languages already (including German and French) without wanting to learn another one for the purpose of area study.

Still, Kissinger, even in 1968, was keenly concerned with relations between China and the Soviet Union. He had begun to think in his characteristically broad, geopolitical way about required adjustments in U.S. foreign policy to profit from the chill between Beijing and Moscow. Within a year of our first talk, Kissinger would be in Washington. Rockefeller lost to Nixon in the Republican primaries, Nixon became president, and Kissinger his national security adviser. Soon I would have dealings with this German-born wizard in exciting ways, as China became Kissinger's constant preoccupation.

Susan Lubochova, a Czech scholar to whom Henry introduced me, later presented herself to me in Prague as if she had been his girlfriend. I do not know if that was true, but she was a marvelous guide to the exciting Czechoslovakian situation, when I visited East Europe a month later.

After Nixon became president, and Kissinger became national security advisor, Vincent asked Stanley Hoffman, Kissinger's former colleague in the Government Department and other guests to a party. I wrote in my diary, "Stanley said Henry Kissinger is a European-type conservative and a neat match, from the Intelligentsia, for Richard Nixon's businessman's prudence. He is persuaded of doom. Will not give himself to anything remotely approaching humanism." Hoffman, a leading professor of international relations, complained that in recent decades "a readiness to intervene, trampling on self-government if necessary, has blossomed in American foreign policy."

Why had it occurred? I asked the gathering. Vincent called out from the kitchen, "Because of the Chinese Revolution."

With Nixon the new president, Lee Kuan Yew, prime minister of Singapore, during a visit to the U.S. came to Harvard. I had lunch with him and a few China specialists. Afterwards I wrote in my diary, "I think he came to the U.S. to check out two opposite fears: of U.S. disengagement from Asia, and of a U.S. toughening in the wake of the Vietnam defeat, which would provoke China. He probably goes home to Singapore with the conclusion that a measure of U.S. disengagement is on the cards, but probably not enough to make him panicky."

This was indeed how Nixon, closely advised by Kissinger, proceeded in his six years in office, 1968–1974. He was prudent, but fortunately, for the U.S. and China alike, he did not fold America's tent and leave Asia.

NOTES

1. "When America Lost China, The Case of John Carter Vincent," *Atlantic Monthly*, Vol. 224, No. 5, November, 1969.

2. Ross Terrill & Bruce Douglass, eds. *China and Ourselves*, Preface by Edgar Snow, Boston, Beacon Press, 1969.

3. John Maxwell Hamilton, *Edgar Snow*, Bloomington, Indiana, 1988, Prologue.

4. *Let's Go*, Harvard Student Agencies, Cambridge, MA, 1965.

5. Both letters, Paul Evans, *John Fairbank and the American Understanding of Modern China*, New York, Blackwell, 1988, 72, 92.

6. Fairbank, *Chinabound*, New York, Harper, 1982, 285.

7. *New Republic*, "A Trip to China I," *New Republic*, January 2, 1965; "A Trip to China II," *New Republic* ; January 16, 1965; "A Trip to China III," *New Republic*, January 23, 1965; "China Birth Control and Bibles," February 6, 1965.

8. "The Siege Mentality," *Problems of Communism*, March–April, 1967.

9. Ross Terrill, "Whose China Problem?" *Motive*, February 1968, 7.

10. Dinner (attended by the author) at Signet Society, Harvard, May 14, 1969.

11. Service, interview, ADST-LOC.

Chapter Four

Tiananmen Square and Harvard Square

Students of China at Harvard had to peer at the Cultural Revolution through a double curtain. Access to Beijing was minimal. There were no American diplomats or businesspersons resident in China to observe the Red Guards and "class struggle." Virtually the only non-Communist bloc journalists to penetrate the issues and pathologies of the Cultural Revolution were the Japanese. My letters to clergyman Zhao Fusan and other acquaintances from 1964 sank into China without trace. I received a letter of approval for a China visa in 1967, but by the time I reached Hong Kong to claim it, a message arrived: "We regret that your idea of visiting China during 1967 has to be abandoned." The gyrations of the Cultural Revolution made my visit "inconvenient."

Second curtain was Vietnam. The Vietnam War confused the American view of China. Vice-President Hubert Humphrey in 1964 spoke ominously (and with partial truth) of an "Oriental red chain of command" that stemmed from Beijing to Hanoi. Differing, I tried to fit the Vietnam War, China, and my experience in the Australian Labor Party into a framework of public values. This was considered unusual. Many Harvard professors, learned as they were, ignored China or confined it to the realm of the exotic.

My German-born teacher of political philosophy, the eminent Carl Friedrich, said to me one day after class, "Mao's thought is childish. Undigested Marx—he does not understand Aristotelian logic." Another professor of political philosophy, Judith Shklar, reacted badly, chain-smoking her Parliament-brand cigarettes, when my essay for her on the ideas of Edmund Burke and Thomas Paine at the time of the French Revolution made a comparison with Chinese political thinkers. Not only had the brilliant Shklar, author of *After Utopia*, never heard of the military philosopher Sun Zi and the founder of Taoism, Lao Zi; she laughed at the very idea their philosophies could be of interest.

One of my best professors, the Soviet specialist Adam Ulam, told me he thought the crucial context of the Cultural Revolution was that the Russians were aiming to provoke civil war in China. "A strong, Communist China is a terrible threat to Moscow," he said. "You cannot overestimate the desperation Moscow feels about this." Whether at Soviet prompting, out of domestic Chinese political dynamics, or through American military pressure, the Cultural Revolution as a prelude to Chinese collapse was widely supported at Harvard.

I was reluctant to confine China to the realm of the exotic. Innocent, I was eager to find connections between Chinese struggles over power and principle and Western experience of such conflicts. I tackled China studies at the same time as I researched the democratic socialist ideas of the British historian R. H. Tawney for my Ph.D. thesis. I identified twin evils of concentration of power (the drawback of communism) and concentration of wealth (the weakness of capitalism). I believed that social democracy could avoid both evils.

I also favored an American policy in East Asia that accepted a give-and-take with other powers. "We cannot view China any longer as if we, the West, constituted a fixed point," I wrote in my *Motive* essay, "with China merely the object of our attention. China and the West are now together on an open sea."

The late 1960s at Harvard and other schools was a time of wrenching feuds over East Asia policies, quickly-sprouting student politicians, families divided at the dinner table, students occupying university buildings, proliferating committee meetings, tense riots, and smoky bombings. As China's Cultural Revolution unfolded, a small but highly educated segment of the U.S., many on Ivy League campuses, experienced a cultural upheaval of its own. For privileged young people in revolt against authority, the official U.S. hostility to Communist China was itself enough to make them pro-China. In eighteen months, during the counter-cultural phase of 1967–1968, a single firm, China Books and Periodicals in San Francisco, sold 250,000 copies within the United States of Mao's *Quotations*, mainly to young Americans.

At a student-faculty meeting, Fairbank was assailed to his face for "prettifying American aggression in Asia" and being "hostile to socialist China." Another of my professors, hearing my comments on Vietnam, called me a "firebrand."

From Beijing, a real firebrand, the journalist Anna Louise Strong, offered fuel to the campus radicals of her native land. Born to a congregational clergy family in Nebraska, she had been the youngest woman to receive a Ph. D at the University of Chicago, with a thesis on "The Psychology of Prayer."

She transferred her faith from Christianity, to the Soviet Union, eventually to Mao's China. She resided in a wing of the former Italian embassy, now a "Peace" compound, which was as palatial as Anna Louise's spirit was Spartan.

Strong defended every twist of Mao's 1960s madness. She took a "proprietary attitude toward the Chinese Revolution as [she previously had for] the Soviet Union, " said her friend Helen Snow, first wife of Edgar Snow. Locked up in a Russian prison in 1949, she observed, "I just missed the Russian revolution and now I've just missed the Chinese revolution." However, she didn't miss the Cultural Revolution. As chaos mounted in the capital, Strong wrote a "Letter from China" to contacts around the world, including me. Her "Letter" resembled the sermons of her clergyman father in Nebraska, with China substituted for the Gospel.

To Strong and some other Americans a symbiosis existed, with Vietnam as a common ingredient, between the mood of the 1960s in the United States and Western Europe, and the turbulence of the Cultural Revolution in China. A similarity of impulse was detected between the idealism of the newly established U.S. Peace Corps and the apparent idealism of the Chinese Red Guards. Were we Harvard students not natural Maoists in seeing a disjunction of values between authority and grassroots, and in feeling the structures around us had to change if we were to be happy?

However, it was not so. In China, the Red Guards were manipulated and the professors were ordered, "To go to the countryside." And in the U.S., hoped-for alternatives to an "oppressive society" were elusive. American students talked of escaping urban life for rural "communes." Few did so. I wrote in my diary, "Alternative forms of society, locally, nationally, and internationally, are mighty hard to detect."

American leftists seemed to think a change of lifestyle amounted to "revolution." Blue jeans, loud music, drugs, the sport of Frisbee, and organic food grown in communal gardens equaled a new society. A book that became a bestseller, *The Greening of America*, by Charles Reich declared: "Choice of a lifestyle is not peripheral, it is the heart of the new awakening. What is coming is nothing less than a new way of life and a new man." But a new man was slow to appear in either Harvard Square or Tiananmen Square.

Four strands of thinking existed in the U.S. on China. Strand One was the Johnson administration's point of view, less distant from that of the Eisenhower years than usually thought. Washington followed the formulation of the British leader Alex Douglas-Home in believing the "thin" Communists in Beijing were even more dangerous than the "fat" ones in Moscow. Both Kennedy up to 1963 and Johnson thereafter felt the Chinese Communists would have to change their behavior before the U.S. would deal seriously with them. The American embassy to China continued to sit in Taipei, which hampered Washington's policy toward Beijing.

A fear of China intervening in Vietnam understandably worried Johnson. But he ended up with muddle in both Vietnam policy and China policy. He moderated his actions in Vietnam in 1968, yet without gaining any benefit in relations with China. He reduced American support for Chiang Kai-shek's desire to retake the Chinese mainland, yet without achieving a coherent new PRC policy to replace that of Dulles.

Strand Two was that of mid-level China officials in the Johnson administration. I talked with some of them in Washington and in Cambridge. Publicly they were hard-line toward the PRC; they had to be. Some of them felt Johnson, obsessed with Vietnam, was dealing less well with China policy than had Kennedy. Marshall Green, later a senior figure in Asia policy, expressed the private feelings of some diplomat China Hands: "The death of Kennedy in late 1963 put a great damper on all that we were trying to do to bring about a new attitude towards China. Also, things were going on in China [!!!]. And there was our deepening involvement in Vietnam. The new President [Johnson] was totally wrapped up in Vietnam."[1]

In truth, China folk in the State Department were semi-paralyzed in their own thinking. They were anxious at Johnson's policies in Indochina. However, their own preferred China policy lacked an architecture for the overall East Asia situation. They favored "talks" with Beijing, but on peripheral issues little related to geopolitics, which really counted.

Strand Three was the academic Sinologists, my teachers. Most of them were middle-of-the-road liberals. Some senior figures, including Fairbank, had been wounded by McCarthyism and were definitely not inclined to anti-communism. But few had sympathy for the revolutionary left. Most were uneasy at Johnson's deployment of massive U.S. military power on China's doorstep and clung to a liberal hope in the magic words "talks" and "full diplomatic relations."

My professors were oriented to pedagogy and naïve on policy. A key journal, *China Quarterly*, skillfully sifted the limited available data from China, but seemed stalled on foreign policy analysis, simply wishing the horrible distraction of Vietnam would go away. The Sinologists backed Johnson's wariness lest Beijing intervene militarily in the Vietnam War as it had in Korea.

Strand Four was the campus and media counter-cultural left, already mentioned. On campuses, a new crop of young China Hands saw U.S. policy in Vietnam as the trigger of the Cultural Revolution. They believed the U.S. had no right to be in Vietnam and no moral authority to sit in judgment on

Mao's communism. They cried, with little evidence, that U.S. alienation from Beijing was the fault of capitalist America.

The new anti-Vietnam War generation of China analysts, many speaking excellent Chinese from study in Taiwan, lacked any pre-1949 or McCarthy-era memories. To them the PRC was an inspiration, not a threat; the U.S. should welcome and learn from it, they said. They bestowed on China's wretched Cultural Revolution a ray of reflected hope for an America supposedly in darkness.

Strand Four had a major effect (eventually) on Johnson's Vietnam policy, but little direct effect on his China-policy (other than to help shorten his entire presidency). Nevertheless, these radicals captured the attention of America. For several years, they held center stage in the media and liberal urban public opinion, offering a negative view of American society and the U.S. role in the world.

One evening during the Harvard "bust," when police arrived in force to end student occupation of a key Harvard Yard building, I saw the film "The Virgin and the Gypsy," based on D. H. Lawrence's novel, at a nearby cinema. A Christian clergyman, who maintained a very strict household of three generations in the face of a rebellious daughter, says to his wild daughter, "Yvette, this can't go on." She responds: "Yes, it can. Because there will come a time when grandmother will be dead, and you will be dead, and I will still be alive."

Coming out of the cinema into Harvard Square, I saw black-clad police with tight jaws and ugly sticks angrily beating back a crowd. The folk in retreat were mostly young. A lot wore unconventional clothes. Some sang peace songs to the strumming of a guitar. Many smoked marijuana. "Nothing has happened yet," a passer-by said to me, referring to the expected assault on the occupied Harvard building, "It's just that a young guy insulted a cop and they're kicking everyone out of the Square."

I returned to my study in Kirkland House, between Harvard Square and the Charles River, and wrote in my diary, "So Lawrence's lesson goes unlearned. Again, values are defended that cannot long be defended. Again, those in authority confuse moral protest with law-breaking, and the fury over the latter makes inevitable a deepening of the former."

Yvette's words in the film highlighted the foolishness, I felt, of opposing youth root-and-branch, as many officials and professors at Harvard were doing. "The police just don't like the way of life of the youth who gather in Harvard Square," I continued in my diary. "Self-important upholding of 'law and order' is incidental to their aggrieved resentment against a youthful beauty and liberty their generation seldom knew."

Rightly or wrongly, I supported youth's cultural iconoclasm because I saw in it a hope for a transformation of America's role in Asia. "However, much youth lack 'balance,'" I wrote, "they have burst out of the garden of American innocence, and called in question American Prometheanism." I felt the alienation of American youth had become a problem in itself. "I expected it," I wrote in my diary, "because Washington was never going to stop this Vietnam War short of the alienation of its best youth. This has now happened." I found a connection, at the time, between students flinging off the authority of rigid education structures, on the one hand, and Vietnamese and other Third World peoples resisting Pax Americana, on the other hand.

Whether America's radical students resembled China's Red Guards was another question entirely.

Milan Bogdanovic of the Yugoslav news agency Tanjug came to Harvard to talk about the Cultural Revolution with China specialists. A dozen of us, together with two leading American journalists, dined at the Faculty Club. Bogdanovic had been eight years in Beijing as Tanjug correspondent. He was a bright, slightly cynical man. Perhaps as a Yugoslav, offered the competing paradises of Moscow and Beijing, he had to be a skeptic.

Bogdanovic was well informed and very negative about the Cultural Revolution. "I watched a Russian military attaché besieged for four hours, a picture of Mao held within inches of his face," he said tensely. "Afterwards this man, a hero of Stalingrad, wept like a child. I was shocked."

Said Bogdanovic: "Coming from a Communist country myself, where the police are powerful, the *ne plus ultra* of rebellion came when I saw the police minister's name, Xie Fuzhi, preceded by "Hang" and followed by "X." This message was painted on the building of the Ministry of Security. When I saw that, I doubted mankind had a future." The "X" had been written by Red Guards as a kind of "pointing of the bone," a threatening attack meant to signal Xie's doom.

Bogdanovic stunned the table of Americans by saying: "The last United States election campaign, which I came to straight into after returning from China, reminded me very much of the Cultural Revolution. Purges, labeling of enemies, careless stuff about traitors. . . ."

"No, no," interrupted an outraged editor from the *Washington Post*, "there are big, big differences." Dishes of Boston cod arrived, calming the atmosphere.

My view lay in between Bogdanovic and the *Washington Post* editor. "Why should a bout of criticism of Xie, China's equivalent of the shadowy FBI director, J. Edgar Hoover, be the worst thing that could happen in the world?" I said. Bogdanovic pointed out that Chinese parents became afraid of their own children. I said that did not suggest government terror against the people; it sounded more like cultural and generational strife. "We have that here," I reasoned.

Bogdanovic was not impressed. But I had not actually witnessed the Cultural Revolution. He had been in the midst of it.

Speaking about the turmoil, Bogdanovic recalled that once, before the Cultural Revolution, China had excellent security. "Nothing was ever stolen in those days." An American colleague asked Bogdanovic if anything was stolen from him during the Cultural Revolution.

"No."

I persisted in my dissent. "So perhaps it was more a political-moral movement—all this disorder—rather than the disappearance of civil security?"

Bogdanovic knew much about China, and spoke good Chinese, and he realized the impact of the Cultural Revolution had its limits. Each morning, outside the bedroom window in the *hu tong* (lane) in which he and his family lived, he would hear the cabbage seller, the barber, the knife grinder, each with their particular cries, their personal melodies. This life of the *hu tong*, and the loving-kindness of his amah, went on, regardless of the storms at the top. Only for two weeks did *hu-tong* life come to a halt (for that period Bogdanovic and his family moved to the Yugoslav Embassy). This China endures, he said, it is strong, and humanistic. It is what he elusively called the "Real China."

As we left the Faculty Club, one American colleague said to another: "Well, the Cultural Revolution must have been tough. Yet how shocking was it alongside Vietnam, which Bogdanovic never mentioned throughout the evening?" Such were American priorities at that time. Many of us were prisoners of the Vietnam trauma. This twisted our judgments about history.

Few societies understand other societies well, and China and America, despite mutual attraction, have known spectacular misunderstandings, ever since the 19th century. The late 1960s was such a period. I learned much about China at Harvard, from Fairbank, who stressed the wrongness of assuming the Chinese were just like us, and interpreted modern Chinese history in terms of the impact on China of superior Western power. Also, from the former China-diplomat John Carter Vincent, for whom the Vietnam War and the international problem of China's isolation were the urgent features of the China issue. Too, I learned from development theorist Professor Samuel Huntington, who said of Mao's Communists: "Surely one of the most outstanding achievements of the mid twentieth century was the establishment in China in 1949 for the first time in a hundred years of a government really able to govern China."

Yet, in retrospect, at Harvard I did not learn to understand the Cultural Revolution. The focus on China's international position was not open to the pathology of Mao's domestic actions. China's upheaval in 1966–67 could not be explained by the "impact of the West" approach of Fairbank, by China's reaction to the Vietnam War, which preoccupied Vincent, or by the "political order" theories of Huntington. Nor yet from any comparison between Chinese utopianism and Western youth's Christian quest for a "new man." Least of all by equating the Red Guards with radical American students.

Why, then, had Mao become discontented, militant, whimsical, and anti-Soviet? Grumbling toward him after the Great Leap Forward had left wounds; Mao likened senior colleagues to nit-picking old women. Mao was trying to differentiate himself from a Soviet Union that disappointed him; Soviet-style socialism had not produced the glories for China expected prior to the capture of power. In response to new complexities, Mao treacherously discovered ever more "class enemies" as scapegoats.

My view of "class struggle" was far more limited. Class theory, I felt, suited occasional moments in history when polarization between social groups becomes extreme. This was true in China during the first half of the 20th century. Other times, talk of struggle between classes tragically loses individual responsibility in collective abstraction. Such class talk, and purges that follow, elevates the appeal of hate over the appeal of love; everyone loses.

At over seventy years of age, Mao was in a race against time for the Chinese Revolution, and for himself; he sought quick renewal at once political and personal. A semi-Daoist trait of questioning even his own successes seemed to surface within Mao. The "monkey" in him got the better of the "tiger," as I later wrote in my biography. Most of these factors were outside Western democratic experience and the American agony over Vietnam. Tiananmen Square really was different from Harvard Square.

NOTE

1. Marshall Green, interview, ADST-LOC.

Chapter Five

Chinese Friends in the Cultural Revolution

At first, in the 1970s, Chinese said little to foreigners about the Cultural Revolution. Eventually, nearly everyone—cab driver, scholar, barber, office worker—shared stories of life during the storm. How they were treated, how they coped, the price they paid. Yet silence reigned on large issues of the Cultural Revolution: Who exactly was the enemy? What outcome did the Cultural Revolution yield? Nevertheless, after the CCP criticized Mao in 1980, tongues loosened and a stream of opinions emerged.

I came to know diplomat Zhou Nan during the summer of 1971, in a month of traveling together around China. Over dinner in Xian, I asked the future deputy foreign minister and Xinhua news agency chief in Hong Kong, if he witnessed book burning in the late 1960s. "Not mine; I still have my classics," he said with a broad smile.

"Did you lock them up during the violent years?"

"No."

"What if Red Guards had come to your house and said your books should be burned?"

"I would have quoted Chairman Mao and persuaded them of their error," he said grandly.

Poetry was the magic cave in which Zhou Nan hid from the storm. He blocked out horrors by mentally emigrating to Tang Dynasty verse. Zhou was a very private man, close to his family, and an avid reader. He hated being turned inside out by questioning Red Guards. Still, he was skilled at coping. In his memoir published in 2007, he wrote of the Cultural Revolution as "Cultural Revolution " or "so-called Cultural Revolution."[1]

Many others failed to steer an even path. Pastor Zhao Fusan, whom I had met at Rice Market Church in 1964, did not communicate with me again until the 1970s. On the acknowledgements page of my book, *800,000,000,*

I mentioned Zhao, "whom I did not see in 1971, but often thought about." Much later, when Zhao had come back from internal exile to Beijing—though not to being a pastor—he drew me aside from a group of colleagues. "Thank you for that note about me in *800,000,000*," he said. "I read the book while I was in the countryside. It helped keep me alive, and your mention of me especially helped. "

One friend in political science at Peking University was led on a roller-coaster by the Vietnam War and the Cultural Revolution. "I was so enthusiastic for Beijing-Hanoi solidarity," she told me. "I even applied to go to the battlefield." But she fell afoul of the Red Guards at her university. "My crime was to read Milton," she said of an English poet she admired. With the later falling out between China and Vietnam, she was sobered. "I lost a double trust," she said sadly. "In Vietnam and to a degree in my own government."

This political scientist said to me of the Cultural Revolution, "There was a false public opinion." She grew silent as if recalling difficult experiences and Mao's grandiose boasts. "We just didn't realize how dangerous it would be for China to fight the imperialists. . . It was all very well to just shout 'Down with Imperialism.'"

Sad days arrived for those caught in a family of "bad background." One case was Sun Muzhi, a young teacher whom I came to know well from the late 1970s. Sun's father was felled in 1967. During the 1950s, the father had written two articles on archeology and sent them to Guo Moruo, himself an archeologist, as well as Mao's favorite intellectual. "After my father's disgrace," Sun told me, "the articles were published under Guo's name—but we still have the two letters from Guo which make it clear the writing was my father's work."

Despair engulfed Sun, a thin, bright, tense man in his thirties. "If you were in my situation," he asked me one afternoon at the Temple of Heaven, when he was feeling all doors were closed, "wouldn't you simply kill yourself?"

When the Gao family in Hebei lost its elevated "poor peasant" ranking, their world crumbled. They became "the enemy" up and down town, an approved target for the mob. Frequently, people like the Gao's judged "counter revolutionary" were refused medical treatment, even if they were terribly beaten.

Years later, Gao Yuan returned to Hebei Province to see former classmates, most of who, like Gao himself, had been Red Guards. Many were in business. One classmate "had gone crazy and burned himself to death while yelling, 'I want to go to university!'"[2]

For Tian Hua (not his real name), a teacher of English literature in Shanghai, his membership in a family denounced as "bourgeois" derailed his life. I met him at a college in New York State, where he became an early PRC student in 1981. I was at the college to give a lecture and Tian lingered to ask questions. We became friends. He visited me in Boston and I took him sightseeing in New York.

Tian's father had worked for the KMT in the 1940s and later became a professor of economics at Fudan University. His mother was also a university teacher. From the Anti-Rightist Movement of 1957 onward, the family was harassed. "My brother was sent to Xinjiang," Tian said. "He lived like Robinson Crusoe." In the Cultural Revolution, Red Guards ransacked the family house. "Got any gold?" one sneered. "Where are your American dollars?" cried another. They found none of either, but this did not halt the bullying.

Tian's education was interrupted, his health was undermined, and his faith in human nature shriveled. It was the sort of comprehensive disaster that in the West might come from a horrendous car accident, a long wrongful imprisonment, or the loss of both parents.

After his parents were classified as "class enemies," his father fossicked in the streets for bits of food, brushing back the leaves at his feet to look for something to eat. Once when Tian came from Shanghai to see his parents in Beijing, his mother was ill in bed, rolling with pain, but there was no money to see a doctor. "The neighborhood committee had taken nearly all our funds," Tian explained, "on some pretext of having to supervise us." Tian never forgot these terrible moments.

Because of his family background, it was impossible for Tian to join the Communist Youth League or the Communist Party. "It was as if here, in Boston, your son was not allowed to join the Boy Scouts," he said.

Tian's case revealed the twisting of character that occurred when injustice from above was allowed to stand. When I told him a cleaning person was coming to my apartment, after I left to lecture at Harvard, Tian said: "How can you trust a stranger with a key, to come in by herself like that?"

Tian stressed how much he had suffered. I believed him. Still, the total effect was to make him suspicious of many things. "My passport to come and study in U.S. was delayed a month," he told me. "I think people at the Foreign Languages Institute where I was teaching held it up. They were raising one more time the issue of my bad family background." As we walked around Harvard, Tian said: "I can't seem to find out the truth. That is why I think it may be better to believe in God."

One evening in New York we dined at the Harvard Club on 44th Street and went upstairs to our room with its two single beds. After a long day I fell asleep. Suddenly Tian Hua sprang out of his bed and into mine. It was like an attack. But that was not my Chinese friend's aim and we were both half naked. "Guys don't approach each other like that," I said gently. But Tian meant well.

He taught me that disliking Mao and liking the West were not the same thing. He loved Chinese tradition, preferring historic Beijing to newer Shanghai. He was an elitist, finding many features of the U.S. vulgar, including the TV ads. He looked at black people as folk from another planet. One day after we had disagreed on a couple of matters, he looked at me sadly. "You just haven't been through what I've been through," he complained. Another day in New York he amused me by looking up at some Manhattan skyscrapers and saying, "They really look quite old, some of them," he said. "Just like in Shanghai."

Shen Chunyi, a 28year old with shortcropped hair and solid build, came to the West a decade later than Tian Hua. For him, sex and Western ways inter-related closely. "We knew that in the West a hug leads on to sex," Shen Chunyi said of the assumptions of his upbringing. "But we regarded it as a capitalist activity." Two years study in Australia adjusted his view both of capitalism and sex. Back in Beijing, Shen and a young lady spent the night in a borrowed room. He told me next day, "I was amazed, Ross. It's really so easy."

When we traveled together in Sichuan Province, Shen met a pretty, brightly-painted young woman. She came back to his room at Chengdu Hotel for the afternoon. At dinner, Shen told me she explained she was a virgin and could not do much. "I suggested one or two things and she asked each time, Why do you want me to do that?" Said Shen as we ate noodles, "She really didn't know much. I replied to her questions, Well, the Americans do it that way." After they finished, she said to him, "Of course, you're in foreign languages. I suppose Chinese in foreign languages become rather open-minded."

The girl spoke the truth. Western ways and a Chinese person's sexual ways had interacted in Shen's life. He had become an autonomous individual. Tian Hua had not (yet) done so.

In the 1960s, people became adept at lying. The saying was, "Wave the Red Flag to Oppose the Red Flag." It was one way of saying the opposite of what one means. "In the U.S.," Tian observed, "people bad-mouth a person in private, but praise him in meetings. In China, it's the opposite. People attack another person in meetings, but treat him kindly in private." It is something precious for us to cling to." Shen Chunyi was scrupulously honest, even in public, which was one reason he moved to the US, married a Japanese woman, and found success at business in Minnesota.

If Mao had understood the private-public dualism of Chinese people coping with the Chinese state, he might have realized the futility of his puppet-show. Politics was a fringe realm for ordinary Chinese, still is for most.

Loudly-proclaimed public campaigns have nowhere deep to lodge in Chinese minds.

A Beijing University student named Yang Bingzhang, tall, lean, and bespectacled, was tossed like a salad by the Cultural Revolution. Later he came to Harvard as a graduate student and research assistant on my book *Madame Mao*. For all its horrors, the Cultural Revolution gave Yang a political education.

He left Shandong Province to study at Beijing University in 1964. At first, he found the Cultural Revolution an exciting opportunity to express the Marxism he studied in class. His task as a Red Guard was to write periodic reports to the central authorities on the turbulent situation at the university. Witch-hunts fueled by "class struggle" were uncovering "enemies" behind every bush. Yang felt himself in an epic battle between darkness and light and he saw communism drawing closer each day.

Later in Cambridge, Massachusetts, Yang told me the following story, as he puffed on a cigarette and we drank coffee. Jiang Qing, wife of Mao and mistress of the arts, visited Beijing University in July 1966 and addressed a small group of which Yang was a member. Next day he wrote a report addressed to Mao that among other things criticized Jiang Qing for failing to understand socialist theory. He took a bus to the reception office of the headquarters of the Communist Party and told the desk clerk he had a letter for Chairman Mao.

To Yang's surprise, the charming but lethal Jiang Qing, hearing of his arrival with a six-page letter for Mao, sent word she would see him. "I hadn't asked to see Jiang Qing," Yang said lamely. When Jiang read Yang's letter, her largesse in receiving an ardent young Red Guard turned to fury. Within a week, Yang was in prison.

"It was lonely," he told me, under a brilliant blue sky in bustling Harvard Square, of his fifteen months of incarceration. "I was the only person in a room meant for four people. I learned to play chess with myself, using dirt and soap to make a black and white chess board on the floor of the cell." Later, Yang was given a cellmate. "He was a high school senior from Hubei Province," Yang said, "and his crime had been to put up a poster in Xidan saying that Lin Biao [defense minister and Mao's heir apparent], despite appearances, was not a loyal supporter of Mao. This young man played chess with me."

Yang and I traveled by train in southwest China in the 1980s, when I was writing a feature for *National Geographic* and Yang was assisting me with interviews. He told me about advancing his knowledge of Russian while in prison, "I had only one book in my cell, Mao's *Selected Works*. With my knowledge of Russian from two years of courses at Beijing University, I roughly translated Mao's writings from Chinese into Russian, using a cut open toothpaste tube as a pencil."

Early in 1967, Yang was taken from his cell "to meet the masses" at his campus, Beijing University. In a reception room, he was pushed down in the "jet plane" position, arms yanked high behind him, head thrust forward toward the floor. Students, teachers, and staff built up political credit for themselves by denouncing him. "It was agonizing," he recalled as he puffed on a cigarette and our train rolled toward the Sichuan Province capital of Chengdu, "and I was on the verge of fainting. I begged them to let me straighten up, or lie on the floor. I said I would listen to all the attacks, but I couldn't bear this 'jet plane.'"

His fellow members of China's premier university, formerly intelligent folk but now zealots, did not agree. After hours of "jet plane" treatment, the crowd trampled upon Yang and he lost consciousness. "The guards from the prison truck rescued me," he said softly, "put me on the back of the vehicle, and drove me home to prison. I was so glad to be back in my cell!"

Around this time, three female students from Yang's campus, indignant that an ex-landlord was living in their neighborhood, rushed off to confront the old man. They burst through the front door of his home, in the lawless manner sanctioned by the Cultural Revolution, and screeched that the landlord had been a bad element since birth, opposing Chairman Mao day and night. This old man had reached his limit. He came out of his kitchen bearing a carving knife, and mustering strength almost beyond his capacity, he lunged at the first student and stabbed her to death. He had time also to kill a second before he was captured. Two days later the old man was shot dead.

When the leftism that Mao promoted in 1966 broke itself on the rock of factionalism by 1968, Yang Bingzhang, like millions of others, experienced loss of idealism, puzzlement at doctrinal hairsplitting, and struggle to align private values with a public realm that no longer seemed rational. Who was your enemy, who was your friend?

Coping with loss of faith in the Communist Party was tough. "After I came out of prison, I had lost much hope," he said one night at our hotel in Chengdu, southwest China. "I decided to write a critical book about the party and the arrogant authorities, and send it to Chairman Mao. A strange thing!" he said of his own action. "It seems like what a mad person would do." Yang by the late 1960s adopted the opposite view on any topic to that of the Chinese government.

Yet he distinguished "the authorities" and Mao. "Still at that time Mao was my idol," he said. "I felt he had weight, he would analyze things, and if something was wrong, he would change his mind, that is why I wrote a letter to him, and a whole book for him." From the village where he was dispatched after leaving prison, Yang made a package of his 600-page work entitled "Chinese Politics" and posted it to Mao in Beijing. "The postage cost me 10 yuan," he said, "which was a quarter of the annual allowance I was getting in the village."

"There was no reply," Yang went on with a laugh. "But after writing the book, I felt I didn't owe the damned authorities anything."

Yang's method of coping took a bizarre turn. He resolved to try life in North Korea. "A friend of mine went to the China-Korea border to check the landscape," he recalled of his one year of preparation. "Then I went, and later my friend went to the border again. I bought clothes, did research on Korea, and planned what to say if I was caught at the border."

The day came. Yang proceeded a little beyond the frontier and the North Koreans captured him. "Kim Ilsung's prison was worse than Mao's prison," he said without rancor. Yang never showed any rancor.

Relations between Beijing and Pyongyang were strained, but later they improved and within a year, Yang was released and sent back to China. As we dined together at a Chinese restaurant in Boston one evening in 1988, he could laugh at the two huge slogans erected on either side of the border he had furtively crossed two decades earlier. On the Chinese side, the slogan was Mao's slap at North Korea's friendship with Russia: "TO COMBAT IMPERIALISM, YOU MUST COMBAT REVISIONISM." On the Korean side, the slogan was a defense of North Korea's agenda in the face of China's political fever: "NATIONAL INDEPENDENCE!"

Yang remarked that after the Cultural Revolution there was a tendency among some to "talk big, but do little." He believed it was a result of the "empty bombast" of the 1960s. "During the Cultural Revolution, righteous rhetoric soared, but actual conduct declined in quality."

Guo Moruo, eminent writer, multi-purpose intellectual, and friend of Mao, asked me to the Great Hall of the People in 1971. Nearly eighty years of age, Guo said, "You are like the rising sun at eight." 32 years old at the time, I did not know how nice the remark was.

"We have a three-in-one combination in China," Guo explained, "young is up to 35, medium is to 55, and old from 56. I said to Zhou Enlai there should be another category, 'Super-old,' for those over 75!" Yet, maybe, Guo quipped, that would sound too much like "Superpower."

Guo asked about John Fairbank, "my old friend from Chongqing during the anti-Japanese War, and later from Shanghai," and about Edwin Reischauer: "He speaks Japanese so well," Guo said of my senior Harvard colleague, "because he was born there and his father was a missionary to Japan." Guo himself lived for years in Japan and knew the country better than he knew the West.

Figure 5.1.   Guo Moruo signs one of his books for author as staff look on, Beijing, 1971.
Author's photo.

Guo had troubles in the Cultural Revolution, but he did not talk about
them. He slid around the entire subject with soothing platitudes. The Cultural
Revolution, he said, "blocked all channels for the restoration of capitalism."
He cited Lenin on how socialism can be re-infected with bourgeois ways. He
explained how Mao had carried Lenin's ideas about preventing the return of
capitalism to a new height.

I wondered if the price was worth the suffering. Guo's own son met a
horrible death in the Cultural Revolution, a topic not brought up during our
conversation.

Yet it was exciting to hear snippets about Mao. He was studying English
hard, Guo said, as China had decided to replace Russian with English as first
foreign language. Two of Mao's favorite new phrases were "law and order"
and "anti-Mao." Mao had recently read the classic historical novel *Dream of
the Red Chamber* for the fourth time, Guo remarked.

I asked him about authors he translated early in his career, including
Goethe and Nietzsche. "We don't read these people nowadays," he said.
What about Chinese novels? Guo mentioned only the old classics, *Dream of
the Red Chamber* and *Romance of the Three Kingdoms*. Contemporary writers had not yet made a big mark, he suggested lamely.

Guo did become excited in talking of romantic Western writing: "The man
I really like is Shelley." He praised another romantic work: "The Rubaiyat of

Omar Khayyam is also wonderful." Guo added quietly: "We do not read any of these people nowadays."

Perhaps Guo really believed the leftist Cultural Revolution had rescued the true spirit of the Chinese Revolution. Only Mao, he insisted, had found the secret of consolidating revolution. "Lenin died too soon to carry it through. Stalin lacked time for the research necessary to spell it out."

In a *Motive* essay I mentioned a problem that Guo did not broach. "China re-enters world history, but world history will also catch up with the redness of China's revolution," I wrote. "The attempt to perpetuate militancy seems doomed. History bestows the blessing of permanence on no revolutionaryregime, no revolutionary mood."

I questioned some efforts to re-enact heroism. "How can a towering epic like the Long March be simulated by sending Red Guards marching from Chongqing to Peking?" I asked. "How can communism prevent the advent of banality, when its very aim has been to make everyday and universal the benefits that once were the possession of but a few? Modern China will not be exempt from the apparent laws of modernity."[3]

Guo Moruo, whose dramatic style of expression held in thrall his aides at the session, spoke about language reform, a topic of special interest to him. "Latinization is the ideal solution, but it's very difficult," he said. "Children were taught in the 1950s to put the Latin version beside the characters, but when they started character-writing, they forgot the Latinization!"

Of course, literacy was now much greater in China than at Liberation. "It is probably better to just continue simplifying the characters," Guo said. "We won't think of Latinization again until Mandarin is completely popularized. Otherwise, China might turn into a number of different states, each with its own language."

Before I took my leave from Guo Moruo, I pulled out my copy of his classic book, *Zhongguo gudai shehui yanjiu* ("Research on Ancient Chinese Society"), which I bought in Hong Kong. I had been told that Guo, in a sop to Red Guards, said it should be burned. But, opening the book, Guo smiled and autographed it for me with a flourish.

As it happened, despite the Cultural Revolution, the Chinese people's impulse toward individual freedom, hard work, family values, and property rights was to revive fast in the years after Guo's death (1978) and Mao's (1976).

Mao unified and strengthened China. He did not change human nature. He did not cancel the sense of honor, taste for materialism, and family-mindedness of the Chinese people.

A thoughtful travel official, Jia Aimei, quiet but sharp, asked as we strolled in the Xiang Shan hills, "Do you understand the Cultural Revolution?" I replied, "Not completely." She went on, "Nor do us Chinese. It must be harder still for foreigners. Some told me they think the Chinese went mad during the Cultural Revolution." On one of my later trips to China, Mrs. Jia took the unusual step of coming to see me at my hotel. She was guiding a group of art lovers from Arkansas. On her blouse was pinned a large badge: "See Arkansas First."

Legendary French diplomat Etienne Manac'h told me of Mao's words about a high (low) point of the Cultural Revolution: The violent ransacking of the British Office in Beijing in 1967. While Manac'h was accompanying the French leader Couve de Murville at Zhongnanhai in 1970, Mao turned to Ambassador Manac'h, "Were you here when the British were attacked?" In fact, none of the existing French Embassy staff were in Beijing at that time. Mao clung to the topic, "Well, have you heard about it?"

Of course, Manac'h and every diplomat in Europe had heard. Mao proceeded to denounce the violation, the smashing of everything in sight, and all the ultra-leftists who caused it. "That was a completely indefensible way to carry on politics," he declared. Mao went on to criticize "ultra-leftism" and say to Manac'h, "I, myself, am a center-leftist."

NOTES

1. Zhou Nan, *Zhou Nan kou shu: yao xiang dang nian yu shan guan jin,* Jinan, Qi Lu shu she, 2007, 152.

2. Gao Yuan, *Born Red*, Stanford University Press, 1987, 360.

3. "Whose China Problem?" *Motive,* February, 1968, 11, 12.

Chapter Six

Neighbors View China

China's politics affected many nations. Close neighbors wondered if the Cultural Revolution would alter Beijing's approach to Asia. Fraternal countries in the Communist Bloc saw definitions of socialism change before their eyes. Chinese in Hong Kong felt close to the turbulence, yet also distant, given their status as a British colony.

In Saigon, a crumbling regime called to mind the last years of Chiang Kaishek's government in China. During the summer of 1967, the Cultural Revolution spilled into Hong Kong like an opera bursting from the performance hall into the street. In Hungary and Czechoslovakia, the differences between Mao's "to-rebel-is-justified" socialism and the stability-minded socialism of Moscow was sharp. Having resolved to specialize on China, I became curious about how countries physically or politically close to China viewed the emerging giant.

In arguments about the Vietnam War at Harvard, two issues stood out. Was the National Liberation Front in South Vietnam a mere arm of Hanoi, or was it an indigenous movement that, if it won military victory, would form a separate regime in Saigon? Was Hanoi, in turn, part of Hubert Humphrey's "Oriental red chain of command" stemming from Beijing? On the answers to these questions hinged one's view of American policy in East Asia, and one's view of the impact of the Chinese Revolution on Asia.

On a Pan Am flight from Singapore to Saigon, I realized how much the war had affected life in Vietnam. With tourism drying up, I was the only passenger in an entire Boeing 707. Amusingly, a steward objected when I put my umbrella in the overhead compartment. "It could fall and hit a passenger," she reasoned, standing amidst row after row of seats without a single human being. I thought if my own umbrella was all that hit me on a visit to South Vietnam, I would be lucky.

At Tan Son Nhut airport, the sky and ground were astir with helicopters. A military police jeep escorted our Pan Am bus into the city. As gunfire crackled, the driver told us to duck our heads or crouch on the floor of his bus. As the war pushed out tourism, the modest Tan Loc Hotel into which Pan Am had booked me had become a brothel.

Drunken American GIs, unable to speak Vietnamese or French, the two languages of the city, enlisted my help in the corridors to interpret between French and English. "I paid 2000 pesos for a girl and she left her clothes on all night!" one complained. As beautiful girls in tiny dresses paraded, I tried to help soldiers negotiate with "hotel" staff.

"Heh, you look like an Aussie," gurgled another GI, "how come you spoutin' French ?" Next morning, thanks to the Australian ambassador, I found a hotel, the Majestic, which overlooked the Saigon River.

Saigon was a leafy, stylish place, a nearer match for the accolade "Paris of the East" than the usual choice, Shanghai. On all sides, France came to mind—scrambling Renaults, "Le Bar" and "La Brasserie" on every block, lunches spun out with red wine and Citane cigarettes.

The atmosphere was fashionable and cosmopolitan, despite an air of impending violence. I wrote in my diary, "The French taught their colonies how to live, even as they failed to teach them governance."

However, politically I had the impression of a regime near the end of its span. "Saigon is like China must have been before the Communists took over," I wrote in a letter to a Melbourne friend, president of the Labor Party in Victoria, "demoralized, without a purpose any bigger than anti-communism, corrupt beyond description, dominated by generals squabbling for power, a school of idleness and vice."

I was still in my twenties, excitable, woolly-minded about communism, imbued with guilt over Western colonialism, and embarrassed by Australian racism toward aborigines and Chinese and other non-white immigrants.

The American journalist Robert Shaplen, in his 1965 book *The Lost Revolution*, wrote of the need for "truly revolutionary social techniques" in Vietnam to produce "a meaningful alternative to communism." These words paralleled Fairbank's comments, during a State Department Round Table of October 1949 that dissected the American "loss" of China. The theme of social purpose linked the Vietnam issue, for Fairbank, and for me, with China's civil war in the late 1940s.

"The whole vocation of the Western world hangs on Vietnam, it seems to me," I wrote in my letter to Melbourne. "Do we believe enough in ourselves, and have we enough faith, to strive for something positive, that we know to be right, in Asia?"

I compared Saigon with Canton (Guangzhou) which I saw in 1964. Each nested by lush fields of brilliant green under the glare of a tropical sun. Each lay around a muddy river alive with a thousand boats large and small. However, Saigon was economically ahead of Guangzhou. "The Saigon River has more motorized craft than the Pearl River," I noted in my diary, "and the street scenes of Saigon are more modern than those of Canton." I saw a difference between an Asian city prospering in the risky arms of the West (Saigon) and an Asian city poor yet independent from foreign intervention (Guangzhou).

As American influence eclipsed French, Saigon was becoming a tougher, richer, more dangerous city. It was a cauldron of opportunity, injustice, cruelty, humor and love. When American and Vietnamese culture met, the encounter was far from one-sided. The Americans had the resources, but the Vietnamese were very clever.

American diplomat Peter Tarnoff, later president of the Council on Foreign Relations in New York, invited me to a French lunch in his apartment. He said of his ambassador, "When [Henry Cabot] Lodge came back to Saigon, I met him at the airport, and he said it was good to be back because in Saigon he would have power. In America, he said, he had missed out on power when he failed to be elected vice-president, but in Saigon he will effectively be vi-cepresident of South Vietnam." The remark called to mind the presumptions of such American envoys to China during the 1940s as Ambassador Patrick Hurley, special envoy of President Roosevelt. Hurley tried to tell Mao how to handle Chiang Kai-shek. I felt Washington was making the same mistakes in Vietnam that had led to its "loss" of China.

"The Americans are fifty years ahead, so no one understands them," a Viet-namese official said, turning my mind back to China some decades earlier. "They have good intentions," he added, with a shrug of the shoulders. "The Chinese [residents] play a bad role in Vietnam," said the nationalistic Minister of Education in his small office. "You know, they have two photo IDs, one Red and one Nationalist, just in case. They have no feelings." I realized the Vietnamese were strong-minded people, critical of everyone.

"The VC [National Liberation Front] is not independent of North Vietnam," diplomat Peter Tarnoff argued. "That issue is now dead; anyone who wants to raise it is refusing to discuss Vietnam seriously." I concluded that Tarnoff was right. The war was Hanoi's war, and if Hanoi won it, Vietnam would be a single entity ruled from Hanoi.

My conclusion to a second question that led me to Saigon was that no "Oriental red chain of command" bound Beijing to Hanoi. No link existed between the Vietnam War and the prospects for "people's war" in Japan or most other Asia countries. Hearing the Chinese talk about solidarity with Vietnam in China in no way prepared me for hearing in Saigon of Vietnamese resentment at one thousand years of dealing with China, or hearing Vietnamese criticism of Chinese as materialistic and anti-foreign. Vietnamese fears of China made some of us wonder if the war against the USA would be enough to guarantee Hanoi-Beijing friendship.

However, I persistently saw the Americans "trampling" on Saigon, just as the British had trampled upon Canton (Guangzhou) at the time of the Opium Wars. "Having once been isolationist," I said of the Americans in a feverish letter to an Australian classmate, Tony Staley, later a conservative cabinet minister, "they now have sprung to the opposite extreme, and think they ought to control much of the world. It involves them in a vulgar replacement of other nations' wishes and interests by their own. They cannot seem to break through to mutuality in their international relations."

It seemed the South Vietnam regime would lose as the Chinese Nationalists lost, forfeiting the nationalism issue to Communists, and lacking a social purpose to match communism. Saigon seemed a "heap of loose sand," as prerevolutionary China was described by Sun Yatsen. Could such an incoherent social order endure?

I wrote to Andrew Peacock, soon to be Australia's foreign minister (and Shirley McLean's boyfriend), that "the National Liberation Front will eventually win (unless the United States totally destroys Vietnam), since the choice, in political terms, almost has been narrowed down to the National Liberation Front or the United States Embassy." I predicted the social crisis within America that I later witnessed at Harvard: "I fear that the Vietnam War may do something terrible to the United States."

However, I should have distinguished between American goals (reasonable) and American methods (poor). In addition, I should have been more worried about a possible American withdrawal from Asia in the event of defeat in Vietnam. Such a sweeping withdrawal would have been bad for a number of nations, including China.

The South Vietnamese lived very close to a Communist regime. A Vietnamese official named Tien, with an aunt and uncle and cousins in Hanoi, told me, "If the free forces had lost World War Two to the fascists, Communists would not be ruling in China and East Europe." I asked Tien which was worse, fascism or communism. "Both are worse!" he replied passionately in accented English. "If I had to choose, I suppose I would choose fascism—it's dictatorship by an upper class; communism is dictatorship by the lower class."

"Anyone living under communism becomes a slave," Tien said. In Saigon, a bleak view of communism from people whose nation had experienced it directly, planted new thoughts about China—where no one was free to speak their minds as in Saigon. "The Chinese will rebel against the Communists," official Tien predicted, showing me to his office door. "It will be feelings about family, that will do it."

"I am holding two ideas without fitting them together," I confessed in my diary. "I favor social democracy—I call it the socialism of happiness, as opposed to socialism by a collective design. Plus, I hold a second idea, which comes from the fact that my home is in the Asian region: a sense of the decline of the West, the return of China, and the historical importance of Vietnamese resistance to America."

However, in reality, the rise of the East would not necessarily be at the expense of the West. U.S. leadership in East Asia would continue strongly. There would be room both for a strong China and a strong America in the coming Age of Economics. Chinese prosperity and Chinese socialism would not necessarily evolve in tandem. Nor would my social democratic values prove relevant beyond the West—and not long in the West.

Figure 6.1. Author with his boatman on the Yangzi River, heading for Wuhan. Author's photo.

In the hot summer of 1967, Hong Kong, a territory usually a-political, was at political fever pitch. Mao's portrait smiled down from shops, banks, and offices. The Cultural Revolution had spilled out upon this last jewel of the British Empire. The people of Hong Kong were "rebelling" against their British overlords. Or were they?

I saw leftist demonstrators, neat and wellgroomed like bank clerks, arrive at the scene of a protest against a British company or government office, with bandages ready in their pockets and cans of red paint under their arms. Within an hour, they were lying "bloody" and bandaged on the sidewalk, "beaten" by the "oppressive imperialist authorities of Hong Kong."

True, there were a few local roots to the Hong Kong crisis of 1967. Mainly, however, the Hong Kong leftists had their eyes on Beijing, trying to be more Maoist than Mao, for political safety. Moderate Hong Kong business-persons who had spoken well of China in 1964 and 1965 fell silent. "Beijing has lost Hong Kong public opinion for five years," an executive told me.

Meanwhile, 400 GIs were arriving each day at Kai Tak airport from Vietnam for R & R (Rest and Recreation), and Beijing was warning that if America interfered in Hong Kong, China would fight America. The political advisor to the British governor of Hong Kong did not feel Beijing was trying to reshape Hong Kong politically. "If they wanted it back," he said, "they would write a letter to London and ask for it." That Beijing was not trying to take back Hong Kong, but rather encouraging it to salute Maoism under Britain's nervous gaze, suggested the Cultural Revolution was a campaign of political indoctrination, not a drive for institutionalized political change.

A left-wing medical friend, Dr Wu, spent half the day seeing patients, half following the Cultural Revolution. At his dinner table, we used knives and forks, not chopsticks. I wrote in my diary, "Hong Kong leftists seem more modernised in daily habits than non-leftists. Chopsticks are a contrast with knife and fork. The fork is explicit, as is the knife; its purpose is to spear the food; it is shaped accordingly. The purpose of the knife is to cut the food, and it is shaped for that. However, the function of chopsticks is ambiguous. With them you can cut, lift, spear, and separate. Differentiation lies in the movement of the hand." I felt it might be similar with Chinese thought and Chinese foreign policy, in contrast to Western thought and foreign policy. "Differentiations on the Chinese side are not explicit, and are missed if one expects Western ways."

A Harvard graduate student friend was doing anthropology research in Hong Kong, making a film of the Hungry Ghost Festival. This is a major Buddhist and Taoist event in summertime Hong Kong. The ghosts are restless spirits of people who lacked a funeral. No one visits their graves; they do not receive the gifts that Chinese people give ancestors. To stop aggrieved ghosts causing problems for the living, Hong Kong folk provide them with food. They build Altars from bamboo poles. Taoist priests recite passages from sacred books to appease the ghosts. They pray to the ghosts for peace and happy living. They hope the hungry ghosts will not disturb them in the future.

Here was clear-cut superstition, backed by Chinese business-persons and popular with ordinary Hong Kong folk. Semi-feudal superstition could co-exist with modernisation seen in purely economic terms. By contrast, the kind of social modernisation afoot in China would make a ghost festival impossible. My friend illustrated the abundant superstition in Hong Kong. We were talking to four women in a lane when a duck came by. The women were terrified and started whispering and pointing. They wanted to run away. The lane once had a name that included the word "duck."

I alluded to China's social modernization in *Motive*. "There is no worship of cows in China, as in India. There is no longer traditional dress, as in Japan. . . . In China the peasant becomes a worker." At that time, I thought the U.S. felt threatened by such a modernization. "The believer hates the heretic more than he hates the unbeliever," I wrote. "The historical function of communism—to rapidly modernize backward societies—is quite akin to the historical function of capitalism in the 19th century. Yet the ideologists of liberal capitalism today smile more readily on Asian traditionalism than on Asian communism."[1]

On balance, the summer of 1967 was unhappy and damaging for Hong Kong. I felt more admiration for British rule there after 1967 than I had done in 1964. Then, after some weeks amidst the purposefulness of Beijing and Canton, I was struck by Hong Kong's gaudy commercialism. Now it was different. "The main hope for Hong Kong," a businessman friend said as we picnicked in the New Territories, "is that China itself will settle down." Yet China was far from settling down.

In the spring of 1968, I visited several East Europe cities for *The New Republic*, to write about Alexander Dubcek's "New Course" reforms in Prague and reactions to them.[2] Czechs were cynical about Marxism, unlike the Chinese. They considered Mao's China very strange. When they dismissed China as a faroff curiosity, naive in its socialist extremism, my sympathy for China rose.

I wrote a letter to a Harvard classmate: "I sense relaxation in friendly officials at Prague airport, uninhibited street scenes, and bustle in key hotels. Everyone is keen to read the newspapers; what a change! There is excitement in Susan Lubochova's [Kissinger's friend] voice, as I wrest her from the TV to talk about Dubcek and his ideas—'I don't want to miss the latest developments,' she explains breathlessly."

Some Czechs criticized "Eurasian" Marxism. They felt that the further east you went, the less progress and culture you would find. "Remember Stalin was not a European," sniffed a Prague editor in a reference to the tyrant's Georgian origins. How could "Eurasian" socialism sit smoothly on Czechoslovakia, a pretty brooch on Europe's bosom?

European socialists seldom grasped the importance for world history of the Chinese Revolution. In my 1966 essay in *Motive,* I wrote, "Part of Russia is part of Europe. Prague and Budapest are historic European cities, where Western music, languages, literature, cuisine are rooted. China, by contrast, is not one nation within a civilization: she is herself a civilization, comparable not to Russia or Hungary or France but to the whole of Europe." I tried to see the Cultural Revolution as a struggle pertaining to this historic separateness of China.

The Czechoslovakia of Dubcek's "Socialism with a Human Face" was an exciting place. A sophisticated land, where Europe's first railroad was built, Czechoslovakia had been held back for years by Stalinism under Antonin Novotny. In the 1940s, Czechoslovakian president Edward Benes had raised the cry "East *and* West," but the Cold War stifled the idea of Prague being open equally to Paris and Moscow.

I wondered if Dubcek might be able to achieve what Benes could not. A vital condition—European detente—seemed within reach. The center of world tension had shifted to Asia, as Moscow was deeply anxious about China and Washington was whoring after false gods in Vietnam.

Moscow's response to Dubcek showed that Russian power outweighed socialist ideas. Mao saw this, but he exaggerated how far President Johnson "colluded" with Brezhnev over the crushing of Dubcek; and Mao had no sympathy at all for the ideas of what he called "Dubcek's revisionist clique."

In Budapest, a Hungarian friend, Karoly Toth, asked about my impression of Czechoslovakian events. He remained haunted by the memory of 1956 in Hungary. Remember," Toth said, "Hungary is very close by." Of course, he meant close by the Soviet Union, as well as close by Czechoslovakia.

One saw in Prague an early attempt at "political reform" in a Marxist state. Dubcek felt Lenin and even Marx had thrown little light on the problem of the political system in a post-class struggle society. What kind of political system would follow the dictatorship of the proletariat? According to Marx and Lenin, the state would begin to "wither away," but no one expected that, so Dubcek was treading on virgin soil.

Visiting a magazine's offices, I looked into the censors' room and saw them with their feet on their desks reading comics. "They have nothing to do," an editor said with a smile. The press began to reflect the real life of society. The Czechoslovakian Boy Scouts, long forbidden, reappeared. "We begin to see that socialism as interpreted here in the past," said an editor of *Literarny Listy*, the magazine of the writers' union, "is not an aim in itself. Freedom is the more ultimate aim."

"The Czechoslovakian progressives," I wrote in my diary of Dubcek's circle, "are in the process of qualifying Lenin's communism as much as John Stuart Mill and William Beveridge qualified Adam Smith's capitalism." Dubcek was taking the first steps toward a democratic political system while trying to cling to a Marxist economy. Visiting a Czechoslovakia that the Chinese Communists called "revisionist" suggested the Cultural Revolution in China might be less about rescuing socialism than about power and Mao's personality.

The sculptor Auguste Rodin called Prague the "Rome of the north" for its seven hills, and on an April afternoon, I climbed the one topped by Hradcany Castle, on a path winding by churches and courtyards. The Vtlava River flowed silently behind, and peach and pear blossoms shone in the sunshine ahead. Moments later, I was in a gloomy alley; the blossoms were gone; the chill of stilldamp stone walls gave a foretaste of winter. Four months later in August 1968, Moscow invaded Prague and put an end to Dubcek's New Course. Soon, it seemed the blossoms of the Prague spring had never been.

The Czechoslovakian crisis of August 1968 affected Mao's view of the Soviet Union in a way momentous for ties between China and the West. If "the new Czars" in Moscow could invade Prague to "rescue" Czech socialism, Mao reasoned, maybe they would fish in the "troubled" waters of China and seek out a "pro-Soviet" faction in Beijing to support with Soviet force? My Soviet-specialist professor at Harvard, Adam Ulam, expected just this.

Mao's top colleague, Liu Shaoqi, felt China and Russia should mount "joint action" to counter America in Vietnam. However, Mao was already looking beyond Vietnam; he saw the Soviet intervention in Czechoslovakia as a signpost to Moscow as his biggest headache. That would change his view of the USA, too.

Mao, although excessively anti-Dubcek, made an acute observation on the Czechoslovakian crisis when he pointed out that American-Soviet relations were not damaged by Moscow's invasion of August 1968. The world learned that an issue of peace and war could produce a certain alignment of international forces: the U.S. gave the Soviet Union a green light to occupy Prague. Yet during the same event, an issue of justice within societies could produce a different alignment of international forces: American sympathies lay with Dubcek.

Visiting Saigon, I had witnessed gunfire and a taxi driver robbed me. "It's funny," I wrote in my Vietnam diary, "that I feel much less safe in Saigon than I did in Beijing—or the Red cities in Europe." Here was a basic point that Professor Samuel Huntington made in his lectures at Harvard.

The 1950s and 1960s were in many countries an era of state building. There was more trust in government in this period than during later decades. A problem of the time was that the end of colonialism in the Third World often left a vacuum. However, China avoided that problem; Mao built a strong regime. In South Vietnam, anti-Communists and the U.S. were trying to build a state. Yet it wasn't clear whether the main aim was establishing democracy, or just making the south stronger in the face of the power challenge from Hanoi.

"The most important distinction among countries," Huntington wrote in *Political Order in Changing Societies*, "concerns not their form of government but their degree of government."[3] He feared a political vacuum above all else. He admired the CCP for its ability to "create new institutions of political order." He did not admire Mao's remarks to Andre Malraux of France in 1965, doubting this, undermining that, as the monkey in Mao pushed aside the tiger.[4] Huntington liked regimes that shored up the state, not regimes that tore it down. When the Cultural Revolution arrived, its worst feature for Huntington was that it squandered, at least for a time, the Communist Party's capacity to maintain political order. Huntington expressed the state-building caste of mind of dominant modernization theory. At least it explained why I felt safer in Beijing than in Saigon.

Still, in 1968, I obstinately stuck with social democracy. I clung hopefully to its central role for individual self-realization, and its objection both to "tyranny of wealth" (capitalism) and "tyranny of power" (communism).

NOTES

1. Ross Terrill, "Whose China Problem?" *Motive*, February 1968, 8, 9, 12.

2. Ross Terrill, "Czechoslovakia's New Course," *New Republic*, May 18, 1968.

3. Samuel Huntington, *Political Order in Changing Societies*, New Haven, Yale, 1968, 1.

4. Jacques Andrieu, "But What Exactly Did Mao and Malraux Say to Each Other?" *China Perspectives*, Hong Kong, December 1996.

Chapter Seven

Turning Points

During the 1960s, China took almost 30% of Australia's wheat exports. Still, no order came after 1969. Beijing said the conservative Australian government, headed by William McMahon, was in the grip of "anti-China sentiments." Meanwhile, Canada in October 1970 dropped diplomatic links with Taiwan and recognized the PRC.

Wheat was a symbol of Australia's self-image as a rural nation, and farmers took it for granted that the world desired Australian wheat. But in a communiqué at the end of Canada's first trade mission to the PRC, Beijing stated, "In accordance with Canada's wishes, China will continue to consider Canada first as a source of wheat as import needs arise."[1]

Australian governments had a record of hostility to the PRC. During the 1950s and 1960s, China was threatening to Australia largely because it was unknown. McMahon's government and earlier conservative governments going back to 1949, all reflected this sentiment.

In 1967, Canberra passed a note to the Australian Wheat Board, a marketing authority supposed to be a–political, instructing it to inform Beijing that an existing contract for the sale of Australian wheat to China would be void unless Beijing intervened to stop the riots going on in Hong Kong.[2] In 1969 in Hong Kong, the Australian foreign minister spoke of "serious questionings of conscience in Australia about how far we're justified in trading with China."

Canberra put support for the Vietnam policy of Washington squarely in an anti-China context. "Suppose the Americans withdrew from South Vietnam," said a predecessor of McMahon, conservative prime minister Robert Menzies, "does anybody with his five wits doubt that before very long Chinese communism acting through North Vietnamese communism would sweep down through South Vietnam, would put itself in an early position to control Thailand, to render the position of Malaya almost intolerable, and in the long run we would find ourselves with aggressive communism almost on our shores."[3]

From Canberra, the Leader of the Opposition Labor Party, Gough Whitlam, in April 1971 asked me to urge Beijing to invite him for talks on China-Australia relations. Whitlam, a tall, strong-minded lawyer, saw a chance to push the China issue—and win power as prime minister—in Beijing's apparent 1970 decision to discontinue wheat purchases from Australia and give the orders to Canada instead.

The Labor party of Whitlam thought Australia should have as good relations as possible with all four powers that dominated Australia's region: U.S., Japan, China, and the Soviet Union. Whitlam possessed the rationality of a bright lawyer; he wanted a logical, solve-all-the-problems Australian foreign policy. He felt this did not exist in the 60s and early 70s. The British writer Robert Stephens commented in 1967: "Australia is dependent on America for its defense, on Europe for the mainsprings of its culture, and increasingly on Japan and China for its markets."[4] Whitlam wanted to tie all three strands together into one package.

Nevertheless, the Labor Party's China initiative in the spring of 1971 was risky. Whitlam announced his appeal to Beijing for a visit before he telephoned me to try to make the invitation occur! He seemed more confident than I was that I could pull a few strings. He rashly predicted publicly that China would not buy one more grain of Australian wheat until Australia had a Labor Party government that recognized the PRC.

Doubts about the Vietnam War influenced Whitlam's approach to China. I knew the current French ambassador in Beijing, Etienne Manac'h, from interviewing him in Paris about Vietnam while on assignment for *Atlantic Monthly*. I explained to him that the Australian Labor Party's policies on Vietnam and China were close to France's; could he smooth Whitlam's path to Beijing?

Ambassador Manac'h involved Premier Zhou Enlai in the matter, via the senior diplomat (later ambassador to Washington), Han Xu. I soon received a cable from Whitlam that read simply, "Eureka. We won." He was invited to Beijing for talks with Chinese leaders.[5]

The invitation was extended against the advice of Ted Hill, head of the "Australian Communist Party (Marxist-Leninist)," rival to the pro-Moscow Communist Party of Australia. The London *Sunday Times* detailed Hill's representations to Beijing. Hill recommended that Whitlam not be invited and that I not be given a China visa to go with him.[6] However, fortunately, it seemed the Chinese government did not wish the Australian self-proclaimed Marxist-Leninists to have a veto power on all interactions between China and Australia.

On a sun-drenched Memorial Day at the end of May 1971, the Chinese embassy in Canada phoned me at Kirkland House on the Harvard campus. "You should come to China immediately. We think it would be a good idea for you to arrive two weeks before Mr. Whitlam." I spent the next seven weeks in China.

My first retirement event as a faculty member in the Government Department was for the political philosopher Carl Friedrich in December 1970. During the dinner, Henry Kissinger, back from Washington for the evening, asked me about Wilfred Burchett, the Australian left-wing journalist, and his views on China and Vietnam.

"Burchett's an extremely intelligent man," said Nixon's national security advisor. "I know that." He'd heard Burchett was well-informed on Hanoi's mind as well as Beijing's.

"I saw Wilfred at Thanksgiving," I said. "He had in his hand a copy of your recent backgrounder on the Paris Vietnam negotiations."

"Leaked by the State Department," said Kissinger tartly. I told Kissinger that Burchett admired his backgrounder for its realism and its skepticism about Japan. We discussed whether Vietnam was most concerned with China's power or Japan's power in the region.

All this time we were leaning together behind the back of the wife of a colleague who was in conversation with Adam Ulam, the Soviet Union specialist, seated opposite. But Kissinger wished to continue; he edged his chair further away from the table.

I told Kissinger that Burchett said Hanoi was considering breaking off the Paris negotiations. "Because of our bombing?" Kissinger asked. I said it was because the Vietnamese thought leaving Paris would embarrass Nixon politically at home.

Kissinger said of Hanoi and the Chinese: "I think the reason why Hanoi is active in Cambodia is to prevent the Chinese dominating it." Trying to veil my amazement, I related that [North Vietnam premier] Pham Van Dong recently said: "We have conquered the French and just about conquered the Americans; next we will have to face the Japanese."

After a while Kissinger had to slip away to fly back to Washington. "Send me a memo on all this," he said in parting.

Sometime later, after Kissinger's pioneering trip to China, Burchett wrote to me: "I have a few things to tell Kissinger about Hanoi's current view. He's met Zhou Enlai and found he can do business with him. The same could occur with Pham Van Dong."

I informed Kissinger that Burchett would like to meet him. "I may be wrong," I wrote in a note to the White House, "but I think he has more than a casual chat in mind." A Kissinger aide named Campbell quickly phoned me to say Henry would see Burchett for breakfast at the White House. Would I convey the invitation?

Burchett was a round-faced, cheerful man. Like me, he was from the hills and trout streams of Victoria state. We shared an Australian nativism, yet were drawn to Asia. Beginning in the late 1960s, we corresponded and talked regularly, whether in Paris, where he lived, at the Xin Qiao Hotel in Beijing, or in Cambridge, Massachusetts.

Burchett helped me with contacts in China and Vietnam in the 1970s. I sent him books from the U.S. not easily available in Paris. I helped him get his Australian passport back—lost through his disloyalty over the Korean War—when Gough Whitlam came to power as prime minister in 1972.

The evening before Burchett was to fly from New York to Washington to see Kissinger in October, 1971, he phoned me in a panic. His U.S. visa, given for the purpose of him covering the drama of Beijing 's seating in the UN for the American Communist newspaper, *The Guardian*, did not permit him to travel more than twenty-five miles from New York City.

I phoned Kissinger's office. "Tell Burchett to forget the restriction and get on the plane," Campbell said.

After the breakfast, Burchett phoned me at Harvard. "I think he wants to get out of Vietnam," he said of Kissinger. "It's a case of finding the right framework." Burchett said Kissinger seemed to indicate it would be useful to have Le Duc To or Pham Van Dong on hand in Beijing when Nixon is there. He wanted me to find out if that indeed was his meaning. "It certainly could be arranged," Burchett said, "to have a Vietnamese leader 'on hand.'"

Preparation for my 1971 trip to China included listening to Chinese language tapes. Having studied Chinese while working on my doctoral thesis on political philosophy in the late 1960s, I had learned to speak hundreds of words that I could not remember how to write. I copied each damn ideograph onto a "flash card," and carried the pack of square white cards around the Harvard campus, like a thief bearing the code of a safe he hoped to crack. Although my mind became modestly stocked with Chinese characters, my tongue was far from fluent.

I practiced with Chinese readings in a shrill Beijing woman's voice of essays by Mao including, "Serve the People," "In Memory of Norman Bethune," and "The Foolish Old Man Who Removed the Mountains." Today, I can still recite phrases in Chinese from these three pieces.

The Chinese language is tyrant, mistress, and illusionist at the same time. Hugh Dunn, who was at different times Australian ambassador in Taipei and

Peking, told me his tutor at Oxford said of the Chinese language, "Studying Chinese has a tendency to make you think you possess something no one has ever had before." The tutor advised student Dunn. "If you get that feeling, put your Chinese books away for a week and play golf."[7] When the Chinese characters made my mind soar too much, I turned to the political philosophy of R. H. Tawney, which pinned me back to my identity as a citizen of the West.

But my mind was to soar in the summer of 1971 when Zhou Enlai asked me where I learned Chinese. "In America," I replied. The premier beamed and said, "That is a fine thing, for an Australian to learn Chinese in America."

I did wonder if a China so ideological would readily grasp the outstretched hand of the West. Still, much had happened to the Chinese, and to Americans and Australians, in the years since my previous visit in 1964. I could hardly wait to see post-Cultural Revolution China. One-half of me thought Whitlam would succeed in his diplomatic mission; the other half feared he might fall flat on his face.

The editor of *Atlantic Monthly,* where I was the youngest contributing editor, had urged me to try to return to China and now he commissioned articles on the "new China." I also looked forward to first-hand observation of China's reactivated foreign policy for a course I was starting on China's foreign relations (a first at Harvard) as a new faculty member.

"How long will I stay?" I asked the Chinese official on the phone to Ottawa. "As long as you wish," he replied. I said seven weeks, dividing my time between investigation of China's domestic condition in the wake of the Cultural Revolution and interviews on China's outlook on the world. The plan was to visit eight cities and cover 7000 miles. In June 1971, I walked across the wooden bridge at Lo Wu that separated Britain's colony of Hong Kong from the PRC.

This reversed the direction of my journey in 1964, when I arrived from Siberia. However, the Chinese foreign ministry insisted I immediately leave the south and come to the capital for "discussions," which postponed my plans for Guangzhou. On the flight from Guangzhou to Beijing, a steward of the Chinese airline CAAC recited a quotation from Mao as preparation for take-off. Half way through the trip north, items from Beijing revolutionary operas were played. I took a nap, and as we descended upon Beijing, the steward cried solicitously into my ear, "We've arrived. Stop sleeping." Foreigners were few, and each was treated individually.

Some ten days later when Whitlam and his aides reached Beijing, Chinese Foreign Ministry officials and I met their plane. On the airport road, trees only three feet high, seven years earlier, now formed a green canopy turning a rural road into a boulevard. Whitlam emerged from the plane in a blue suit and said to Professor Zhang Xiruo, head of the Chinese Institute for

Figure 7.1.   Gough Whitlam (soon to be Australian Prime Minister) with author, at a Chinese commune, 1971. Author's photo.

International Affairs, host to the Australians, "I have been looking forward to meeting you." In informal Australian style, the secretary-general of the Labor Party wore a bright red shirt and the chair of the Queensland Labor Party was in vivid blue floral.

Whitlam's group, now including me, stayed at Beijing Hotel as guests of the Chinese Institute for International Affairs. Following talks with various ministers, one evening we were told by our hosts not to leave the hotel. A film was to be shown that we would find "very interesting." We should "wear suits and ties for the film show." Soon after 9 pm a phone call came: The movie was off. A meeting at the Great Hall of the People was on.

I was excited to meet Premier Zhou Enlai, to whom I was introduced by Ma Yuzhen, later ambassador to the UK. Zhou warmly welcomed his Australian visitors to the East Chamber, with its high ceilings, leaping murals, and crimson carpets. Present also were Ji Pengfei, the foreign minister, and Bai Xiangguo, the trade minister, both of whom we had met in previous days.

Zhou Enlai was slight and handsome, with expressive hands and a theatrical manner. His mouth was set low in his face, and when pushed forward, gave grandeur to his face. Zhou was all in gray except for a red "Serve the

People" badge, black socks inside his sandals, and black hairs amidst his gray ones.

This man had studied and agitated in Europe at the time of Lenin. He had been a member of the Politburo of the CCP since 1927. Four decades ago, he had been a colleague of Chiang Kai-shek's in Guangzhou. Sitting in his cane armchair, Zhou was a loose-limbed willow of a man. By comparison the tall Whitlam, hunched over in his chair, seemed stiff as a pine.

Zhou flattered me by saying, with a finger pointing toward my chair, "This man came to Beijing as your vanguard officer!" In fact, I was not quite a vanguard officer for Whitlam. However, I was a Beijing-lured "vanguard source" for Zhou's staff as they prepared for Whitlam. At a meeting the previous week, Ma Yuzhen asked me, "Are the policies of the Australian Labor Party public?" Zhou Nan asked, "Which members of Whitlam's delegation are left, and which are right?"

When Zhou and Whitlam found agreement on the positive changes occurring within American society about relations with Asia, the Chinese premier again pointed to me and said, "The materials Mr. Ross Terrill supplied to us added to what we knew, because he has lived in the USA." He paused to urge me, like a professor giving an instruction to a student, to study a recent editorial in *People's Daily,* on the occasion of the 45th anniversary of the Chinese Communist Party (CCP).

This essay stressed the importance of the Communist Party's control over the gun and gave stress to air force and navy as well as army. Some foreigners took the second point as a sign of coming professionalism in the People's Liberation Army, since it implied dependence on technology and weapons; you cannot repair a plane without spare parts, no matter which Mao quotation you utter. I still have the text of that editorial, with its red-lettered headline in a July 1, 1971 copy of *People's Daily,* now ginger-colored and crumbling.

Whitlam gave a good account of Australia's foreign policy to the Chinese premier, but he showed little understanding of the impact of the split between Beijing and Moscow on both Chinese and American thinking. The premier spent minutes criticizing former U.S. secretary of state John Foster Dulles for his policies of "encircling China." He reached for his tea mug, sipped, and swilled with deliberation. Then he went on, "Today, Dulles has a successor in our northern neighbor." Whitlam said, "You mean Japan?" This revealed how unprepared Whitlam was to grasp the strategic shift that had occurred in Chinese thinking from the late 1960s.

Zhou was curt in response to Whitlam: "Japan is to the east of us—I said to the north." It was hard for anyone on the Australian left to accept that Mao's CCP might think of the Soviet Union as an enemy. In the exchanges about Dulles, the encircling of China, and the Vietnam War, Whitlam also unwisely said, "The American people will never allow an American president to again send troops to another country." (Of course, they have done so numerous times since 1971).

If Zhou Enlai was tough on the Soviet Union, he was just as tough on Japan. He feared the Nixon Doctrine, asking more self-reliance from America's allies in Asia, would turn Japan into America's "vanguard in East Asia." He said it was "in the spirit of using Asians to fight Asians," or, involving Australia, "Using Austral-Asians to fight Asians." One of his strongest criticisms of Moscow, indeed, was that it failed to stand up against "Japanese militarism." He feared Japan would develop nuclear weapons.

"Look at our so-called ally," Zhou said to Whitlam of the Soviet Union. "They are in warm relations with the Sato government of Japan and in warm discussions on so-called 'nuclear disarmament' with the Nixon government, while China, their ally, is threatened by both of these."

"Is your own ally so very reliable?" the Chinese premier dramatically challenged Whitlam. "They have succeeded in dragging you onto the Vietnam battlefield. How is that defensive? That is aggression."

Later, Whitlam told he me he was surprised Zhou had not raised the issue of American military bases in Australia. In fact, the omission was a sign Mao was no longer as worried about the U.S. as he was about the Soviet Union. However, in a separate session the Chinese foreign minister did raise with Whitlam, China's unease that Australia had troops stationed in Singapore and Malaysia.

Zhou Enlai talked with the grace of an aristocrat even as Marxist doctrine came out of his mouth. "The world is not tranquil," he declared, "because monopoly capitalists want to gain profits." When the Australian Labor Party leader expressed acceptance of the "One China" principle that Beijing asked of foreign partners, the Chinese premier said crisply: "So far this is only words. When you return to Australia and become prime minister you will be able to carry out actions." Throughout the evening, Zhou never mentioned trade or uttered the word "wheat."

The following day *People's Daily* published a photo of our Australian group. Chinese officials made it clear that important business had been done with the Australian side, though only to be consummated by political change in Australia.

In general, the points made by Trade Minister Bai Xiangguo to Whitlam in a previous session were borne out by events. He said China would "deal with the McMahon government" but "only if we have to." However, China's desire for foreign wheat depended on factors other than politics. Bai also said that after Canberra recognized the PRC, Australia would get "the same consideration on wheat that Canada was getting. " At the Canadian Embassy in Beijing on July 5, I was told Canada's exports of wheat to China increased 10% in the first year after diplomatic relations were established between China and Canada.

Bai's mention of Chinese interest in Australian iron, steel, and bauxite turned out to be a sign of much to come. In addition, his indication that as Chinese taste for sweets grew, China would probably seek Australian sugar. However, these fruits lay in the future. For the early 1970s, I was justified in writing just after Whitlam's July 1971 trip, "the results, now the mission is over, seem likely to be weightier in foreign policy than in trade."[8]

"The days roll by and I give scarcely a thought to my prior world," I wrote in my diary during this magic summer of 1971, "I let China flow over me like the ripples of a brook. The only way to know today's identity is to look at my watch and count the days since June 16th, which sticks in my mind as the day I crossed the border from Hong Kong into Guangdong."

Prime Minister McMahon sharply criticized Whitlam's trip to Beijing. Zhou Enlai "had Whitlam on a hook," he mocked. "He played him as a fisherman plays a trout." Of Whitlam's words to Zhou, McMahon said, "I doubt if I have ever read such a damaging and irresponsible series of declarations by any political leader in all my time in politics in Australia."[9] Another government leader said, with more justification, "It is most dangerous to this country when the elected Australian government has a clear policy, for that policy to be undermined by the Opposition, not only at home but abroad."[10] A third government minister called the Labor Party's "exploitation" of the issue of China and wheat "degrading and disgusting."[11]

Whitlam's fairly skillful performance with Zhou, Foreign Minister Ji, and Trade Minister Bai ensured that the China issue would propel him nearer to election as Australian prime minister. It also set in motion new thinking among Australians about China. I wrote in the Sydney magazine *Nation* after Whitlam returned to Canberra: "Surely China will seem just a little less extra-planetary in Australia than before."[12] It happened. A foundation was laid for a flourishing and mutually advantageous relation between the PRC and Australia. It made our uphill struggles at the University of Melbourne during the 1960s for "Recognition of China" worthwhile.

Whitlam respected the traditions, rationality, and humor of Chinese people. He put China in the center of his thinking at this time. Some in the Labor party urged him to go to Japan and Indonesia as well as China on the July trip, but he swept the idea aside. In many years of association with him, Chinese were the only living people I ever saw him in some awe of (he esteemed the ancient Greeks and Romans). However, other Australians in Whitlam's 1971 group took China as they found it. They assumed the Chinese they met were fun-loving, beer-drinking human beings similar to Australians. They did not bring any baggage like me as a scholar of Chinese affairs.

The low-key Australian approach to China differed from the excited American approach to China. Folk from New York or San Francisco were more likely than Melbourne or Sydney people to grow enthusiastic about China, or to denounce China over a late train or a dirty hotel room. Australians were also less ethnocentric in approaching China than Americans. U.S. visitors hearing about wage scales in a commune might start comparing them with those at the Chrysler Corporation; Australian visitors just took note of Chinese wage scales as something new to be digested.

Wheat did not prove, after all, to be the key to the shift in China-Australia relations. Already in September 1972, with McMahon still prime minister, Beijing resumed wheat buying from Australia, with large orders totaling over one million tons. China called this a "purely commercial transaction" with no political significance. Still, non-wheat trade between Australia and China also leapt from A$6 million in 1969–70 to $A37 million in 1971–72.[13]

McMahon's foreign minister, rebuking Whitlam for his China foray, said the new Chinese wheat purchase was no reason for Australia to go "rushing to Beijing like a little puppy dog dragging its tail." In fact, by late 1972, Beijing may have been neutral in the coming Australian election. It is true that in his session with us in July 1971, Zhou Enlai twice said he hoped Whitlam would win the next Australian election. Yet much had changed by the time of the election of December 1972. Mao told Nixon in February 1972 that he liked rightists in certain circumstances. Chinese officials told me they appreciated any foreign leader who understood Moscow's dangerous ambitions.

Some Sinologists at the Australian National University (ANU) suggested the wheat order of September 1972 was in fact a quiet attempt by Beijing to help the re-election of the conservative Australian government. I cannot judge that. However, it was true McMahon was more anti-Soviet than Whitlam. Whitlam was better for Beijing on the bilateral relationship; McMahon may have been preferable on the broad international situation.

After I returned to Boston, I attended a party for the former prime minister of Britain, Harold Wilson, given by *Atlantic Monthly*. The event at the Ritz Hotel was in honor of Wilson's memoirs, edited and put out in the U.S by my own publishers. When the magazine chief introduced me to Wilson, I remarked that the mission of his foreign minister, Douglas Jay, to Beijing in late 1964 had apparently produced no results in China-Britain relations. "True, the Chinese wouldn't budge an inch," the former prime minister said. Of his disappointments with Beijing, while British prime minister, 1964–1970, Wilson summed up: "The Chinese thought I was too close to the Russians."

In Beijing, Whitlam asked Foreign Minister Ji what the Chinese government's attitude to Ted Hill, head of the Australian Communist Party (Marxist-Leninist), would be in the event of a Whitlam government. "Noninterference," replied Ji. "We do not know what is best for Australia." The Chinese press talked of Australia in Marxist terms like "sharpening of class struggle" but in practice Beijing seemed to have little interest in "making revolution" Down Under.

Australian opinion was divided over Whitlam's China visit, but the press was favorable. "Dropping Taiwan, as Whitlam is prepared to do," said a July 8 editorial in *The Australian,* owned by Rupert Murdoch, could be electorally unpopular; not dropping it, as the Government wants, means falling behind events that will decide our place in the region." The centrality of Taiwan to problems between China and Australia was interesting in light of the 3–4 decades of history since.

Incidents were regularly occurring in Australia over Taiwan. One involved the visit of the Chinese table tennis team in July 1972, just one year after Whitlam's visit to China as opposition leader, five months before the Australian election. The players on their second day in Australia learned that a Taiwan women's basketball team was in Australia at the same time. Schedules indicated the two sports teams would overlap in Melbourne and Sydney.

A spokesperson for the PRC team said, "The Taiwan visit is a deliberate conspiracy to promote the idea of two Chinas. Taiwan is an inseparable part of China." Ten minutes before the first match against Australia in Sydney, the Chinese team said it would not play. In an atmosphere of crisis—a crowd of 4000 was already waiting in the pavilion—the Chinese players agreed to do exhibition matches among themselves.

As tensions swirled, McMahon's foreign minister, meeting with the leader of the Beijing team, pointed out the Australian government did not arrange either international tour. Both were in the hands of Australian sports' associations. The PRC team offered to play in Perth and Adelaide, where the Taiwan women were not appearing. The Australian Table Tennis Association rejected this plan. The Australian foreign minister refused a Beijing request to expel the Taiwan women's basketball team from the country.

So, within 36 hours of its arrival in Australia, the Chinese table tennis team packed up and returned to China.[14] Sports lovers on all sides were dismayed.

A month after Whitlam's trip, in August 1971, McMahon's foreign minister Nigel Bowen told me, "Australia needs all the help we can get" from "specialists like you." He seemed to be testing my attitude to communism when he suggested that a blending of capitalism and socialism is "what we should eventually have." I said I didn't see it that way, since I thought communism was only relevant for less developed societies. The foreign minister seemed surprised by my position.

Bowen tried to downplay the wheat issue. "The wheat reserve this year is about 175,000 tons," he said, "compared with more than 100,000 tons more than that last year. It actually would have been embarrassing had we got a large wheat order from China this year." I wondered if he would have said that in public to the wheat farmers!

Throughout 1972, a "Committee for a New China Policy," of which I was on the executive, tried to urge on Canberra a switch of relations from Taiwan to Beijing. We put out an appeal on July 16, 1972, drafted by Stephen Fitzgerald and myself—corresponding and phoning between Harvard and the ANU, where Fitzgerald did research—urging the McMahon government to act.

"The China question is at the center of recent changes in world politics," we wrote, "described by President Nixon as essentially a change from confrontation to negotiation." We argued: "If we recognize Beijing, whatever may be the hopes or fears of the Australian government or of individual Australians regarding future Chinese policies, we will be in contact with the main streams influencing the Chinese people to make wiser and more informed judgments."[15] However, nothing came of our efforts during 1972.

Overall, in the early 1970s, in the view of many people in the U.S., Australia, and other countries, when the torment of Indochina finally ended, the West would have to share the future in Asia with China. Whitlam began a modest contribution to this turning point. Beijing, for its part, seemed ready to ease China's isolation and terminate the risks of its 1960s' double hostility to Russia and America alike. It was a step ahead for all three countries (but not for Russia).

NOTES

1. *Canberra Times*, July 5, 1971.

2. Patterson, House of Representatives, Hansard, September 28, 1972.

3. Ross Terrill, *Facing the Dragon: China Policy for a New Era*. Australian Strategic Policy Institute, Canberra, 2013, 10.

4. *Age*, Melbourne, March 30, 1967.

5. The story is told in the memoirs of Etienne Manac'h, *La Chine*, Paris, Gallimard, 1967, 382–83, 405, 408, 419–20; and the memoirs of E. G. Whitlam, *The Whitlam Government*, New York, Viking, 1985, 55.

6. *Sunday Times* article, carried by *Sun*, Melbourne, August 3, 1971.

7. Hugh Dunn, interview, OHAD, NLA.

8. *Nation*, Sydney, August 7, 1971.

9. McMahon speech, Young Liberals' Rally, Melbourne, July 12, 1971.

10. Hansard, Australia, September 28, 1971.

11. Hansard, Australia, September 28, 1971.

12. *Nation,* Sydney, August 7, 1971.

13. *Age*, Melbourne, September 29, 1972; *Sun*, Sydney, September 29, 1972; *Sydney Morning Herald,* September 29, 1972.

14. *Age*, July 24, 1972.

15. Fitzgerald, interview, OHAD, NLA.

Chapter Eight

Excitement Builds in Washington

One morning, prior to the arrival in Beijing of leader of the opposition, Gough Whitlam, across a coffee table laden with cakes and beer at the old International Club in the Legation Quarter, Peng Hua, head of the foreign ministry's information section, sought information on Kissinger. "Just how much power does he have in Nixon's White House? Is he still Germanic and anti-Russian? Is it true that he is nonchalant about the use of nuclear weapons? What does he think of Japan?"

The next day, Zhou Nan and Ma Yuzhen invited me to the International Club. They asked me questions, some about Australia, but many about Washington and Henry Kissinger in particular. I was puzzled. I also wanted to ask THEM questions about China's foreign policy.

However, since I knew Kissinger while a graduate student for five years in the Harvard Government Department where he was a professor, I was pressed to supply a picture of the man and his views on international relations.

During a further session, Zhou Nan was riveted by the Pentagon Papers case, which was unfolding by the day in the USA. "Who will benefit, the Republicans or the Democrats?" he asked of the illegal release of documents relating to the Vietnam War. He could not believe that Daniel Ellsberg may have acted alone in divulging the Pentagon Papers. "Is it the Morgan's who are behind him?" he probed. "Or the Rockefeller's?" He also asked if the Morgan's, not one single individual, had assassinated President Kennedy in 1963.

Introduced by a letter from Edgar Snow, I met Tang Mingzhao, who had been a journalist in New York in the 1940s, and much later was Under Secretary General of the UN. I walked down the steps of the Xin Qiao Hotel to take a taxi to Tang's office. However, my driver, shown the name and address on the envelope of Snow's letter, said he didn't know where Tang's unit, the well-known Association for Friendship with Foreign Countries, was located and disappeared into the staff booth.

Twenty minutes later, a travel official came out of the Xin Qiao Hotel and said I was wanted urgently on the phone. It was the Foreign Ministry; I was required there immediately. Postponing the delivery of Snow's letter to Tang, I went with my driver to answer the summons.

Zhou Nan and Ma Yuzhen were waiting for me. The meeting about my program seemed routine, until out of the blue, Ma raised Snow's letter. Just what was in it? I explained it was merely a letter of introduction from a "good friend of China." We will deliver it for you," said Ma. When Tang Mingzhao gave me lunch three days later, Zhou Nan was present throughout.

Tang Mingzhao was a wiry, lively Cantonese with opinions on every subject. "Pakistan is a capitalist state, not a socialist state," he declared, "but we like its independence." He said China lets a hundred flowers bloom in scientific debate. "We don't, like the Russians, pass a central committee resolution on whether Lysenko's theories are correct." Tang said China does not kill people who make mistakes, it remolds them. "If you kill people, they can't correct their mistakes," he reasoned.

Relaxing in mid-July, I went to Wuxi to enjoy Tai Lake and the surrounding blaze of mulberry trees. I watched members of a local people's commune swim in commemoration of Mao's famous swim of five years before; a boat followed them in the water, in alternation broadcasting directions and shouting Mao quotations.

Driving back to my hotel after visiting a peach orchard, I heard a stunning announcement on the car radio. Kissinger as envoy of President Nixon had just concluded a visit to China and Nixon himself would visit China within months. Next day, *People's Daily* carried the announcement in seven lines without commentary. Zhou Nan, who was traveling with me, received a phone call from Beijing to brief him on the turn of events.

That evening over dinner, Zhou Nan expressed his pleasure at the step in China-U.S. relations. "Nixon has asked to come to China," he said, "we will see what message he brings and we will respond accordingly." Such caution reflected the low-key manner in which news of the American initiative and Beijing's response broke in China. While the American public exploded with excitement (and some criticism), the Chinese public was of necessity restrained.

Zhou Nan was a graduate of Yenching University, originally founded in 1919 by American missionaries. An English speaker who honed his skills in postings to Tanzania and Pakistan, he felt comfortable with China's fresh opening to the West. He warmly welcomed Washington's live-and-let live detente with the PRC. He was certainly happy that the U.S.-China summit would occur on Chinese soil, not American. He grinned as he pointed out the announcement spoke of Nixon's "expressed desire" to visit Beijing and of China having "granted his request."

Early in July 1971, Nixon gave an interesting but little-noticed speech in Kansas City that praised the Chinese people and predicted a world of "five great economic superpowers" (U.S.A., USSR, Japan, Western Europe, and China). In Beijing, I discussed the Kansas City speech several times with senior officials Peng Hua, Ma Yuzhen, and Zhou Nan.

Kissinger wrote in his memoirs, "Zhou [Enlai] spent some time in our first meeting [in July 1971] . . . expressing his general agreement with the concepts outlined by Nixon in a speech in Kansas City on July 6. This put me at a disadvantage since I was unaware of either the fact or the content of the speech . . .[1]

In his memoirs, Kissinger also said of Zhou Enlai: "His command of facts, in particular his knowledge of American events and, for that matter, of my own background, was stunning."[2] Some of that knowledge had come quite recently. I, too, was unaware of the Kansas City speech until the Chinese raised it.

A cable from the *Washington Post* requesting articles on the breakthrough reached me in Changsha, home city of Mao. I had some background knowledge of the U.S.-China maneuver from my acquaintance with Kissinger, the questions asked by my Chinese minders, and the dialogue between Whitlam and Zhou Enlai.

On July 21, in the ferocious heat of a hotel room in Changsha, I wrote my first piece for the *Washington Post*. Zhou Nan was not happy with my doing the article. He discouraged phone contact by me with Beijing to seek information and reaction.

No typewriter was available. No one at the Changsha telegraph office knew English. Each *letter* of my article had to be identified in their "Alphabet Book" to ensure correct transmission. My only possible method was to handwrite block letters. As I wrote, like a child printing in a homework book, Zhou periodically came to my room, uneasy at my labors, looking at his watch.

"There is a banquet in your honor, given by senior Hunan officials, in a few minutes!" I took the finished article to the Changsha telegraph station for transmission to Washington.

The banquet with Changsha officials was congenial. For some reason Zhou Nan excused himself during the latter part, leaving me to struggle on with the exchange of views in my inadequate Chinese. After the banquet, we boarded a train for the southern city of Guangzhou. My berth had written on it, "Supreme Instruction: Serve the People—Number Nine—Lower." Sitting back on the opposite berth, Zhou Nan's first words were, "An interesting article you wrote for the *Washington Post*. Just two strange points in it." I realized why he excused himself toward the end of the banquet.

My cabled article from Changsha appeared on the *Washington Post's* front page on July 22. Kissinger phoned me at my apartment in Harvard's Kirkland House. "That was the most interesting newspaper article I have read from China," said Nixon's national security adviser. This did not prevent the *Washington Post* making a fuss over the cost of the cable from Changsha, which they had agreed to pay.

Kissinger was pleased to read in the piece that Chinese officials had told me they preferred to deal with Republicans rather than Democrats, because it had been Democrats (Truman and Acheson) who backed Chiang Kai-shek to the end, and who fought China in Korea. In addition, Democrats were too ready for "collusion with Moscow."

Kissinger equally liked to read that Beijing appreciated his skepticism about the Soviet Union's current "peaceful intentions," and saw Kissinger's past non-involvement in U.S. policies in East Asia as a point in his favor.

The day after my article came out Professor Ezra Vogel wrote on behalf of Harvard, "We can scarcely keep up with the new developments in China and are now prepared for practically everything. We look forward at the East Asian Research Center to your return and to getting a first-hand account."[3] Vogel and other colleagues at the East Asian center were all Democrats, and they were confused by a Republican president making a major breakthrough to their favorite country.

Zhou Nan was a wonderful traveling companion. Tall and straight, he walked briskly, carried a fan, and fell silent when something displeased him. He loved history, books in general, and swimming.

"You must study ancient Chinese history," he said one day in Xian as we visited the Big Wild Goose Pagoda. Links between ancient China and other parts of the world always delighted him. "Look, Ross, this Tang Dynasty stele shows a connection to the Roman Empire!" He likened a Buddhist image to a scene from Venice. Once in Guangzhou as torrential rain drenched us, he cheerfully cited Lao Zi: "The heavier the rain, the shorter it lasts."

Zhou Nan's daughter was studying German and Zhou Nan was interested in anything to do with Germany. Familiar with South Asia from his time in Pakistan, he tried to set me straight on how the Five Principles of peaceful coexistence related to China's support for world revolution. "We support revolution only morally," he told me, "we do not export revolution." I expressed the desire to visit Amoy in Fujian Province if the opportunity arose. "Your safety could not be guaranteed there," said Zhou Nan. "You might be shelled by [Chiang Kai-shek's] KMT!"

During a dinner in Guangzhou, I asked Zhou Nan what was the most difficult year since Liberation. "Economically, the worst year was 1961," he replied. "Politically, the year before the Cultural Revolution was the most difficult." I asked him if there could be revolution in Africa, where he had served as a diplomat, just like in China. Shaking his head, he paraphrased Sun Zi: "They don't know themselves and they don't know the enemy, that's the trouble."

At the end of a banquet in Shanghai, Zhou Nan signed the menu for me with a flourish. "I've done it in the old style," he said grandly. I asked if he sometimes used a brush. "At home I practice calligraphy every day," he said with enthusiasm. "I have different brushes for different styles. I have a collection of calligraphy from each major dynasty." I think Zhou Nan was in a good mood because the *Washington Post* article was not anti-China.

At Harvard, we had considered President Nixon calmer about communism in Europe than about communism in Asia. However, he changed. Edgar Snow was pleased when Kennedy defeated Nixon in the election of 1960; he told us President Kennedy, unlike Nixon, was prepared to move on China policy. It didn't turn out that way. I wrote in my diary at Wuxi, "Nixon's acts [in relation to China] seem less out of step with his words than previous Democratic administrations." That was true, and China-U.S. relations benefited.

Having dealt first-hand with both Senator Ted Kennedy and Kissinger over steps toward China, I saw a basic difference in approach between Democrats and Republicans. Kennedy and other Democratic senators who sought to go to Beijing from the late 1960s were concerned with legal and diplomatic issues. The Republicans were concerned with the U.S.'s role in the global power balance. Nixon called it the search for an "overall structure of peace."

The talks between a few of us Harvard faculty and Kennedy dealt with the China seat in the UN, blocked assets of China within the U.S., and formulae for dealing with the sovereignty of Taiwan. Kissinger was more interested in how to cope with the power of the Soviet Union.

I wrote in the *Washington Post* article of July 22, "Beijing takes the change from President Johnson's expansionism to Nixon's prudence very seriously." That was a crucial point.

An incident related to me by Edwin Reischauer, a senior colleague at Harvard's East Asian center, revealed Nixon's change of views on China. Early in 1969, Nixon met Reischauer, who had been President Kennedy's ambassador to Japan, sinologist George Taylor who was a "hawk" on China, and three other sinologists who like Reischauer were "doves." In the Oval Office, all four doves criticized the existing policy of nonrecognition of Beijing and keeping China out of world forums. Then Taylor spoke in favor of the existing policy, saying the United States should wait until China was less anti-American before holding out a hand.

President Nixon broke his silence. "You know, I used to think that way once, too, Mr. Taylor," he said. A new breeze was blowing in Washington.

Late in 1971, I created a stir by saying Washington had decided to look the other way while the UN moved toward seating Beijing in the China spot at the UN and its security council. Year by year the U.S. had been losing ground in its efforts to keep the Chiang Kai-shek regime in the China seat. After Kissinger's July 1971 visit to Washington, the momentum in Beijing-Washington relations predisposed Nixon and Kissinger to let the chips fall where they may at the annual vote on the China membership issue in October 1971. I wrote that Kissinger had intimated to Zhou Enlai that the U.S. would favor Beijing taking the China Security Council seat, but that it would also support some role in the UN for Taiwan. However, I added that Kissinger said the American side "did not know" whether this second effort would succeed. This was a sign of fatalism.[4]

When the vote drew near a second indication of events to come was the timing of Kissinger's visit to Beijing that October. China managed to schedule his visit to coincide with and thus influence the UN vote, and to extend Kissinger's stay by two extra days in case any "slip-up" occurred in the expected Beijing victory in New York. This confluence of events certainly did not help George Bush (later to be president), who was U.S. ambassador to the UN, to twist arms in favor of keeping the PRC out of the UN's China seat. Kissinger's presence in China during the vote was more eloquent of Nixon's real feelings than were Bush's words at the UN.[5]

After the UN vote on October 25, 1971, I wrote a diary entry: "An historic night as Beijing enters the UN. The Albanian resolution wins at last, 76 to 35. I recall the Fall of 1965, listening to Adlai Stevenson's dismal defense of the United States policy of keeping Beijing out. Ever since, I have felt depressed at American obstructionism on this issue."

I visited Zhou Nan at the Roosevelt hotel a few days later. He was enjoying the wave of China-centered diplomacy. He said the Chinese delegation had not expected the margin to be so great in the UN vote to seat Beijing. "But our Chinese delegation cannot sleep well," he complained, "because of the loud sirens in New York; we are all taking sleeping tablets." I asked about the possibility of him coming to Harvard to talk to a student audience. "I would

speak in Chinese," he said, "and my topic would be Tang Dynasty poetry."
The talk did not occur.

The opening to Beijing had been prepared for two years with channels in
Warsaw, Bucharest and Rawalpindi. In 1969, Kissinger told the American
ambassador in Poland to intercept the Chinese envoy at a social function and
tell him Washington wanted to resume Warsaw talks between the U.S. and
China. At that time, American and Chinese diplomats rarely acknowledged
each other at diplomatic gatherings.

A few days later at a Yugoslav reception to launch a fashion show, the
American ambassador suddenly addressed the Chinese charge d'affairs, Lei
Yang. The Chinese diplomat, startled, turned around and walked out the
door. The U.S. ambassador ran down the stairs after Lei Yang to say a few
crucial words. Later in Beijing, Zhou Enlai said to Kissinger, "If you want
our diplomats to have heart attacks, approach them at parties and propose
serious talks."

In the American style, drama surrounded the new moves with China. Kissinger during one conversation with Zhou Enlai, after delivering his carefully
prepared summary of why the U.S. government wanted serious contact with
China, declared that at last the American side had arrived in the land of "mystery." Zhou asked why "mystery" was the appropriate term. Why was China
the land of mystery and what was the meaning of mystery? Of course, it was
a silly remark from a normally rational professor.

Looking towards Nixon's trip, the *Washington Post*, in a February 13,
1972 editorial, "Prospects in Beijing," gave a shrewd summation of the task
from the U.S. side: "the problem is to ease off a generation's devotion to the
'containment' of China without making the American friends on the rim pay
the costs of that change."

Kissinger told me two kinds of folk opposed what Nixon was doing on
China in 1971–72: "People who feel we should be loyal to Chiang Kai-shek,
and people who say we shouldn't upset the Russians." In fact, Kissinger
himself was enthusiastic for the China opening exactly because he had NO
BACKGROUND of commitment to Chiang Kai-shek and he WANTED for
strategic reasons to "upset" the Russians.

My Australian skepticism kept me from going "hot" or "cold" on China.
I felt removed from the American tendency to swing between romance and
hostility. However, I strongly favored the Nixon moves. Washington and
Beijing together had found a basis for a new order in East Asia. True, it was
based on a "negative" to begin with: the greater threat of Moscow to both
sides compared with any threat posed by Washington or Beijing to each other.
Still, as events turned out, the China-USA relationship was to strengthen its

basis over the decades; it moved far beyond an anti-Soviet stance and indeed set the framework for a broad economic leap in East Asia.

Having links with three countries, I saw relationships with China from a variety of angles. Chinese officials asked me about Kissinger's mind ("What does he really think about Japan?") and about the "monopoly capitalist" foundations of American and Australian newspapers ("Are the Rockefellers or the Morgan's behind them?). Kissinger asked me about the Chinese ("Are the Vietnam leaders similar to Zhou Enlai?). Some Australian leftists could not believe the Sino-Soviet split was real ("Ross, are they just pretending to quarrel, in order to trick the Americans?").

In February, 1972, Whitlam, on a trip to North America as Leader of the Opposition, asked me to arrange a meeting at the Chinese mission to the UN. We talked for two hours with Ambassador Chen Chu, a blunt, friendly man, at the Roosevelt Hotel in New York, where the mission staff lived while waiting for their own building.

Whitlam asked what kind of reception Nixon would get in Beijing the next week. "There will be no rotten eggs and tomatoes," Chen Chu said. "But, speaking personally, I do not think there will be vast crowds." The ambassador, who chain-smoked all morning, reaffirmed a relation between politics and trade, as Foreign Trade Minister Bai had done to us in Beijing. He said Canada was getting the preference over Australia on wheat in present circumstances.

The conversation turned to Taiwan. "We will strive for a peaceful solution to this problem," Chen Chu said, "but it's not entirely up to us." He pointed out, "Some parts of China were liberated peacefully—Beijing for example—but other parts were liberated only with a certain amount of violent struggle. Tibet was liberated peacefully, but later a violent struggle arose when feudal elements tried to kick back."

When the Ambassador asked Whitlam his impression of America, the Australian mentioned his visit that morning to the head of the Morgan Guarantee Trust. "I think American business circles are becoming very open minded toward China. For example, these bankers have all read Ross Terrill's articles in *Atlantic Monthly*."

I had reported in one of those articles that Washington, in the interests of the overall relation with Beijing, privately indicated they would pull back from Taiwan as U.S.-China tensions subsided.[6] The *Washington Post* and other newspapers seized upon this. They interpreted my report as proof the U.S. was ready to return to the 1949 policy. That is to say, "Washington was not going to interfere in the destiny of Taiwan."

The newspapers correctly related my conviction that Nixon would begin the process of pulling back from Taiwan before arriving in Beijing in February 1972, just as he had made previous gestures toward China at key moments. Initiating efforts to talk seriously with Beijing in 1969, Washington quietly ended Taiwan-based spy flights over China and removed most of the Seventh Fleet from the Taiwan Strait.[7]

Similarly, Beijing watched to see if the American incursion into Laos in the spring of 1971 meant an incipient threat to China or not. In fact, as the *Washington Post* afterward said, "Nixon did nothing to salvage the South Vietnamese failure in Laos." Chinese officials made it clear to me they noticed and appreciated this restraint. It was an important gesture from Washington at a crucial time.[8]

My *Atlantic* articles were expanded into a book, *800,000,000* in March, 1972. The volume was quickly published in Japanese, Norwegian, German, and other languages. In the U.S. it soon sold 40,000 copies in hardback. The magazine *Nation* noted mischievously, "President Nixon has been reading Terrill's book; with Kissinger excepted, you might have to go back to Alger Hiss till you find any character from Harvard to whom Nixon paid such close attention."[9]

Chinese translation in Taiwan was a curious affair. The KMT newspaper in Taipei, *Zhongyang ribao,* began a series of articles drawn from my book (without seeking permission). The first excerpts were accompanied by a note saying a total of twenty-two excerpts from *800,000,000* would appear. Mysteriously, however, after four articles the series stopped without further explanation.

Some Chinese correspondents raised reasonable criticisms of *800,000.000.* "Why the title *800,000.000*?" wrote a Chinese reader from California. "Yes, China has a large population, but the phrase strikes me as a subtle analogue to Dean Rusk's vision of a 'billion Chinese armed with nuclear weapons.'" This reader had a point.

So did another Chinese reader who objected to my saying China was "isolated." She said the "absence of Coca Cola signs" does not bespeak isolation and in terms of "revolutionary movements around the world," China was well-connected. My stress on China's policies of "self-reliance" was stronger, this correspondent felt, than my description of China as "isolated."

In the early 1970s, a Western writer could only nibble at the edges of China. Because of international tensions, Chinese and Westerners were just discovering each other's humanity. It was true, as the Chinese Preface to *800,000,000* stated, that in 1971–72 I had a "world view"—call it bourgeois—that did not include the life of China within the life of humanity as a whole. Baby steps of accepting "the other" would have to precede larger strides of common endeavor. We Westerners did not yet feel that we could share the world's future with China. That would come later.

An amateur specialist on the Daoist book of wisdom. *I-Qinq*. "Book of Changes," wrote from rural Massachusetts. "Please, Mr. Terrill, does Chairman Mao consult the I-*Qing*?." He inquired: "Would one find a copy of the *I-Qing* in a typical people's commune?"

Simple letters were touching. "I am in grade four at school," wrote a pupil in Melbourne, Australia, "studying China at the moment. I was wondering if you could discuss some questions with me to help in my class assignment." She began her list of questions; "Are Westerners afraid of China? If so, why?" Her next question was equally sharp: "How old are you—I need to know because it helps me analyze your answer to my first question."

The mention of Chinese medical treatments in *800.000.000* evoked letters. A Spanish man wrote about the need for acupuncture for his crippled daughter. "If anything comes of this appeal in the direction of China," he ended his letter to me, "a beautiful and charming girl in Madrid may be able to walk again." A blind man wrote in huge black block letters from Rhode Island asking if "the Chinese through acupuncture have been able to cure cases of blindness that would be considered incurable in the West?" My passage on the Paraplegic Unit at Beijing Chinese Medicine Hospital brought a letter from the Spinal Injuries Centre at a hospital in my home city of Melbourne. "This is the first reference I have ever seen to the existence of a paraplegic unit in China," wrote the physician, who was vice-president of the International Medical Society of Paraplegia. "We eagerly seek contacts with China."

Ambassador Manac'h of France told me of talking with Zhou Enlai as ping-pong diplomacy unfolded. It had been Manac'h, who conveyed to China two points Nixon made to de Gaulle before he became U.S. president: that he would withdraw American troops from Vietnam and improve Washington-Beijing relations. In the spring of 1971, Manac'h reminded Zhou Enlai of these points. The Chinese premier asked what impact China's favorable response to Nixon was having within the U.S. "It helped Nixon in his goals," Manac'h replied to Zhou. "I don't mind that effect," Zhou said. "China is now ready to cooperate with Nixon."

Both France and China feared any "getting together" between the U.S. and the Soviet Union, and both felt this was less of a danger under a Republican administration in America than under a Democratic one.

An opening to China appealed to Nixon for transcending Vietnam with a broad new era in East Asia. To Kissinger, the appeal of China lay especially in its anti-Soviet potential. Chief of staff in the Nixon White House, Bob Haldeman, in *The Ends of Power,* testified from his close observation of events: "When Nixon took office, one of his first priorities was reopening of relations with China. Kissinger was a rather reluctant passenger those first six months. Then came the Soviet-Chinese border clashes [of 1969]. Kissinger and Nixon huddled."[10] From then onward, the president and his national security adviser were on the same page concerning China.

At a Washington Press Club dinner in January 1972, where the menu theme was China ("Snow Peas in Mao Jackets," "Election Egg Rolls") I chatted with Henry Kissinger. After his key-note speech Kissinger said of the *Atlantic Monthly* pieces: "They were the first thing I gave the president to read in preparation for the trip next month."

A British expert on Asia, Ernest Satow, once told young recruits going to East Asia: "Do not waste your time worrying about what is in the Asian mind. The main thing is to be clear what is in your own mind." In this respect, Nixon and Kissinger were ahead of Congress, the Democratic Party, the universities, and the media. They knew what they sought. To get it, they located overlapping interests with China. They would find out in negotiation what China required, align some overlapping interests, and try to satisfy these requirements as well as U. S. interests.

Coming from left of center, I found a striking virtue in Kissinger's open mind about China. "What should we talk to the Chinese about?" he would ask me, a totally different approach from the more usual, "When are the Chinese going to become worthy of our recognizing them?"

An understanding of balance of power politics also made Kissinger a refreshing force in American policy toward Asia. He saw that China and America had a mutual interest in drawing closer to each other as a way of countering Soviet power. He felt the breakthrough with the Chinese would come on broad grounds and he was correct.

James Thomson, head of the Nieman Foundation at Harvard, told me over lunch at the Faculty Club of his talks in Washington in January 1972. "They are starry-eyed towards the Chinese at the White House and the State Department," he reported. Kissinger said to Thomson, who had been a China advisor to President Johnson. "These are the most mature, responsible, humorous leaders in politics today. The only man I could compare Zhou Enlai with is De Gaulle." Al Jenkins at the State Department (later to serve in the U.S.'s liaison office in Beijing), who had churned out the anti-Communism of Dulles in the 1950s, looked Thomson in the eye and said, "It's beautiful, the equality in that country. They are creating a new man. . ."

A week before Nixon's trip, Barbara Waters of NBC phoned with questions about China. "I wanted to get you for our coverage," she said, "but I believe CBS has grabbed you for theirs." Walters' questions ranged from sex and marriage to the price of cabbages. "Do work points operate only in the rural communes or in factories too?" she asked. Clearly, she had been an attentive reader of my *Atlantic Monthly* articles.

A *New York Times* culture critic arrived in Boston to interview me about Chinese food. Raymond Sokolov came with a photographer to my Harvard office to ask about the cuisine Nixon would encounter in China. "Some of Ross Terrill's impressions were on the President's desk last week," the article cried, to buoy the importance of our talk about food.

I described for Sokolov a dinner in Guangzhou, hosted by myself, where *gou rou*—not chosen by me!—was one of eight dishes served. The smell of dog took away any desire to taste this southern delicacy. Later in the article, American readers, accustomed to eating in "China Towns" in U. S. cities, may have been surprised to read my truthful words, "I never saw a single fortune cookie in seven weeks in China."

Sokolov quoted me, "There is egalitarianism at the Chinese table; chauffeurs sit down with VIPs." I also went over the top, "Food is almost sacred in China." A huge photo of me sitting with a map of the PRC in Chinese behind my office chair ran with the article in the *New York Times* on February 17, four days before Nixon landed in Beijing.

Pearl Buck was more immersed in Chinese ways than any living U.S. writer, diplomat, journalist or academic. After decades in China, her first language was and remained Chinese, and she had lived half of her life in China. Within American society, Buck's most famous book, *The Good Earth,* was even more influential than *Red Star Over China*. It was a novel about the human condition in rural China, not a report of war and struggles, like Snow's work and most American books on Chinese politics. So fully was Buck a China hand that, when she won the Nobel Prize for Literature in 1938, William Faulkner, who won the prize himself eleven years later, wrote without generosity that he would prefer not to win the Nobel than be in the company of "Mrs. China hand Buck."[11]

In her eightieth year, Buck invited me to visit her in Vermont, where she lived with her staff among beautiful hills and trees. It was 1971; Nixon's China trip had been announced but still lay ahead. Resplendent in jewels and a long blue dress, Buck hosted a Korean dinner for me. Next day she asked questions for six hours about my summer 1971 trip to China. Some weeks later, her secretary sent me a full transcript of our conversations.

Buck felt she had not really left China, because China was within her. She was nevertheless uncertain about the wisdom of a return visit three decades after she had left her prior world. *My Several Worlds* was the revealing title of her autobiography. Buck had written to Beijing about a Chinese visa. She awaited an answer at the time of our conversations. However, she wavered on whether she really wished to go. She was no longer young, she was a little frightened, and unsure she would fit in with new China.

I found Buck not in awe of any political leaders, Chinese, American, or others. Over our Korean dinner in Vermont, she told me of a party given by President Kennedy for U.S. winners of the Nobel Prize. The president asked her during dinner, "What should we do in Korea?" She made a few points on the history of East Asia. Kennedy said, "I think we'll have to get of there. It's too expensive and we must involve the Japanese to play their part in Korea."

Buck gave me a smile that had no warmth. "It was the only time an American president—and I've known them all since I returned from China in 1938—the only time one has asked me a question about Asia." And Buck thought Kennedy's remarks showed ignorance of the history of Japan-Korea relations.[12]

"There's a generation gap among nations," she said as we sat in the sunlight of her living room facing golden Vermont trees beyond the window. "Many of the differences between the U.S. and China are because the U.S. is young and China is old." Buck did not believe in democracy. "Rather I believe in great people and their benevolence and virtues toward other people." Buck was a lover of China who transcended the political struggles over China-policy of the Roosevelt, Truman, Eisenhower, Kennedy, and Johnson years.

NOTES

1. Henry Kissinger, *White House Years*. Boston, Little, Brown, 1979, 748.
2. Kissinger, *Ibid.*, 744.
3. Vogel, letter to author, July 23, 1971.
4. *Atlantic Monthly*, January 1972, 47.
5. *Washington Post*, March 19, 1972.
6. *Atlantic Monthly*, January 1972, 48.
7. *Washington Post*, January 6, 1972; *New Nation,* Manila, January 7, 1972.
8. *Atlantic Monthly*, January 1972, 43–44; *Washington Post*, January 6, 1972.
9. *Nation*, weekly, Sydney, March 4, 1972.
10. Haldeman, *The Ends of Power*. New York, Times Books, 1978, 91–92.
11. Sheila Melvin, "Pearl's Great Price," *Wilson Quarterly*, Spring 2006, 27.
12. Conversations with Pearl Buck, Danby, VT, December 26–27, 1971, unpublished memo prepared for Ross Terrill by Buck's secretary.

Chapter Nine

Nixon "Changes the World"

Nixon and his entourage of eight hundred arrived at Beijing airport on the wintry morning of February 21, 1972. It was the first time a U.S. president was to negotiate on the soil of a country lacking diplomatic relations with the U.S. Nixon's eight-day trip was the longest foreign stay a U.S. president had ever made. Premier Zhou Enlai was at the airport to greet the president as the Stars and Stripes played. But there was no crowd of Chinese people; Nixon's party of 800 outnumbered all the other people at the airport.

I was in a CBS studio in New York as a commentator. For a week, morning (evening in China) and night (morning in China), I made remarks on large matters and small to tens of millions of Americans about the visit, in dialogue with Walter Cronkite, the kingpin of American television news. It felt like history hour by hour.

After a dialogue with CBS anchor Charles Collingwood on Nixon's first day in Beijing, I wrote in my diary: "I felt excited as Nixon's plane 'Spirit of '76' drew up at Beijing airport with the American flag fluttering in the north China sky and the melody of Stars and Stripes echoing over the wintry scene. I tried to keep my commentary sober and balanced, but I am not sure I succeeded."

China now held Americans in thrall. During that week, had I told American viewers that every Chinese child was an angel and Mao was the greatest man in history, they would have believed me.

It was new in the U.S. for China to be a topic of daily conversation. Chinese clothes, Chinese cuisine, Chinese history—all aspects of the topic were scrutinized. An athlete phoned the CBS studio to ask if I could help him get permission to run across the top of the Great Wall. A Chinese-American in California wrote asking me to write an essay about her father who once worked with Zhou Enlai in the wartime capital of Chongqing.

The Cleveland Museum of Art sought assistance to set up cultural exchanges with museums in Chinese cities. A professor in North Carolina cabled to seek a cassette of the musical "Red Detachment of Women" for his next class on Chinese society. The Kettering Foundation in Ohio asked my help in setting up "substantial communication between Americans and Chinese on scientific and cultural questions."[1] The requests kept coming.

At Harvard, some enthusiastic students wished to plan two canoeing trips with Chinese counterparts, one along the Yangzi, the other along the Mississippi. "We have located a China Watersports Association in Beijing," the leader of the Harvard group wrote to me. "Also, we've seen magazine pictures of canoes and kayaks on Chinese waterways." The students had written a score of letters to Chinese organizations and anxiously awaited replies.

One viewer of our CBS coverage watching from Northampton, Massachusetts wrote, "I was very offended at [reporter] Eric Sevareid for making so much of the regimentation of Beijing–ers sweeping up snow, when we have the regimentation of standardized food like McDonald's hamburgers and Kentucky Fried Chicken." A professor at the University of Massachusetts who knew of my immigration struggles as an Australian trying to get a green card in the U.S. wrote: "I hope Immigration Department officials watch CBS!"[2]

Some felt the networks overdid non-stop attention to elusive China. CBS boss Richard Salant told *Newsweek* he cancelled the planned final broadcast from the Forbidden City. "I just thought we'd had enough picture postcards [from the previous day at the Great Wall]."[3] CBS's penultimate session from China, complained *Newsweek*, "found the correspondent team huddled together in the Beijing press room, speculating on events they didn't understand. When the CBS broadcast switched to New York," *Newsweek* went on, "a bright young scholar named Ross Terrill cut through the fog with succinct answers to specific questions."

Although the American left suddenly grew cooler on China, the American foreign policy establishment grew warmer. Sympathetic China commentators sprouted like bamboo shoots after rain. Kissinger from the White House and media princess Barbara Walters from a TV studio became overnight China enthusiasts. Both stood to the left of me in commentary on China. "No other world leaders have the sweep and imagination of Mao and Zhou," said Kissinger after his Beijing experiences in the early 1970s. "Mao radiates authority and deep wisdom."[4]

Walters of NBC invited me for China-talk on her popular show "Not for Women Only," which came on each weekday. Our five segments were taped during one morning in New York. We changed the color and style of our clothes five times, so each day's show would look different; the NBC studio was like the fitting room of a department store.

In between segments, Walters sprayed me with pro-China observations. She had fallen head over heels for China. "The people all say their life is better now than it was in the days of the landlords," she declared. Walters felt able to generalize, sometimes correctly, about the views of 800 million people—after eight days in China.

"The planes which took Mr. Nixon, his official party and American correspondents to China," the *New York Times* wrote, "were in effect air-borne Universities," catching up on the study of China. Reports that Mao was brushing up with English lessons suggested to the *New York Times* that "a similar effort to learn about this country has been taking place in Beijing."[5] In fact at a Washington Press Club speech in early February I had conveyed this news, learned from Mao's friend Guo Moruo, who said two of Mao's favorite English phrases were "law and order" and "anti-Mao."

During Zhou Enlai's banquet for Nixon in the Great Hall of the People, Cronkite, from his chair on a balcony above the head table asked me in the CBS studio in New York, "Why have the Chinese hosts served Nixon a plate

Figure 9.1.   Author snapped premier Zhou Enlai after their chat, 1971. Author's photo.

of Jell-O for dessert?" When I looked into the screen beside me, I saw before each guest a white plate holding a brilliantly colored tangerine. "Is it Jell-O, Walter?" I murmured. "Or are those tangerines?" A heavy silence came from Cronkite in Beijing. Such was the technology—and triviality—that filled the moments of a historic event.

What struck me during Nixon's trip was the American capacity for renewal and enthusiasm in dealing with China. It was as if the years of fear and hostility between the United States and Mao's China never existed. The normally calm columnist James Reston declared: "China obviously has a manner, a purpose and an ideal which touch something deep in the American spirit."[6]

Nixon himself on leaving Washington compared his trip to China with his compatriots' voyage to the moon. In Guam at a refueling stop, he said to the crowd: "Join me in this prayer, that with this trip to China a new day may begin for the whole world."[7] In Beijing he quoted Mao's poems as if they were the Bible. "A trip to China is like going to the moon," he told *Time* magazine in a Man of the Year interview.

I wrote in my diary after the week at CBS: "I think the way of life of the Chinese people is starting to come into focus for Americans. Maybe a new relationship between the two peoples will blossom, wherein each remain themselves, but also become a little different by virtue of understanding the other."

Nixon eventually said his trip added up to "a week that changed the world." As summit meetings go, the trip did indeed change the world. China emerged with a half-reassuring smile from the Cultural Revolution, triangular diplomacy was born, the Russians were agitated like ants on a hot stove, and most of the domestic critics of both Zhou Enlai and Nixon were (for the moment) silenced.

Even for those too young to recall the Nixon opening to China, the trip of 1972 lives on five decades later, in China and across the world, as a symbol of political audacity; a scintillating maneuver pulled off by the wrong person opening the right door.

Nixon in China sparked vivid moments. He vigorously shook the hand of Zhou Enlai on the tarmac of Beijing airport, canceling John Foster Dulles' unreadiness to shake Zhou's hand at the conference on Indochina in Geneva in 1954. American (and perhaps some Chinese) officials clinking glasses of *maotai* in the Great Hall of the People sensed a revival of what they fancied to be a unique chemistry between the two nations.

The columnist Henry Owen wrote an Op-ed saying Nixon's trip "should be viewed as an exercise in American public education," to end "unrealistic American judgment about China for the last hundred years."[8] This did not really happen. Some old myths died but new ones lay ahead. Parallel to a funeral, Owen aptly said, Nixon's trip did not change reality but forced people to acknowledge reality. That meant accepting an East Asia in which tentative partnership between China and the U.S. was a centerpiece.

The Chinese premier later looked back on the Nixon visit: "In the communiqué with the American president the five principles of co-existence were mentioned as a common point," he told the deputy prime minister of Australia. "This shows that after twenty years of John Foster Dulles policies, the result of their observation has been that there has been a change in their ideas."[9] The Chinese were naturally satisfied at this switch by Washington.

It was equally remarkable that the shared section of the Shanghai Communiqué stated of the U.S. and China: "Neither should seek hegemony in Asia-Pacific."

Ten hours ahead of Kissinger's secret pre-Summit arrival, Prince Sihanouk of Cambodia, then resident in Beijing, was told personally by Zhou Enlai of the impending events.

China had persuaded Sihanouk and Pham Van Dong to work together in uneasy harness. Orchestrated by Zhou Enlai, Sihanouk and Pham met. Sihanouk told me, mixing bits of English with his French, that on crucial questions Zhou said he consulted Mao. Sihanouk related that Mao eventually said to him directly: "You can have anything you want from China."

Sihanouk didn't want Vietnamese troops to remain in Cambodia, as Zhou didn't. Zhou said to Sihanouk: "We do not support the so-called Maoists in Cambodia. China is one country; Cambodia is quite another—you should remain neutral." Zhou also told Sihanouk, "It is better not to have Chinese troops on Cambodian soil."

Sihanouk told me he was very happy when Pham said to him: "After Liberation, we'll go together to the Vietnam-Cambodia border and plant frontier marks, at the existing borders, with the international press present, to indicate the complete integrity and independence of each country."

I asked Sihanouk his assessment of China's international strategy. "Russia is China's biggest problem, and Japan is Asia's biggest problem," he replied. How did Sihanouk's style as a royal figure and a Buddhist go down with Mao? "The Chairman told me he likes princes when they're not reactionary, but with their people, and against imperialism—like me."

I wondered whether Sihanouk's beloved land would be able to secure true independence. "So long as Vietnam is independent-minded, Cambodia will not be dominated," the Prince said. He realized the future depended, not only on Japan, but on whether China respected smaller countries in its neighborhood. "I don't think it's in China's interests to make Cambodia a satellite. First, it's a poor country, and would be a burden. Second, because if the

Chinese subjected Cambodia, they would not be able to convince Africans and Asians that China respects small nations."

Sihanouk's main frustration with Zhou Enlai was over travel around the world to put the case for a truly independent Cambodia. Sihanouk was on the edge of his chair: "I told the premier, 'You should help me travel outside the triangle of China, North Vietnam and North Korea. Some people say I'm a prisoner. It's not good to have this believed.'" The Prince's face pouted. "The CIA may kidnap you," Zhou explained. "He says he is preparing a plane for me. But he does not seem keen. I don't know why. . ."

Zhou assured Sihanouk of China's "total solidarity" with him despite a changed situation. "We are not like the leaders in Moscow," the premier said. "We will not sacrifice our friendships and principles for the sake of détente." Sihanouk recalled that Zhou also said: "Even if we get the necessary concessions out of the Americans, we will not be finished with imperialism in our region. For the Japanese are ready to take over."

"It was a stroke of genius by the Chinese side," Prince Sihanouk said cheerfully of the Chinese invitation to Nixon. "It will isolate and disconcert the U.S.'s allies in Asia—above all [Cambodian rival] Lon Nol."[10]

In planning for the trip, unusual excitement within the White House led the U.S. side to defer to Beijing. U.S. territory only for refueling stops—Hawaii and Guam on the way and Alaska on the way back—to avoid stops at U.S. air bases like Okinawa, lest Chinese objections be raised. U.S. air bases in the Far East were not even on the emergency list in case Shanghai airport should close. Nor was Hong Kong listed, only Guangzhou, a nearby city within the PRC.

Nixon was also deferential to China's values (far more so than, say, the second President Bush). "You believe deeply in your system and we believe just as deeply in our system," he told Zhou Enlai in his toast at a dinner for the Chinese premier. "It is not our common beliefs that have brought us here, but our common interests."

Such was the positive mood about the trip in the U.S. that even the left-of-center newspapers treated a Republican president with respect. "We wish his undertaking well," the *Washington Post* wrote uncharacteristically on February 13. A few days later the *New York Times* editorialized: "Millions of Americans must have been thrilled last night as they watched the President arrive and heard the Chinese band at the Beijing airport play 'The Star-Spangled Banner' while the American flag fluttered overhead." It even gushed: "Through the magic of television, Americans and the world at large now have a chance to see China as it has never been seen before."[11] Those were the days.

Mao Zedong seemed eager to meet Nixon. Plagued by a congestive heart, he rose early the day Nixon flew in, dressed in a new suit and shoes, his hair cut for the first time in five months. Sitting restless on a sofa, he kept in touch with Premier Zhou by phone.

When President Nixon reached Zhongnanhai, among Mao's first words were, "Our common friend, Generalissimo Chiang Kai-shek, doesn't approve of this."[12] Mao's wife, politburo member Jiang Qing, escorting Mr. and Mrs. Nixon the next evening to see "Red Detachment of Women," was less mellow: "Why did you not come to China before now?" She was reminding Nixon of his anti-Communist past in the 1950s.

In the preliminary Beijing-Washington negotiations, China had sought to stick to the single issue of Taiwan, while the U.S. wanted to broach an "overall structure of peace" in East Asia. However, at Zhongnanhai Mao said to Nixon, "Taiwan is not an important issue; the international situation is an important issue."[13] With that remark, he had temporarily compromised on Taiwan because of alarm at the Soviet Union. Broader issues were on the table. The Americans exulted.

In U.S. official thinking about China, realpolitik had pushed ideology aside. Gone was the Republican Party's across-the-board anti-communism. The Vietnam War and the Cultural Revolution were both transcended by the "realism" of Nixon and Kissinger.

In the Shanghai Communiqué, Nixon gave China guarantees against the use of force, interference, or any bid for hegemony in Asia. China, apprehensive about the Russians ("John Foster Dulles's successors" as he described them to Whitlam, objecting to their "interference"), agreed to move toward "normalizing" relations with the United States even while Washington retained full diplomatic ties with Taipei. It was a good deal for both sides.

The president of Hofstra University in New York organized a panel on the trip in April 1972, with my colleague Reischauer and the senior international relations specialist Hans Morgenthau. In his letter of invitation, the Hofstra president explained why he had chosen me: "Fairbank wrote to me, 'We have a man here, Ross Terrill, who spent five weeks in China and gave us the best report I have ever heard from a traveling academic observer.'"[14]

Reischauer complained to the Hofstra audience that Washington's new China position "is extremely confusing and upsetting for most of [the U.S.] and for some other countries too." On the Nixon trip itself, the former ambassador to Tokyo grumbled about "Hollywood habits" that made too much drama of the occasion. He mistakenly thought Taiwan would suffer: "We don't want to move from the myth that China doesn't exist to the myth that Taiwan doesn't exist."

Morgenthau, a gruff German-born scholar, rebuked me for my approval of Nixon's step. He said, "The bipolar world on the nuclear level" has not been changed a jot. "There still exist, as before Nixon's trip, just two superpowers, two nuclear powers."[15]

Many Democratic Party figures and liberals in the media and academia, wounded by Vietnam, felt American power had reached a low point; Nixon was scraping the barrel out of weakness, they said. At Hofstra, I acknowledged this argument. "The Guam doctrine of 1969 was the real turning point," I told a large audience of students. "It was taken more seriously in Beijing than among Nixon's critics at home." But it was not weakness that Nixon expressed in Guam. Rather it was a new vision of give-and-take in East Asia that did in fact produce peace and prosperity.

I wrote in the *Boston Globe* on March 5, 1972, "Mr. Nixon has accepted, to his great credit, that a cooperative world is not a luxury but a necessity."

At Harvard, the Center for International Affairs sponsored a large public meeting in March 1972 at which Zbigniew Brzezinski, Reischauer, and I spoke. The future national security advisor to President Carter spoke critically of Nixon's trip to China: "An extremely large cost Nixon paid by going to China was intensified political anxiety felt by the Japanese." Reischauer agreed with Brzezinski: "Japan is undoubtedly beginning to wonder about American intentions." I took a different view. Soon Prime Minister Tanaka's trip to Beijing bore out my point that Nixon's damage to U.S. relations with Japan was temporary.[16]

Brzezinski claimed that China, by gaining a freer hand on its American flank, could see itself free, if it chose, to resume good relationships with Moscow. He spoke of the absurdity of the Panmunjom situation in Korea. "Here is China facing off against the UN, even though she now belongs to the UN." I doubted both points.

At Princeton University, the venerable Soviet expert George Kennan grumbled that the trip "cannot fail to raise hopes and anticipations at home that no one could seriously expect to satisfy." However, the retired diplomat was wrong on many points. Wrong in saying Nixon's trip was "abrupt" and "little prepared" and "cannot have enhanced America's reputation for steadiness and reliability." Wrong to predict that the trip would "in one way or another spell the end of the [KMT] regime in Taiwan."[17]

Yet Kennan, unlike many other Democrats, did see the potential of Nixon's new policy in putting the Soviet Union—which he knew well—at a disadvantage. The *New York Times*, in an editorial the day Nixon's trip ended, did not. It entirely overlooked the beneficial effect of the Mao-Nixon summit on both Beijing's and Washington's relationship with the Soviet Union.

Instead, the *New York Times* lamely called the Shanghai Communique "a renunciation of force, in favor of diplomacy," oblivious to the seismic shift in world power balance under way. It focused on old issues stressed by the Democratic Party such as cultural and technical exchanges with China. It wrongly said (as did most American liberals) that U.S. military withdrawal from Japan, Korea and Thailand would result from Beijing-Washington ties.

The *Boston Globe* conducted a triple interview about the trip's outcome with Reischauer, James Thomson, a China Expert under President Johnson, and myself. "The trip was as important for its negative gains as its positive gains," I said. "It's now less likely than before that the U.S. and China will either fight each other or grossly miscalculate each other's position."[18]

Reischauer worried with some reason about possible excesses. "Throughout history we Americans have tended to overreact to China, and once again we've done something in a spectacular way toward China, which gets the public over-reacting in ways that have given us problems in the past." Like a few other distinguished journalists or China specialists, including Stanley Karnow, Lucian Pye of MIT, and Richard Walker of the University of South Carolina, Reischauer, as a former ambassador in Tokyo, thought the "China fever" of 1972 went too far.

Asked by the *Boston Globe* to peer ahead a decade, I replied: "The real tragedy of American–Chinese hostility has been that small countries in between have been swept up, like iron filings in a magnetic field, into military alliances. This has resulted in a distortion of their economic and social development." Thus, I foreshadowed the Age of Economics that soon proved a great benefit for East Asia—made possible by better China-U.S. relations.[19]

Japan's initial nervousness was acute. Consul-General Tajime came from New York to Boston for dinner at the Colonnade Hotel. He was absolutely beside himself over the new China-US relationship. Tajime was no longer the carefree man I knew in Hong Kong, where he had been consul-general. He said he was on a tour of the U.S. to find out what he could about America's "crazy" course of action over China.

Tajime stressed that Japan is "not capable diplomatically." This was his only rejoinder to my point that at any time Japan could itself normalize relations with China. He just kept saying, "We don't have the diplomatic experience and ability for these kinds of moves."

I told Kissinger at the White House some months after Nixon's trip that I thought he had brilliantly enabled America to ease out of its messianic posture toward Asia. "Well, we've done it with China," he said, "but not yet with Vietnam."

Some of my left-wing friends did not approve of my dealing with Kissinger and supporting Nixon. "What a fine socialist you've turned out to be cavorting with Tricky Dick [a pejorative nickname for Nixon]," quipped a scholar of political philosophy who had been a fellow graduate student with me at Harvard.[20]

Radical friends from Harvard were also nervous. Jim Peck, an editor at Pantheon Publishers in New York, came to Boston for lunch on May 20, 1972. He said New York left-wing salons believed Wilfred Burchett and myself had gone cold on the Vietnamese and hot on the Chinese! It was amazing how rumors circulated on the New York grapevine. The root of our views on China was different. Mine sprang from a social democratic world view. Peck's was rooted in wounded hope in a savior. My fear was that he would transfer his frantic hope from Beijing to Hanoi and tomorrow, perhaps, to somewhere else.

In *Ramparts,* a radical magazine based in San Francisco, David Kolodney wrote of Nixon's days in China: "Face beaded with feverish ambition, [he] rose to speak and soiled, with his resonant banality, phrases coined in sacrifice by the revolutionary veterans he addressed." Kolodney's opaque prose matched his opaque thinking. "To our radical sensibilities it was an obscene, insupportable insult. The China that we supported or opposed was an illusion. We allowed that illusion to define for us a model of true revolution." It was as if Kolodney's own promising son (China) had smiled at the father's sworn enemy (Nixon). Kolodney's only true statement was that *Ramparts'* China was "an illusion."

Cultural Revolution extremism had been irresistible to Kolodney and other ultra-leftists. "We drew upon the slogans emanating from China and from local Maoists," the *Ramparts* article continued, "and on the slanderous animosity of our own government, and, largely independent of the objective reality of their politics, we internalized a most compelling conception of the significance of China and Maoism." What an admission! The facts in China were irrelevant to what fiery American leftists "internalized" about China. Beijing's betrayal was unbearable. Kolodney experienced verbal indigestion in having to swallow both Beijing's perfidy and Washington's success.

Of Maoism's excesses Kolodney was able to say: "Even the epithets it evokes: reckless, quixotic, intransigent, all imply a grudging respect, almost as if they were just too good for this world." He came right out with the hatred of the West that was the springboard for the American hard left's enthusiasm for the Cultural Revolution. "Their [the Red Guards] unbending hostility to the West and to backsliders in their own camp showed how unshakeable they were." Actually, Kolodney's words showed only how unshakeable dogmatism could become.

"The real importance of the Chinese Revolution to the American Left," wrote Kolodney sadly, "was that this revolution was really revolutionary. Now we have been abandoned by history." In his tantrum he condescended in a nasty way to China: "they are so backward, how could we have expected them to be reliable revolutionaries!" The article read like boiler-plate propaganda out of Moscow.

Kolodney moved to his inevitable "Blame America First" conclusion: "It is, after all, our failure to make our own revolution which has imposed the encumbering burdens of imperialism on theirs [China's]."[21] This kind of leftism led to despair.

The moderate left, including my graduate student friend who mocked "Tricky Dick," gave a grudging approval to Nixon's handshake with Mao. But the entire hard left was bitter about the turn of events. Focused on the Vietnam War, these radicals were chagrined that China, in talking with Nixon, was not primarily interested in Vietnam, but in China's interests and the world balance of power. Understandably, Beijing told visiting American radicals that any domestic political motive Nixon had in going to China was not China's concern but that of the American people.

Nixon's China step caused confusion also among conservatives. Many Republicans supported him out of hostility to the Soviet Union, seeing a shared purpose with China. A few did not. The most prominent was William Buckley, founder of the influential magazine *National Review*.

Buckley feared Beijing had played Nixon like a violin. He attacked me for supporting Nixon, complaining that in my writings and CBS TV commentary I was "making excuses" for China. In a reference to the defeatism over America's power in Asia of Senator William Fulbright, chairman of the powerful Foreign Relations Committee, Buckley laughably called the fevered pro-China spirit of February 1972 the "Fulbright-Terrill-Nixon offensive."

Buckley heard Nixon's announcement of his plan to go to China while sitting alongside Ronald Reagan in his residence as Governor of California. Buckley said of that evening's atmosphere in *National Review* circles: "The [conservative] dissenters were much more than helpless; they were paralyzed." Yet, as Governor Reagan sat contemplating what Nixon had said, a phone call from Kissinger reassured Reagan that Nixon was not changing his fundamental principles and asked Reagan to go to Taiwan and explain this to Chiang Kai-shek.[22]

That autumn, Buckley debated me passionately on his TV show, "Firing Line. Afterwards, 200 letters flowed in from viewers, including one from the chief editor of the left-of-center *Boston Globe*, who wrote extravagantly, "I've waited years to see someone get the best of Buckley—now you've done it."

Another viewer wrote, "I have never seen anyone handle Buckley so expertly in refusing to be interrupted before adequately dealing with a subject. I should think your blood pressure must have risen despite your apparent calm." This man had studied Chinese in Beijing during 1940 and later worked in a leprosy clinic in Guizhou Province. His letter continued: "It was no surprise to me that the Mandate of Heaven was withdrawn from Chiang Kai-shek in 1949."

I felt Buckley was mistaken about the Nixon summit. Kissinger was rightly concerned with structures in international relations, rather than moral postures, as Buckley was. If equilibrium could be achieved, Nixon's national security advisor believed, nations would behave better—would have to—than when disequilibrium prevailed. This made him alert to any possibility of "warning" Moscow by means of U.S.-China entente. Nixon was not "giving in" to China, as Buckley feared, but finding some overlapping common interest with China.

Still, Buckley was humorous and generous as a person. In his 1973 book *Inveighing We Will Go,* he wrote of "the celebrated articles by Professor Ross Terrill . . . a writer of great literary skill whose two very long articles, published in the *Atlantic,* have been by far the most influential document on China of the season."[23] Years later just before his death in 2008, he published a book with the arresting title, *Cancel Your Own Goddam Subscription.* The title came from a letter he wrote to a viewer of his "Firing Line" TV show and reader of his magazine *National Review.* The viewer and reader, a Mr. Morris of Arizona, wrote to Buckley: "Three cheers to Dr. Ross Terrill. He slashed you to bits on the program. Cancel my subscription." Buckley wrote back: "Dear Mr. Morris: Cancel Your Own Goddam Subscription. Cordially, William Buckley." So, a book title was born, and Buckley's ability to laugh at himself was displayed.

Two famous veterans of U.S. historical dealings with China were absent from the Beijing summit. Three days before Nixon left Washington for Beijing, Edgar Snow died at his home in Switzerland, with several Chinese doctors by his bedside. I wrote to Lois, his widow, "It is hard to accept that Ed has gone, for, like many others, I had come to take him for granted as THE Western voice on China and her people."

Even as he lay desperately ill, Snow played a role in Nixon's trip to China. Snow had not felt comfortable in the U.S. during the years of Senator Joseph McCarthy's influence; in the mid-1950s, he moved to Switzerland. However, he never ceased to be a U.S. citizen. It was fitting that he played a role in Beijing's signaling that Nixon would be welcome to visit China. The president wrote Snow a gracious letter on January 31, 1972: "your distinguished career is respected and appreciated." This was true both in the U.S. and in China.

John S. Service, the former diplomat in China in the 1930s and 1940s, now at the University of California, observed: "How tragic that Ed could not have gone [to Beijing for the Nixon visit]!"[24] Maybe not. Snow could not have fitted easily with the huge press party that accompanied Nixon. Theodore White, another American China Hand from the 1940s, went on the trip, but he did not fit in.

The political context had changed and Snow's death coinciding with Nixon's trip made the change poignant. In 1972, China as an issue in international relations had become unhooked from the issue of the nature of the Chinese political system. Nixon was not visiting Mao because he was pro-Mao and anti-Chiang—to recall the biting choice of the 1940s that divided Snow and McCarthy. His reasons were geopolitical. The China Hands of the 1940s, including Snow, Fairbank, and Service, wrestled with how Chinese society would emerge from war and chaos after 1945 and which party might lead it toward peace and justice. Nixon had his eye simply on the balance of power.

Pearl Buck was also absent from Beijing for the Mao-Nixon summit. Her decision on whether to make the February 1972 trip with Nixon was made for her. "In view of the fact that for a long time," read a letter from the Chinese government in reply to her request, "you have in your works taken an attitude of distortion, smear, and vilification towards the people of new China and its leaders, I am authorized to inform you that we cannot accept your request for a visit to China."

It pained Buck that Beijing rejected her return to the land of her birth. However, her sense of identity was intact. Being half-Chinese and yet American was a dualism she carried with serenity. She thought the Nixon opening was entirely natural. I think she would have liked to observe it close up. Thoughtful Americans would have enjoyed her report, not least because she would neither have denounced Nixon's trip, nor swooned over it. I think China feared her candor.

NOTES

1. Kettering Foundation, letter to author, February 21, 1972.
2. Prof. Eric Einhorn, letter to author, February 24, 1972.
3. *Newsweek,* March 6, 1972.
4. Cited in James Mann, *About Face,* 1999, 60–61.
5. *New York Times*, February 21, 1972.
6. Reston, column, *New York Times*, February 21, 1972.

7. *New York Times*, February 21, 1972.

8. Owen, column, *Washington Post*, February 17, 1972.

9. Deputy Prime Minister James Cairns, communication to the author, Fall, 1973.

10. All words of Sihanouk, spoken to the author, Beijing, July 28, 1971.

11. *New York Times*, February 21, 1972.

12. Kissinger, Ibid. 1060.

13. Ibid. 1060, 1062.

14. President Clifford Lord, letter to author, October 26, 1971.

15. *Long Island Commercial Review*, May 19, 1972.

16. *Harvard Crimson*, March 17, 1972.

17. *Observer*, London, February 20, 1972.

18. *Boston Globe*, March 12, 1972.

19. Triple interview reprinted by *Boston Globe*, sent to high schools across Massachusetts; editor Timothy Leland, letter to author, May 11, 1972.

20. Charles Bahmueller, letter to author, September 7, 1971.

21. Kolodney, "Et tu, China?" *Ramparts*, May 1972.

22. Buckley, "To China with Nixon," *Playboy*, January 1973.

23. Buckley, *Inveighing We Will Go,* New York, Putnam, 1972, 92.

24. Service, "Edgar Snow: Some Personal Reminiscences," *China Quarterly*, April 1972; Service, interview, ADST-LOC.

Chapter Ten

Twilight Years as Mao Declines

By the mid-1970s, "Welcome to the people of the five continents" was a typical urban billboard, no longer "Fight the class enemy to the end." In Shanghai, a welcome sign said, "Serve the Chinese People and the Whole World's People." Chinese flights began less often with a quotation from Chairman Mao and usually with the even-handed, "Comrades and passengers, welcome!" Almost no one wore a Chairman Mao badge.

Chinese officials mentioned a new goal, "In twenty-five years, China expects to be a powerful socialist country at the level of advanced countries." Signs of the impact of foreign trade were evident. Whereas five years before there were only Russian and Polish vehicles, now there were Toyotas, Fiats, and trucks from Germany and Japan.

In Jinan, a primary school was abuzz with science and language classes; the joyful cries of sport came in through the windows. But school administrators spoke of evil influence on the school of "class enemy" Lin Biao, the fallen defense minister. I found a chance to ask one pupil directly in Chinese: "Is there class struggle in your school?" The headmistress hissed "yes" to the boy across a silent room. The boy eventually gave a clever reply: "It's difficult to say there is class struggle in our school, but it's also difficult to say there is not."

At a bathroom in the Jinan Municipal Ensemble building, the toilet tissue consisted of recent issues of *Red Flag*, the Communist Party's political journal. It was one of the few places I ever saw the magazine in use.

Tying Lin Biao to Confucius, as all China propaganda did, was hard to understand. I was confused to read in *People's Daily* in early June, 1974 that Lin, Confucius, and the Dalai Lama were all "scorpions from the same nest." The visitor got no help getting clarity. At the Waiwen shudian (Foreign

Books Store) in Shanghai I came upon a "Criticize Lin and Criticize Confucius Browsing Room," but as a foreigner I was denied entry. I thought of a remark Edgar Snow made, in exasperation at a briefing in a steel factory, "Figures don't lie, but liars figure."

Soldiers on duty in factories and schools symbolized the grip of military authority, canceling a Red Guard-driven society that had not "rebelled" according to Mao's formula. A certain recovery from the Cultural Revolution had occurred; there was order in the streets. Still, the political gymnastics of the late 1960s had damaged the economy, knocked stuffing out of intellectuals, and lost China good will in Asia and Africa especially.

I felt I was being shown around a house still being renovated. I was ushered into selected rooms. I was taken to fancy areas, ignorant of how much of the whole they represented, or what lay behind curtained-off sections. The mystery in part sprang from the deceptive nature of "normalcy" in China, while Mao still ruled. Yang Bingzhang, the Peking University student imprisoned in 1966 for criticizing Jiang Qing, was sent to rural Shandong Province after his release. "Were your rights curtailed during this period?" I asked him years later. "Were you supervised as an ex-prisoner?" Yang burst out laughing. "Rights in the countryside?" he cried. "There are no rights in the Chinese countryside. What rights could be curtailed?" The "normalcy" under Mao was not that of civil society, but a political creation.

Each week I saw and heard two things that could not be aligned. In streets, factories, parks and communes, I saw large piles of bricks, pipes, and other supplies. Robust economic progress, surely. Inside briefing rooms, I heard supporting statistics ("More steel produced in Beijing last year than in the entire decade prior to Liberation"). However, there was a mystery. With handsome rises in output, why did China have a low standard of living, decade after decade?

The piles of supplies all over the place hinted at the mystery. A kiln would produce bricks to meet its state quota, but there was no requirement to dispose rationally of the bricks. Profitability was not the coin of a factory's existence. The pile of bricks with no use still counted in the statistics for GDP. It was "production" with no result other piles of unused bricks and barbed wire.

A foreign policy change marked Wangfujing, the shopping epicenter of international Beijing. An air-raid shelter was being built from the ground floor of a bookshop, a double brick tunnel leading downwards and sideways. Part of the shop closed while construction went ahead. Of course, it was a measure taken against the threat from the Soviet Union, now an urgent priority for Beijing.

Rewi Alley, in his 45th year of living in China, after leaving his native New Zealand, sprawled on a couch in an apartment that was an island of colonialism in a sea of socialism. High ceilings, an elderly Manchu servant, heavy carved wooden furniture, a secretary who brought in mail that included *Time* and *Newsweek*.

The Cultural Revolution sobered Alley. "I do not try to pontificate anymore," he said a little sadly. "There are plenty of others to pontificate." He began to talk about the countryside. "It's the Chinese way to go on working through flood and famine and war," he observed. "The Cultural Revolution era was an example of how farmers can do this."

I mentioned Peking University and Rewi said, "I haven't been there since they were killing each other with spears." He recently tried to translate new poems. "They were untranslatable," Alley said with a sigh. "Just a string of slogans." I asked him whether Marxism had lodged in the minds of the Chinese, as the party wished. Deadpan he replied: 'Well, my driver is reading *The Gotha Program* and *The Civil War in France*."

The Swedish ambassador told me Scandinavian "Maoists" visiting China is a very good thing. "The Chinese can see what sort of supporters the Cultural Revolution attracts in the West," he observed, "and the young Swedish Maoists can see how hard the Chinese people work."

One wondered how long the military role in "Revolutionary Committees" would continue, in places such as colleges that were distant from soldiers' expertise. At Peking University, I asked Robert Winter, a long-time American resident on the campus, if I could phone him later to talk. As two PLA men sat in the room, he slipped me a note: "I can't rely on being called by phone. A letter is safer."

It was difficult to read Zhou Enlai's report to the National People's Congress in February 1975 and recognize the Zhou Enlai I met in 1971. The speech was a hymn of praise to the Cultural Revolution and a warning about the inevitability of war. Abstract policy principles dominated; concrete realities were few. It seemed Zhou had political difficulties as well as health difficulties. As Ford and Kissinger were pressured by Reagan on the right in an election year, Zhou Enlai was pressured by ultra-leftists maneuvering for their future. I doubted his words expressed his real thoughts.

In his beautiful living room, Thai Prime Minister Kukrit shared a story of Zhou Enlai, whom he admired, as the premier ailed physically and politically. Zhou told Kukrit he could tell his children and grandchildren in Thailand that China will never attack Thailand. "I said, Prime Minister, these are very, very comforting words. Could you write them down in Chinese script for me? I will have a million reproductions made and hung around our children's necks." The elegant Kukrit paused and looked me in the eye. "But Zhou En-lai declined. Either he didn't have the authority or he didn't want to put the promise in black and white."

"The Chinese are very loyal to their friends," Kukrit told me as a servant showed me to my car. "They will do anything for their friends. So, if Communists did ever overrun Thailand, I'd become a refugee, and go and live in Beijing. They would accept me."

Overall, having observed the Cultural Revolution from Harvard, it was China's partial recovery from the chaos of the 1960s that struck me in Mao's final years. It was a mild relief to find social calm and keen curiosity about foreign countries. Fifteen Western journalists were based in Beijing, compared with two in 1964.

One December night in 1972, I heard the Australian election result. The Labor Party, after 22 years in opposition, was the government. I sent an enthusiastic cable to Prime Minister Whitlam. The next day he received a cable from Premier Zhou Enlai.

A few weeks before the election, John S. Service sent me a copy of *Amerasia*, a book on his confrontation with McCarthy over the "loss of China" two decades before. In my reply, I posed a question: "Jack, Do you think your reports in the 1940s from Yanan [on talks with Mao and others] would on balance have been more worthwhile, or less, had you written them as a journalist not connected with the government, aimed at influencing the government via public opinion?"

I was thinking of my own plans in the wake of the political change in Australia and my success with *Atlantic Monthly* articles and *800,000,000* in the U.S. To shape policy from the inside, or push for it from outside?

Jack wrote back, "IF [sic] one is a well-known, respected journalist with an established publication outlet, one is going to be more influential than someone writing for (and to) the government. There was some circulation of my reports from Chongqing and Yanan in Washington among lower working-level people. But MOST [sic] of them never reached beyond the 'China desk.' If I had been Ed Snow and writing for something like the *New York Times*, they would have had more impact."

Service's opinion was reinforced by William Buckley, whom I had debated on "Firing Line" earlier in the year. In a Nieman Foundation conversation at Harvard, a reporter asked the conservative writer whether being a columnist was enough for his high talents. "Do you have something else in mind for the future? "

Buckley was aroused. "Three hundred and sixty-five newspapers print my column three times a week," he said. "Where could you go from that but down? What is a Senate seat, much less a House seat, compared to the influence of 365 papers?"

As a Harvard faculty, I found it a mixed blessing to have my book a popular success. Some senior Harvard colleagues were uneasy to see a junior professor—only two years on the faculty—being widely read on a popular current topic. I was pleased, yet I also winced in consideration of my academic career, when the *Christian Science Monitor* said in its review of *800.000.000*: "No Harvard professor ought to write so colorfully and entertainingly."

Some crusty political scientists, not all of them wizards with the pen, thought the solution to that anomaly was to ensure the offending author did not forever remain a Harvard professor. It is better for a young academic not to win journalism prizes and attain big book sales while still a junior professor.

However, the envious whispers did not stop the popularity of the book even at Harvard. It was used as required reading in a number of courses from 1972 onward. The large "Social Sciences 11" course in 1974–75, for example, in its final exam asked the following question linking my book with the history of Chinese communism: "To what extent can the society portrayed in *800,000,000* be described as a realization of the ideals of the Yanan experience?"

Days after Whitlam's election, at a lunch at Harvard Law School for visiting Chinese scientists, an aide traveling with the scientists had a message from Huang Hua in New York. "The ambassador thinks that your recent talk with him was very important." I was able to assure Huang Hua, through the aide, that Whitlam had already begun steps to recognize China and establish an Australian embassy in Beijing.

It was a Saturday morning and Henry Kissinger wore a green tartan jacket and gray slacks. We planned to talk about China. However, as I entered, Henry, once my teacher at Harvard, was waving a cable from Prime Minister Whitlam protesting Nixon's renewed U.S. bombing of North Vietnam. "It's unforgivable for this new Australian government to put Hanoi and Washington on the same footing. Australia is supposed to be our ally!"

I submitted that the ANZUS alliance (linking the U.S., Australia, and New Zealand) was "unshakeable" despite this disagreement over Vietnam. "You can't apply the alliance on some issues and not on others," Kissinger snapped.

Nixon's national Security advisor added—knowing I would relay this to Whitlam—"No government, perhaps other than the British, has been given the intelligence information that Australia has received under [conservative]

McMahon and his predecessors. Whether that can continue under Whitlam remains to be seen."

Kissinger rasped: "We're going to pretend this cable from Whitlam never came. I'm not even going to show it to the State Department."

I congratulated him on the U.S.-China relationship and, calming down, he said, "Now I hope we can sustain it for four more years." He was thinking, of course, of Nixon's second term about to begin, and perhaps of domestic issues bubbling up both within the U.S. and China. He went on: "But I won't be here four more years. I couldn't."

"But I doubt you would go back to Harvard," I said, probing.

"It's impossible to go back to Harvard. No job could be as important as this one. There is nowhere to go."

After a pause, Kissinger said, "In my discussions with Harvard, it's always about whether Harvard would have me back, never about whether I want to go back."

Vietnam was naturally a preoccupation at the White House, but Kissinger took a refreshingly broad view of East Asia. "For American policy there are two phases," he remarked. "In the first, Thailand has to be linchpin. But that will give way to a second phase, when détente with China will be the best guarantee of security in Asia."

Although Kissinger now had a Voltaire-like awe for the Chinese, and deep respect for Zhou Enlai, he saw the North Vietnamese as stubborn obstacles to Nixon's strategic plans in Asia. "The Vietnamese, south and north, are all the same, and impossible to deal with," he complained. "They deeply distrust everyone."

Had the Chinese hinted agreement with his complaints about the North Vietnamese? "Yes, they have," he replied. "They know how difficult the Vietnamese are." Later events would suggest Kissinger was correct.

Kissinger took a dim view of Japan. I said it would be a nightmare for Australia if the U.S. and Japan should ever fall out. "That need not happen," he replied. "But Japan is a very strange country. They live only by hierarchy; an equal relationship is something they cannot stand." Kissinger said it amazed him that our liberal colleagues at Harvard, such as former ambassador Edwin Reischauer, could be pro-Japan.

Agitated, Kissinger asked, "Have you ever had to deal with the Japanese? With the Chinese, there are principles. In the case of the Japanese, there's no framework, no intellectual content to the discussion or negotiation. You can't get a proposition from them; you can't get a response; it just doesn't work that way."

I remarked that by the end of the 1980s, China might have gained considerably in strength and the U.S. could be in a new situation. Kissinger agreed, but he added, "There is no reason why the U.S. and China cannot be friendly. Beijing doesn't think in terms of military adventures."

Marshall Green, assistant secretary of state for East Asia, was nervous about the new Australian government. It had been 22 years since Washington last dealt with a Labor Party government in Canberra.

The phone beside Green rang; on the line, a voice whispered, "Your visitor talked with Henry earlier today." Green put down the phone and turned back to me, perhaps unaware I had heard the alert.

"Neither China nor the Soviet Union wants us out of Asia completely," Green said, "because they would not like the ensuing vacuum." He summed up the policy as he discerned it in Beijing's mind: "Go Home Yankee, but gradually."

After I left the State Department for a plane to New York, while making a phone call in a booth at Washington's National Airport, I noticed a be-spectacled man with an intense expression in the next booth. On the Eastern Shuttle to New York, I saw this same man. As I entered the Chinese mission on Manhattan's East Side, to visit Ambassador Huang Hua, I glimpsed him yet again on the sidewalk.

The Australian Embassy in Washington gave a dinner party in honor of Green and his wife Lisa, before they left for Canberra, where Green was to be ambassador. I sat between Admiral Moorer, Chief of the General Staff, and Mrs. Nelson Johnson, whose husband in the 1940s was successively ambassador to China and to Australia. A conservative from Wyoming, Mrs. Johnson declared: "It is terrible that we've abandoned Taiwan." She also re-marked that John Service and other U.S. diplomats who served in China had an "easy ride" when faced with their mistakes in "losing China."

Moorer remarked, as roast lamb arrived, that the U.S. should have invaded Vietnam with an army long ago. "It would have been all over quickly," he said with a shrug. What exactly would have been over, the distinguished Ad-miral did not explain. "Do you disagree, then," I asked, "with Eisenhower's opposition to sending American forces to the Asian mainland?"

"Yes, when a country is as thin as North Vietnam is around Vinh. That narrow strip is where they're vulnerable. There, also, lie the routes into Laos and Cambodia."

In Sydney on a brilliant summer day, Whitlam was buoyant in a floral shirt. He said the negotiations with the Chinese in Paris over recognition were sub-stantive. "They first proposed the same formula as for the Maldives. We put forward the Canadian formula. There was some table thumping by the Chinese side. In the end we had to go far beyond 'taking note' of their claim to Taiwan."

Whitlam asked, "What am I going to say at my press conference about Nixon's Hanoi bombing?" I explained to him Kissinger's view of "two phases." In the first, Thailand was the linchpin; in the second phase, détente with China would be the best guarantee of security in Asia.

China did not bestow trade favors on Australia, despite Whitlam's hopes. The transcript of discussions between Chinese and Australian finance and economic officials during 1973, given me by Deputy Prime Minister Jim Cairns, showed the two countries far apart on trade.

Problem was Chinese foreign trade was handled by the government, which stymied Australian business. "It is impossible to ask us as visiting government officials," said an Australian minister in a discussion with a Chinese trade minister in Beijing, "to list what businessmen in Australia want to buy!"

A Chinese vice-minister of trade inquired: "What kinds of Chinese machinery would Australia care to buy?" An Australian minister responded: "Buying decisions are made by individuals on the basis of price and quality. People from all over the world are pushing goods at Australian businessmen constantly. To sit back and ask, what do you want to buy from us will get no results."[1]

Prime Minister Whitlam fulsomely praised China. "Where the USA went wrong in its revulsion against the change of government in China 23 or 24 years ago," he said, "and where Australia went wrong in America's wake— was in believing that China was an aggressive country. It never has been. It isn't now."[2]

Whitlam became anxious that President Nixon had not yet agreed to see him on his forthcoming trip to North America. Some officials in Washington were dragging their feet, furious that Australia and Cuba had begun talking about exchanging consulates.

The Australian press was insinuating that Whitlam would not be welcome to visit Nixon. The Sydney newspaper *National Times* wrote on March 26: "The White House has rejected two requests for the Australian prime minister, Mr. Whitlam, to visit Washington officially."

Whitlam asked me to mediate. On April 14, 1973, his chief aide, Dr. Peter Wilenski, phoned me, not from the PM's office, but from a dinner party in Canberra: "The PM agrees with you that the [Washington] embassy's access to the White House is not very good. He wants you to arrange a meeting for me with Kissinger." Whitlam felt a middle-man was necessary because he was unsure of the outcome. He was desperate to secure a date with Nixon. If he failed, that mustn't "come out."

I asked Kissinger if he would receive Wilenski to thrash out issues between Nixon and Whitlam. I felt confident because, although he was unhappy with

Whitlam on Vietnam, he thought the State Department had bungled relations with the new Australian government.

Kissinger quickly agreed to see Wilenski. It happened I would be dining with the Australian ambassador a few days later. Wilenski said, "Give no hint to the ambassador of what is afoot. I will tell him just before I go to Kissinger," Peter said, "and after leaving the White House I will return to the embassy to send my cable to the PM from there." Our entire maneuver infuriated Australian bureaucrats.

Some months after the Whitlam-Nixon talks, Whitlam went to China in November 1973. It was satisfying to all Australians when thousands of color-fully dressed Chinese youth danced in welcome at Beijing airport as Zhou Enlai and Whitlam walked slowly among them. As the motorcade drove through Beijing, the emotional Australian songs "Click Go the Shears," "Waltzing Matilda," and "Advance Australia Fair" blared from loudspeakers.

People's Daily carried a photo of Whitlam on its front page. An editorial stressed Australia's role in the South Pacific. Both China and Australia were "washed by the Pacific," the newspaper noted. "After Prime Minister Whitlam took office, he promptly pulled Australian troops out of Vietnam," the editorial went on, "voiced his opposition to the U.S. war of aggression there and advocated letting the Indochinese people settle their own questions without outside interference."

At a banquet in the Great Hall of the People, Whitlam declared, "Now, Australia's foreign policy concern is with all nations, particularly with nations who share a common environment, common interests, and with whom we seek relationships of equality."[3] In Australia, some interpreted these words as anti-American. I had failed to persuade Whitlam to include "common values."

Whitlam later told me Zhou Enlai was tough in their talks. He urged Whitlam to persuade Singapore, to which Australia was close, to resist Moscow's pressure to gain shipping facilities in Singapore. He asked Whitlam to help stiffen the backbone of the British on apartheid in South Africa.

Zhou Enlai used the term "American imperialism" several times. He complained about Kissinger: "We asked Kissinger about Chile, and he answered that the U.S. was not involved in the downfall of Allende. Now, China has proof that, not only the CIA, but also the State Department and other branches of the Washington government were involved. I'm going to raise it with Kissinger next time I see him."

Zhou showed an amused interest in the generally friendly rivalry between Australia and New Zealand. "New Zealand told us in December 1972," he told Whitlam, "that they would like the announcement of China-New Zealand diplomatic relations to be made one hour before that of the new China-Australia tie. I studied the facts and found there was actually a one-hour time difference between Canberra and New Zealand at the time. If we separated the New Zealand statement by one hour from the Australian, the two would in fact come out at the same time—which is what China wanted. This we did.

Zhou Enlai laughed at one of his subsequent mistakes about Australia and New Zealand. "I once thought a single Chinese journalist could cover both Australia and New Zealand," he said to Whitlam. "I found out how wrong that was!" New Zealand, in fact, is as far from Australia as China is from Japan.

During the third round of talks between Zhou and Whitlam, a message came for the Chinese premier. Zhou whispered to his aides. Soon Whitlam was in the presence of Mao Zedong.[4]

Whitlam's first questions about youth and women in the new political leadership of the recent Tenth Party Congress did not interest Mao; he turned them over to Zhou. Whitlam, persisting, asked the Chairman: "Where did you find Wang Hongwen? [youngest of Gang of Four]"

Mr. Wang himself sat nearby. "I don't know," Mao grunted. Wang remained silent. Mao raised the topic of nuclear tests, to which Whitlam was opposed, whether by China or by France. "Japan, Australia, and New Zealand seem to be the most concerned with this," Mao said. "These protests are a necessary routine."

"It is not a routine matter," objected Whitlam. "Australians feel very strongly about nuclear testing." Still, both Mao and Zhou seemed dismissive of the whole topic. The Australian tried to be conciliatory by saying: "I do see a distinction between Chinese tests and French tests, because China is testing on its own soil, and it is threatened, whereas France is testing in a colony in the South Pacific, and France really isn't threatened."

Appeasement failed; Mao was freshly aroused: "I don't agree at all. France *is threatened* by the Soviet Union. It needs an independent nuclear deterrent. It should have one. . . [more calmly] But I still think men matter more than weapons."

Mao asked, "Would your Labor Party dare to make revolution?"

"We stand for evolution rather than revolution," said Whitlam, using a formulation I had often heard from him.

"That sounds like the theories of Charles Darwin?

"I feel Darwin's ideas relate to fauna and flora rather than to social development," suggested Whitlam.

Mao asked if Darwin ever visited Australia and whether the country's northern port of Darwin was named for the botanist. Alas, the prime minister did not know. Later, Canberra sent a letter informing Mao that Darwin had indeed gone to Australia and the small tropical city's name honored him.

Whitlam raised a fresh topic: "Deng Xiaoping told me he was at the eighth and tenth CCP congresses, but not the ninth [in 1969]. Why was Deng absent from the ninth?"

"Because the problem of Lin Biao still had not been solved," replied Mao. "I worked with Lin Biao for many years. Sometimes there was cooperation; more often we were opposed."

"Was it really true," the Australian prime minister inquired, "that Lin Biao was in cahoots with the Soviet Union?"

Mao left the matter in no doubt. "We suspected it for some time. He'd spent much time there during the anti-Japan War, instead of being in China fighting against the Japanese." Mao continued: "His flight north was proof of it. Then after his death, we found documents that made it perfectly clear."

The last part of the session was about mortality. Mao complained of limits and the passing of the days. "My body is riddled with diseases," he told Whitlam. In the awkward silence, Zhou Enlai said, "He has rheumatism in his knees." Mao struck a direr note. "I have an appointment with God," he said to Whitlam.

When Whitlam tried to counter the pessimism by saying China's sturdy youth would guarantee the "future of the revolution," Mao deflated him. With a gesture toward his premier across the room, he added, "Neither Zhou nor I will be around for the conclusion of the Chinese Revolution."

Zhou looked at his watch. Mao pointed to Wang Hairong, granddaughter of his cousin Wang Jifan, "She will never let me talk for too long," he said. Unaided, Mao rose and escorted Whitlam to the door.

Overall, Mao and Zhou saw Australia in the context of its heritage from Britain and its links with the USA, not, as Whitlam did, as a country within the region of Asia.

Harvard hoped to follow-up my trip of 1971 by sending a delegation of Sinologists to China in 1973. Letters flew between Cambridge and Beijing. Fairbank, wary of how moods change, wrote to Qiao Guanhua urging the Harvard trip, "The American public are still capable of great long-term swings of sentiment. . . We need permanent connections that cannot be altered by shifts of public sentiment." Eventually, approval came.

Preparatory sessions occurred, including a dinner meeting at the home of Professor Dwight Perkins, Harvard's leading China economist, author of *Agricultural Development in China, 1368–1968* and other works. Raised in the Mid-west, Perkins was a broad-ranging scholar, a generous colleague, and fond of Australia. "I want to retire in Australia and raise sheep," he said after one trip there.

Alas, Beijing canceled our Harvard trip. Some said the reason was an essay of Fairbank in *New York Review of Books* about the book *Prisoner of Mao* by Bao Ruowang. I wasn't sure. I had met Bao in Europe and found him modest and thoughtful. In the USA, his book was hyped as an expose of Chinese prisons, but it was a simple, moving grass roots memoir. The title may have been over the top.

American Sinologists were too jumpy about their writings being acceptable to Beijing in the early 1970s. Our every word was hardly scrutinized by senior Chinese officials. Also, China was not ready for the full range of exchanges Americans expected. "At present," remarked Fairbank (a man not without his own contradictions), "you can't expect that Americans will be able to have a free run of China." Like some other countries, China did not want to be smothered by American enthusiasm.

Americans visiting China dropped sharply. Making the chill personal, I myself was denied a visa to visit China in the summer of 1974. At Harvard, I tried to convince my colleague Ezra Vogel that the effort to keep the door open for academic exchanges with China was important. Vogel responded skeptically on October 15, 1973, "My impression is that they [the Chinese side] are balancing a go slower policy with a few handshakes and ceremonial good wishes to try to keep us from saying to hell with the exchanges."

Some East Asia specialists, notably Vogel, made a contrast between the "fantastic" relationship with Japan and the "almost non-existent" relationship with China. I felt he misinterpreted the significance of the many-stranded tie between Japan and United States. Could governments change each other's minds by constant intercourse; did they understand each other's interests better as a result? Not necessarily. Actually, a "thin" relationship could be an important one, given the consequences if the balance of power went in the wrong direction. This was grasped by Kissinger about China.

Zhu Muzhi headed the first PRC Chinese journalists' group to the USA in May 1973. During a Nieman Foundation party at Harvard, editors of *Boston Globe* and *Christian Science Monitor* welcomed the visitors. The Chinese reporters, including Mr. Zhu, director of Xinhua News Agency, were disarming, not out to preach, quite professional in sharing ideas, and full of curiosity about America.

One had to pinch oneself, after the chills of the 1950s and 1960s, to behold a convivial party with Chinese media at Harvard in 1973.

I lectured at forums around the United States, including the esteemed Fortnightly Club in Chicago, a huge audience at the Main Line Forum in Pennsylvania, the elegant Crichton Club of Columbus, Ohio, the Washington Press

Club, and the American Academy of Arts and Sciences. At these lectures, I learned more about America and its views of China.

People high and low were welcoming and open-minded even though I remained a foreigner. I felt a growing attachment to the U.S. Was I losing my valuable Australian skepticism ? Americans were more idealistic about China than Australians were, more readily swept by enthusiasm. I saw dangers in this ardor, yet I felt some of it myself.

Hubert Liang, a journalism teacher at the University of Nanking, where Edgar Snow once taught, came by. "All these people coming to study here in the U.S.," Liang said, "are sons and daughters of leaders, from Communist families—so the impact will be great."

I told him of Prince Sihanouk's remark to me: the majority of Cambodian students he sent to Moscow came back anti-communist, and those he sent to France came back Communist. Liang laughed, but disagreed with me on the implication.

He knew Zhou Enlai in the fifties and Zhou told him in 1957 that Beijing wanted to keep contact with America through Henry Luce. "He's a reactionary, but stay in touch with him," Zhou said to Liang.

John Fairbank hosted a dinner at the Ambassador Hotel in Cambridge for Professor Ivor Richards, the English literary critic, and his wife Dorothea. The Richards' moved among Beijing, Cambridge in UK, and Cambridge in Massachusetts.

Ivor, with a sharp British accent and darting bird-like eyes, sparkled despite his age of 82. He knew pre-1949 China and returned to Beijing in 1950 for six months to lecture on Plato at Peking University. His students liked the extracts from *The Republic* and asked if they could publish them in the student magazine, "Words of the Week." Richards said "fine," but the director of studies said "no." "The ironic thing," Ivor told us, "was that the extracts from *The Republic* were uncannily similar to CCP style and line."

Richards announced as we rose from the dinner table, that he was soon leaving America, where he was professor emeritus at Harvard, to live in England. "I don't like the smell and feel of this country anymore," he said sadly. "Especially a country that bombs Vietnamese people from B52s when, nine times out of ten, the pilots are running no risk at all."

American and European religious organizations, especially Protestant Christian, saw a fresh chance to return to China, the "richest mission field of them all," as one clergyman friend put it. I was deluged with requests to help Christian organizations "get back into China."

I had doubts about the China hopes of Western Christian leaders. Historically, Christian missions in China had piggybacked on Western power. Spheres of influence, extraterritoriality, British ships in the Yangzi—these were the context in which Western Christians evangelized in China from the 19th century until the 1940s. The PRC was a brand-new context.

American and other Western Christian leaders failed to understand that Christianity would no longer have special privileges within China. After a talk in New York with Ambassador Huang Hua, I reported to the China Panel at the National Council of Churches: "When I raised the question of the churches with Huang Hua, I must tell you he launched into a denunciation of missionaries. He mocked the Christian diplomat, US Ambassador Leighton Stuart, whom he knew in 1946–1947, as a 'specialist in love.' Huang Hua was also hostile to the claims of some American churches to regain lost property assets in China."

In an essay, "The Chinese Present as World History" in *Motive* magazine, I wrote: "The return of China to world power mirrors the decline of Christianity in the 20th century. The Chinese revolution is the first great revolution to occur in a non-Christian country, and it occurred after a hundred years of Christian missions had converted a mere 1% of the Chinese people."[5] This seemed difficult for ex-missionaries to grasp.

Another problem was that American Protestantism diluted its message. Some of the horrors of 20th century politics had been associated with Christianity. Europe, as the source-spring of modern Christianity, had lost its leading role in the world after 1945. In the U.S., secular modernity and the prosperity of the post-WW2 decades reduced religious adherence among youth.

Protestant leaders embraced anti-imperialism, opposition to the Vietnam War, hopefulness about the Soviet Union, and zeal for racial equality and women's rights. Some of these positions may have been justified, but they did not spring from Christianity. Many Chinese could see this.

Christian doctrine made the dichotomy, sin-or-virtue too tight. Lost was the truth that freedom is not only a matter of human will, but also conditioned by social structures, the work of politics. Because political systems matter, I chose to study political science at Harvard.

Christianity does not offer a political system. It offers a transcendent worldview and the power of prayer. It supplies a belief in the universal worth of human beings. These a-political treasures enrich millions. Mystical books now interested me more than theology books. I remained a Christian believer, but from the 1970s received influence also from Buddhism, Daoism, and Islam. I seldom talked about Christianity in China.

Still, issues relating to China were of potential importance for theology. At Yale University in February 1975, I lectured on "The Theological Significance of New China." The discussion chaired by the leading Yale China historian Arthur Wright was first-rate, with the young historian Jonathan Spence and others asking questions and offering comments. Weighing "tyranny of wealth" carefully against "tyranny of power" seemed to me of potential importance to all societies.

In Beijing, intellectuals reappeared from the shadows. Hu Sheng, author of *Imperialism and Chinese Politics,* a book I prescribed to Harvard students, said as we met: "This is the first time I have ever had a talk with a foreign scholar visiting China." I told Hu Sheng my students were struck by the light stress in his book on Japanese imperialism and heavy stress on American imperialism. "After all, Japan did far more damage to China historically than the USA did," I suggested. The historian explained that he wrote the book in the late 1940s. "By then Japan's imperialism was clear to everyone. But not enough attention was being paid to American imperialism."

We talked of mutual friends; Hu Sheng knew Nikolai Fedorenko from Chongqing in the 1940s, years before I met the Russian at Harvard; we spoke of Guo Moruo's works, and named our favorites. Yang Gongsu, head of the China International Travel Service and former ambassador to Nepal, gave a banquet for me at Sichuan Restaurant. Hu Sheng, Zhou Yiliang from Peking University, diplomat Lin Lin, and other officials and intellectuals were present. "Two kinds of Americans are coming to China," Ambassador Yang remarked. "Those who have studied China and come here to find out if China measures up to their expectations. Second, those who are dissatisfied with the USA and come because they think China will have lessons to teach them." Both starting-points, I suggested, were American-centered. Why not come to China to explore whether Chinese socialism was proving satisfactory to the Chinese people?

In his toast Yang Gongsu quoted a Chinese saying, "When people are bosom friends, a thousand glasses are not enough. When people have not met, half a sentence is too much." I asked Lin Lin about the overall impact of the Cultural Revolution. He pointed to two accomplishments: "Things were done that the Party had not previously cared to do. Second, we achieved a major turnaround with the Soviet Union."

As the 1970s unfolded, American officials arrived in Beijing. In August, 1973, David Bruce, the newly-arrived chief of the U.S. Liaison Office, invited me to lunch with his wife, Evangeline. Ambassador Huang Hua had made a cynical remark about David Bruce's appointment: "I suppose they tried to find a dignified figure to make the office higher than it actually is."[6] I doubted such a motivation.

Workmen were hammering at the walls and unpacking the Bruce's boxes. David looked a tree of color in purple trousers, crimson shirt, and blue shoes. With laser focus, he tackled his chopsticks and his *maotai*.

I asked Bruce, who was one of the U.S.'s most senior diplomats, which world politicians most impressed him. "Harold McMillan, among those I got to know well," Bruce replied, recalling his service as American ambassador in London. "A great conversationalist with a deep knowledge of history." Bruce added, "One weakness in McMillan was a tendency to be an actor playing roles."

Bruce said from his contact so far he considered Zhou Enlai "probably the most accomplished statesman in the world [as of 1973]. He's clearly above any of the current European leaders. Looking back, [Germany's] Adenauer was very good, but intellectually, in debate, in conversation, Zhou Enlai is the best."

Bruce had seen Jiang Qing a couple of times and found her "utterly charming." On one occasion, Qiao Guanhua was with her and, "like everyone else in the room, showed her deference. Qiao even knelt beside her chair to talk to her!" New to China, Bruce was unaware of Jiang Qing's devious ways and ultra-leftist views.

President Nixon told Bruce before he left Washington that he should "keep a low profile" in Beijing. I was surprised. Evangeline thought this meant she couldn't have a party for Chinese women. I suggested otherwise. "Why not have a lunch for Chinese women who've been on trade, journalist or other delegations to the U.S. since Nixon's visit to Beijing?" This she soon did with success. Often Chinese diplomats said to Bruce, "when the Liaison Office becomes an embassy"—not if—leading him to think it was only a matter of time before the U.S. and China established full diplomatic relations.

When dessert time arrived, the effervescent Evangeline Bruce produced a bag of macaroons bought from an old German baker in Beidaihe, a coastal resort. At one end of the dining table sat a paperback copy of *800,000,000*. "We fight over it," Evangeline said of my 1972 book, "because sometimes both of us want to look at it at the same time."

Moved to see American diplomats in Beijing, I wrote in my diary: "One remembers the Korean War. One remembers the Vietnam War. The movies on American TV about the millions of red ants in China. The long desert of the Warsaw Talks. The bitter letter from Beijing to Pearl Buck denying her a China visa in the last year of her life. And here in the big new building of the Liaison office, Americans and Chinese bustle around, cooperating with each other in happy routine."

Australia and New Zealand already had a fruitful relationship with China. I lunched with the ambassadors of both countries at the New Zealand Embassy on September 1, 1975, to review three years of evolving cooperation with China.

Both Stephen Fitzgerald and his New Zealand counterpart, Bryce Harland, had good access to the Chinese government and felt the Chinese leaders took Australia in particular quite seriously. Fitzgerald was in the middle of trying to persuade Qiao Guanhua—at Whitlam's instruction—to re-classify Australia as part of the Third World. The Chinese foreign minister was resisting, but he told the Australian ambassador: "The categories are not hard and fast. And of all the countries in the Second World, Australia is, in China's judgment, the one nearest to the Third World." A tactful response to a silly question.

"Deng is quick and decisive," said Harland as he recalled a recent conversation with the vice-premier. "Zhou Enlai will spend six months and two heart attacks to bring people around to his position. Deng will decide on something and sweep the matter out of everyone's hands except the person told to implement the decision."

In 1971, Fitzgerald and I had a friendly disagreement about whether China wanted all American troops out of Asia. The Australian envoy thought Beijing did; I felt not. Now in late 1975, Fitzgerald had changed his mind. "Beijing is content to have American troops remain in Korea and elsewhere," he said at the lunch table. The Australian ambassador noted that Qiao Guanhua had recently rebuked the Danish ambassador, in the presence of the other Nordic countries' ambassadors, for saying, "It is good that the U.S. was flattened in Indochina."

On another occasion, Harland asked Qiao Guanhua whether some West European countries might capitulate to the Soviet Union. "But they have their relation with China," Qiao pointed out. Qiao felt there were "four crucial countries in Western Europe—Italy, Spain, Greece and Portugal—where a danger existed of great social change that would benefit only the Soviet Union." It was clear that Australia and New Zealand had profited from the tie with the PRC and gained a higher profile in the Asian region.

Fitzgerald took me to the opening of a splendid "Exhibition of Australian Landscapes" at the Palace of Nationalities. The minister of culture, Yu Huiyong, made warm remarks. Affable and charming, ultra-leftist Yu had firm views on many of the paintings. I liked the show, but there were too many works in the 19th century British style, not showing the Australian Outback's bright hues and vast spaces. Of course, in the nature of the exhibition, there were almost no Australian people visible. But Chinese visitors seemed to like the art and Minister Yu was enthusiastic.

Studying Chinese materials at Harvard, I saw that prominent victims of the Cultural Revolution were back at important posts. The huge case was Deng Xiaoping, who reappeared as a vice-premier in April 1973.

One evening in Hangzhou at Pacific Cinema, a documentary of the celebration in Beijing of May Day flashed on the screen. The huge audience, packed close on varnished wooded seats, was quiet, except for cheering during sword fights between small children. Suddenly, a loud audience reaction. Deng Xiaoping, beaming in a gray-blue tunic, was welcoming a Chinese delegation back from a trip to Japan. "Ooohs" and "Aaas" erupted across the auditorium.

For years, these Hangzhou folks, like all Chinese, had not seen Deng on TV or in the cinema. They did not exactly cheer him, but the reaction was strong. It was reminiscent of a pantomime audience responding to the sudden re-appearance of a favorite villain.

Certainly, some struggles of the mid-1970s were about important policy issues: How open should New China be to the world? What was the proper relation between ideology and economic development in mapping China's progress? However, such questions were not clarified by the fights and slogans. Contradictions abounded.

Relations between China and the U.S., too, cried out with unresolved issues. "Vacuum" years of diplomatic "idling" between the U.S. and China displayed two issues: Sharp differences between Washington and Beijing over "détente-or-no-détente" with the Soviet Union. Second, the challenge of promising but long-neglected U.S.-China cultural and trade ties. The opening to the U.S. promised much for China, but posed problems for the Chinese in the Third World.

Washington took a live-and-let-live approach to Moscow. Beijing believed this approach strengthened the Soviet Union. On his trip to China in October 1975, to prepare President Ford's summit, Kissinger spoke differently from his counterpart Qiao Guanhua, an old friend of Fairbank. In his welcoming toast, the Chinese foreign minister said, "The danger of a new world war is mounting. We do not believe there is any lasting peace."

Kissinger began his remarks: "No relationship is more significant for the U.S. than that with China." Important words. But he continued: "Each country must pursue a policy suitable to its own circumstances." The secretary of state then reached the guts: The U.S. will "resist hegemony," he said, but it will also resist "needless confrontation when it can do so." Kissinger insisted it was better to talk than fight.

Kissinger told me privately that he thought Chinese rhetoric exceeded what China could do in practice. Kissinger was worried that Zhou Enlai seemed to be "losing his influence and changing his tune."

Figure 10.1. Firemen wash a Mao Zedong statue in Chengdu. Five decades after his death, Mao still hovers over China. Cary Wolinsky/ Trillium.

Back in May 1970, Mao had said that U.S., "which looks like a huge monster, is in essence a paper tiger, now in the throes of its death-bed struggle." The death throes were slow-moving.

In May 1974, as Zhou missed a string of banquets for visiting foreign leaders, *Beijing Review* ran an article about Fan Sui of the state of Qin in the third century BC. This ancient prime minister favored a policy of "keeping friendly relations with distant states and attacking the nearby states." Fan Sui realized he was "sitting on top of a volcano that could erupt at any time" and he "asked to return the seal of prime minister because of illness." Dead and gone, Fan Sui was Zhou Enlai.

On his eighth trip to China, Kissinger arrived in China via Vladivostok. When they reached Beijing, the U.S. party found in their hotel rooms an article noting that Russia had taken portion of Siberia from China and the appropriate name for Vladivostok was the Chinese, Haishenwai. No doubt Beijing was expressing irritation with Kissinger's route into China and giving him a history lesson to boot.

Brezhnev added fuel to the flames of Chinese discontent with U.S.-Soviet "détente," by flying direct from a summit with Ford in Vladivostok to Ulan Bator, where, 100 miles from Beijing he gave an uncompromising speech on China-Soviet Union border issues.

In the mid-1970s, the potential big step was U.S. de-recognition of the government in Taiwan; but Washington under Ford was not ready to take it. Losing Thieu in Saigon was difficult enough to sell to the American people;

losing Chiang Kai-shek as well would be too much. As Kissinger said privately, "We have used up our ration of betrayals this year."

The editor of *Atlantic Monthly* applied to China through Washington to have me accredited for the press plane with Ford to Beijing. However, the Chinese government, as usual, put foreigners into national "boxes." I was associate professor at Harvard teaching American students on China. However, I was not an American. Beijing told the *Atlantic Monthly* the American president's media party must consist only of American citizens. As I was still an Australian citizen, China judged me ineligible.

One frosty evening in 1975, on my way home from China via Canada, American officials in Montreal, handling formalities for entry into Boston before leaving Canada, asked where I had been. When I said " China," they nodded knowingly, took me to a side room, and said I had broken the laws of the United States and forfeited my right to reside there. I had forgotten Ms. McKeon's pamphlet when she gave me a green card!

As a resident alien, I was required to seek Washington's permission before visiting "hostile" countries. The exact phrase was "the Communist portions of China, Vietnam, and Korea." I thought after Nixon's visit to "the Communist portion of China," and given the thickening China-U.S. relationship, China would no longer be on that hostile list with North Korea and North Vietnam. Not true.

I had indeed visited China without seeking permission. My green card was taken away from me in Montreal. I was allowed to proceed to Boston "on parole," after signing a paper acknowledging that I had one month to leave the U.S. for good. An appeal was allowed. I sought the help of Senator Edward Kennedy.

Then a vigorous man of enormous charm, Kennedy had met with several China Hands on the Harvard faculty, including me, as he sought in 1969–70 to outflank Nixon on China-policy by making his own trip to Beijing. Kennedy told the director of the immigration and naturalization service in Boston—with a certain exaggeration—that I was necessary to China debate in the U.S. and should not be deported. My appeal was granted. I did not have to resign from the Harvard faculty and return to Australia.

About this time, as I later learned from my FBI file obtained through the Freedom of Information Act, the Boston office of the FBI faced a cross-road. "At this stage," Boston wrote to Washington headquarters, "we either interview Terrill or we have to close the file."[7] They closed the file. Surveillance of this left-wing Australian immigrant, begun in 1966, came to an end.

The term "Communist portion of China " summed up a myopia that I had naively imagined to be over. Yet the problem was less U.S. wariness of

Beijing than exaggerated swings of American views of China. I do not blame the American authorities for spying on me from 1966 to 1974, as the FBI file proved they did. On China and Vietnam, I had indeed been a dissenter on some current U.S. policies. At the same time, trying to define a "pro-China" sentiment within American society involved the FBI in distasteful politics of ideological loyalty.

I guessed tension in Chinese foreign policy-making from talks with Ambassador Huang Hua. Foreign Minister Qiao Guanhua gave a leftist speech at the UN late in 1972. A few days later, Huang Hua asked me, "What were the views of your colleagues at Harvard about the speech?" I could say little as opinions in Cambridge varied. The ambassador insisted on some response. I mentioned one or two of Qiao's points approved by Harvard China specialists. The conversation turned to the upcoming Australian election. But Huang Hua suddenly switched back: "What DIDN'T you like about Qiao Guanhua's speech?"

Anti-American sentiment existed in some "Nixon-Kissinger poems" discovered by chance in China. In the early 1970s, a group of Dutch left-wing students, visiting a factory in Xian, were shown a *dazibao* by their Chinese guide. The guide explained that the poster included poems about Kissinger's visits to China in July 1971 and subsequently. Happily, the Dutch students, who knew no Chinese, took photos of the *dazibao*. A Sinologist at the University of Leiden, Netherlands, sent me the poems.

One verse began:

> Blazing fires of revolution burn the world over
> Boiling oil is poured on the Pentagon
> The raging fire in Coconut Grove [a Nixon hideaway in Florida] startles the universe
> War drums along the Equator shake the heavens
> As the economy takes a further turn downward every day
> The tide of rebellion rises up in waves.

This grim picture of President Nixon's America was followed by a solution from Beijing:

> A visit to China is the only way out
> For a brief respite from blazing fires that singe the eyebrows.

A second poem presented the dilemma of the U.S.'s 1972 election:

> For next year's national presidential elections
> Two promises made have not been redeemed
> The key to capture votes is a visit to China.

The trenchant lines went on:

Kissinger is off to Beijing with his joyful message
He drinks fine wine and eats crab's legs, pulling his happiest grinning face. . . .
With painted face-mask, disguised as a beauty, he comes to negotiate
But the demons-demasking-mirror in the city of Beijing is truly inexorable
There must be fear that our true image is revealed and our great cause will fail
There is no way out but to go to church, and in profound worship
To pray to high heaven and beseech God: Protect us through this difficult passage!

I sent the poems to Kissinger at the White House and he dryly replied, "It is always gratifying to see that one's efforts inspire verse, even when it includes some poetic license. I can't say I recall eating crab's legs in Beijing, but the food was delicious." Later I asked him if I may publish them. "Why not?" he replied with a smile.

Thin and eloquent, assistant foreign minister Zhang Wenjin was a thinker as well as a diplomat. Each session with this foreign policy Mandarin yielded signs of the times. Zhang could soften a harsh pronouncement with his grandfatherly air. He had an architect brother living in the United States and knew the West well. Kissinger was escorted by Zhang to Beijing from Pakistan on his first secret trip in 1971 and afterwards referred to Zhang's "austere elegance and understated intelligence."

At my meeting with Zhang Wenjin in August 1973, he was tough.

"Colonialism is about control," Zhang said, when we talked of stages of colonialism and imperialism in Asia. "After WW2, Asians understood Japan's imperialism; they had experience of it. But not American imperialism. So, they welcomed the USA. Now, twenty-five years later, they understand American imperialism, but not Soviet Union imperialism. Moscow walks around under a signboard of Marxism-Leninism. Some are deceived."

Zhang Wenjin saw Moscow "overreaching itself" just as the U.S. had done before it. "They step into any vacuum. Into India; into Indochina, as the U.S. leaves; into the Persian Gulf. During Tsarist days, Moscow's fleets only occasionally went into the Indian Ocean. Now they regularly go from Siberia to the Indian Ocean, and on to the Persian Gulf." I was puzzled that Zhang saw the U.S. and the Soviet Union as two peas in a pod,

He urged Washington to admit reality and depart from Indochina. "How can there be "honorable retreat," he mocked, citing a phrase used by Nixon and Kissinger. "Be like de Gaulle in Algeria," Zhang said with spirit. "Admit the mistake, admit the defeat." Zhang was equally scornful of American insistence on sticking by "old friends" such as Thieu in Vietnam, Lon Nol in Cambodia, and Chiang Kai-shek. "They say they are disengaging," the assistant minister complained of Washington. "How, then, can they also stand by 'old friends'?"

I told Zhang of Kissinger's remark that the situation over Taiwan will "evolve" in the direction of American withdrawal "after the death of Chiang Kai-shek." Dismissing the idea that Chinese policy can be based on the life or death of one individual, Zhang Wenjin said, "Of course, American withdrawal from Taiwan will take time, just as it takes time for withdrawal of troops from Vietnam to occur."

In Cambridge, Korea proved tricky for Fairbank and other Harvard colleagues when money became available to further Korea's visibility in teaching and research. A businessman friend, Jeff Coolidge, from the well-known American political family, initiated a project in 1975 by hauling in one million dollars from the Korean Trade Association and a further 2.8 million from American investors in Korea, including his own Back Bay Orient Enterprise company. It was a splendid scheme that promised to bring Korean studies into the fold of East Asian studies at Harvard. A massive increase of Korean-language books was planned for the Harvard Yenching Library.

Two problems jumped out. Harvard scholars were divided in their judgment of the current South Korea government. Jerome Cohen, head of East Asian Legal Studies, was a sharp critic of Seoul's human rights failings, as was former ambassador Edwin Reischauer, head of Japan studies. Fairbank on the other hand felt criticism of an East Asian government was a lower priority than academic study of that country's history, society and literature. This was in keeping with Fairbank's long-standing approach of "pedagogy-first, politics-maybe."

Fairbank agreed with Kissinger's idea that it was overreaching for Harvard professors to tell a foreign government how to run its affairs. How can professors know the details of domestic political decision-making in China, Korea or anywhere else, Kissinger would say. To which Cohen at the Law School would retort: Research by Harvard professors throws light on political and legal issues and eventually produces better governance and wiser U.S. foreign policy.

Fairbank and Reischauer clashed on this matter, as they had done on some similar issues over the years, always within the bounds of friendship. Reischauer often expressed frustration that Japan had to take second place to China at the East Asian Center, with the implication that he had to accept the lead of Fairbank. This affected arguments over the Korea project.

Just after Mitsubishi donated a million dollars to Harvard for a professorship in Japanese Law, I ran into Reischauer at a party. "Appalling food was served at the lunch [Harvard President] Bok gave to celebrate the Mitsubishi occasion," he complained. "Just noodles! I almost curled under the table in shame. When you think of the dishes the Japanese serve at such events!" Reischauer compared the lunch unfavorably with that for Chancellor Brandt when Germany gave half a million dollars for Harvard's work on European affairs. Reischauer often gave the impression he felt Japan was slighted at Harvard by comparison with Europe and China.

Beyond Fairbank-Reischauer tension, the South Korea embassy in Washington made it clear Seoul expected its million-dollar gift would damp down the criticism by Cohen, Reischauer and others at Harvard (including me) over Seoul's domestic policies. It was known to us colleagues that Cohen and Reischauer also favored reduced American military assistance to Seoul and withdrawal of U.S. troops from South Korea. This added to Seoul's displeasure with them.

Of course, it was, and is, a mistake, for people on both sides of such an issue, to think that a scholar's mouth can be opened and shut with power or money.

Fairbank and Coolidge realized the same issue could arise with China, Taiwan and Vietnam. Were scholars to keep their heads down at research, or were they to be prophets ushering in a brighter world? To Fairbank it was a crucial issue. He and Coolidge, together with a few "traditional" scholars working on Korea, issued a watery statement: "It is necessary to study and understand the culture, society, economy and politics of Korea and the U.S., rather than to criticize politics excessively."

There were two sides to Fairbank. One was soft, even vulnerable. When former diplomat John Carter Vincent died, Widow Betty showed me a letter Fairbank wrote from Tokyo a few hours after he heard of Vincent's death. "I cannot convey the feeling of love which is all that counts at this time," he wrote to Betty. "We have to try to love each other as best we can." Betty's voice broke as she read these touching sentences from John.

The other side of Fairbank was a fierce, hold-no-prisoners approach to the protection and expansion of historical academic study of China, especially, and East Asia in general. This was the aspect of Fairbank that Reischauer and Cohen came up against over the Korea project in 1975.

Looking back to the earlier 1970s, as a China scholar who also spoke up in public, I was fortunate in my timing. On China, the interests of "purists" and "activists" were largely aligned in 1971–72. Both camps appreciated the fresh access to China. And because it was a Republican president who opened the door to Beijing, China specialists were extra lucky; Nixon's boldness provided protection against attacks from the right. The picture became more complex as the 1970s wore on.

Chinese and Americans in the arts, business, technology, and academia enriched each other for the first time in thirty years. However, crosscurrents existed. Visiting China, a former classmate Andrew Nathan, then at Columbia University, presented a history professor at Fudan University with a copy of his scholarly book *Factionalism in Early Republican China.* The book was returned. "Fudan found an item in my bibliography that referred to the Chinese Communist Party as 'bandits,'" Nathan explained when our paths crossed in Hangzhou. "They were not pleased." Nor were Nathan and I pleased to read in *People's Daily* that day, "Music, like all other forms of art, must be an instrument of class struggle."

The U.S. curtailed a Chinese entertainment troupe's visit to American cities in 1974, because of a song whose lyrics vowed to liberate Taiwan. Beijing was upset that Washington allowed a Tibetan song-and-dance troupe to play coast to coast. Over a splendid Chinese archeological exhibit at the National Gallery of Art in Washington, Chinese officials at the PRC Liaison Office cancelled their cooperation on finding invitations had gone to journalists from Taiwan, Israel, South Africa, and South Korea. The upsets bedeviled both sides.

Many congressmen believed nothing would be lost by the United States' standing pat on Taiwan, keeping an American embassy in Taipei while developing relations with Beijing. This attitude was rejected by Beijing. Yet Chinese officials and media gave congressmen and others the impression that the Soviet threat was the alpha and omega of international life and that the Taiwan issue by comparison was a bagatelle.

"The danger," Lin Ping, head of the America-Australia section of the foreign ministry, told me in Beijing in 1975, "is that the tiger [United States] will go out the front door, and the wolf [Russia] will come in the back door."

Sitting on a silken couch with Zhou Enlai, Kissinger could make American intentions more clear-cut than when viewed alongside aggravations of Congress-White House relations, power of the media, churning public opinion in the American democracy, and the U.S. cat and mouse game with Moscow.

In the Ford period, Congress thrust itself into China policy in a way never allowed under Nixon. Richard Solomon, a senior official on Asia, spoke of his difficulties with congressmen. "One group visiting China was headed by Senator Warren Magnuson on the Democratic side," Solomon said with a sigh. "They were out of control on policy. They did not understand what was behind our China policy."

At a dinner, Zhou Enlai received this delegation. Magnuson said to Zhou that he didn't understand why Taiwan shouldn't be independent. "Al Jenkins [a Liaison Office diplomat] kicked Magnuson under the table, trying to get him to shut up because it was such a disastrous opinion to articulate."

Solomon judged: "Zhou Enlai and others in Beijing were exposed to these views, whether or not they fully understood how our Congress worked, and the challenge of any White House to build a coalition of political support."[8]

Overall, by the mid-1970s, domestic politics in China and the United States caused crosscurrents in the foreign policies of both. Fairbank was correct to write to Foreign Minister Qiao Guanhua as Watergate unfolded: "Watergate is essentially a domestic matter. Mr. Nixon's foreign policy continues to have very general support."[9] However, I wondered how steady the China-U.S. relationship would be without Mao and Zhou in Beijing, and without Nixon and Kissinger in Washington.

NOTES

1. Transcript of talks between Australian Treasurer and Minister for Northern Development, and Chinese Vice-Minister of Trade, Chai Shufan, and other Chinese officials, Beijing, November 3, 1973, supplied to author by Deputy Prime Minister Cairns, December 1973.

2. *Time,* March 26, 1973.

3. Whitlam speech, October 31, 1973, Beijing, Great Hall of the People.

4. The Prime Minister gave the author a verbal account of his 1973 visit to China and showed him a transcript of the Mao-Whitlam conversation.

5. "The Chinese Present as World History," *Motive*, Nashville, December, 1967.

6. Huang Hua to the author, New York, March 8, 1973.

7. FBI File, FOIPA, No 320,947, supplied to the author, August 25, 1995.

8. Solomon, interview, ADST-LOC.

9. Fairbank letter to Qiao, shown to the author, 1975.

Chapter Eleven

Loss and Revival

The editor of *Boston Globe* phoned at 4 pm on January 8, 1976 with news of Zhou Enlai's death. He requested an article by 6 pm. I finished my commentary on Zhou's life at 6.30 pm and the newspaper ran it on the front-page next morning. I wrote, "The anchor of Chinese politics has gone." I cautioned readers, "The fact that Zhou has died before Mao will add tension to the eventual post-Mao months."[1]

I sent a message of condolence to Ambassador Huang Hua at the UN and he replied warmly. Although not a Chinese, I felt grief at Zhou Enlai's passing. His skills made a vast contribution to China and international relations over my lifetime. From Beijing came public reports and messages from friends of emotional reaction to the death of the premier.

At Harvard, we Sinologues were surprised that Mao did not attend Zhou Enlai's funeral. A Shanghai friend, Dr. Dong Fengchong, who cared for the premier during 1975 and 1976, told me: "I was the only non-Party doctor, so when they had a Party meeting, I had to withdraw. Zhou heard about this and criticized it; afterwards I joined in the meetings." According to Dong, an operation on Zhou for cancer of the bladder was unfortunately delayed. "Mao had to sign the approval for it," Dong said in reference to a rule for members of the Politburo, "and the paperwork dragged on and on."

I asked Dong if Jiang Qing had a hand in this matter. "Probably she did," he replied. "I found her an arbitrary person. At the hospital I always had the feeling she might suddenly say to one of us [doctors], 'You're a counter revolutionary!'"

In March, former President Nixon met with Widow Deng Yingzhao in Beijing and declared her husband "a great man." That was a widespread opinion inside China and out. At Harvard, China specialists differed on aspects of Zhou's career. Zhou was a "moderate," said quite a few. Others, including me, saw Zhou as essentially "stage manager" for a production, the Chinese revolution, of which Mao was the director. The idea of "Maoist" versus "Moderate" broke down when it came to Zhou Enlai, I believed. Not since 1935 had Zhou made a leadership challenge to Mao.

Qing Ming festival, a Chinese Memorial Day, in 1976 brought a prolonged demonstration in Tiananmen Square. Affection for the departed Zhou mingled with discontent at ultra-leftists. News from the Square was channeled to Mao through nephew Mao Yuanxin. I wondered if Mao was isolated from some truths about the political situation. Those at Harvard who had viewed Zhou as a "moderate" felt vindicated when slogans and poems posted at the Monument to People's Heroes attacked Jiang Qing. If remembering the dead premier became an occasion for opposing Gang of Four, did this not confirm tensions between Zhou Enlai and Jiang Qing, Zhang Chunqiao and the rest?

After Deng's dismissal "from all his posts," I clashed with Chinese acquaintances at the Liaison Office in Washington. I could not accept that Deng was a "capitalist-roader," or a "counterrevolutionary." Hearing this, Xie Qimei said tersely, "If you don't understand that Deng is a counterrevolutionary, you don't understand anything about China."[2]

Being favorably inclined to some Chinese policies, I regretted that Chinese officials preached ideology at me. I realized they were sincerely unsure where events were leading and had little choice but to mouth the tested formulae of yesterday. Yet some of my young friends in China boldly declined to attend the "Victory Rallies" to celebrate Deng's disgrace.

Later, visiting China and wondering how young people viewed the denunciation of Deng as a counterrevolutionary, I talked with a teacher in Beijing. Shen Chunyi, an early PRC student in Australia, was a s 28year old with shortcropped hair and bright eyes. He attended a lecture I gave at Australian National University in Canberra in 1978, lingering afterwards to ask questions about my topic, "Chinese Politics Since the Death of Mao." He liked my view that public opinion was playing a new role in the PRC.

"I had just become a teacher at the institute," Shen related of 1976 as we chatted in Haidian, a university district. "We were pressured to write essays criticizing Deng. People were divided. I felt the case against Deng Xiaoping was ridiculous and, like some others, I refused to write these pointless essays."

"But could you just refuse?" I asked.

"We said we were too busy preparing our lessons," Shen said, "and we pointed out there was nothing new to say about Deng. If necessary, we started an article, then kept saying it wasn't quite finished yet." I asked Shen what happened later to those who denounced Deng in essays. "They're still around," he replied. "They don't like to be reminded that they wrote such stuff; their faces flush if you remind them."

I felt the constant reiteration of Deng's "mistakes" simply aired positions held by Deng that were reasonable. Radical students at Qinghua University mocked Deng's words, "The remarks of the dead cannot be taken as holy scripture. But they can be used for reference." Yet, of course, this was simply common sense to most people.

Mao and Deng had a crucial disagreement on socialism. Mao said capitalism and socialism are like mouse and cat: socialism will devour capitalism as a cat devours a mouse. Deng scoffed at this. He said he didn't care whether a cat was black or white as long as it caught the mouse—progress by whatever means.

My journalist friend Wang Ruoshui said, "Mao was wrong; capitalism is one of the cats, it's not the mouse. Backwardness is the mouse."[3] So it was that China's dissenters had to battle an old enemy (feudalism) but also a newer enemy (Stalinism).

Having spent two years in Australia, Shen Chunyi said, "I doubt that capitalism will collapse in Australia. The capitalists are too strong." He spoke as if entertaining a new idea.

Later at Harvard, I received a letter from Shen in Beijing, which showed how dizzying was two years study in the West followed by a return to one's original unit in China. "I am teaching beginners [in my language institute]," Shen wrote, "and it is very tedious and boring. What I learned in Australia seems of little use."

Deng Xiaoping had just closed the so-called Democracy Wall, a fleeting outlet for written free expression "China cannot afford to allow the kind of democracy you have in the West," Shen's letter went on. "With the bulk of the population backward, there can be no genuine democracy for all. It is always for the few (I mean the ruling elite)." In this 1979 letter, Shen had come to understand China's political dilemma. "I don't reject the introduction of democracy," he wrote. "I merely state that any authoritarian government can't allow it."

In Washington, Assistant Secretary for East Asia Philip Habib expressed pleasure with the prominence given in China to the message of congratulations President Ford sent to Acting Premier Hua Guofeng in February, 1976, following the death of Zhou Enlai. Habib, sunk into an armchair with feet on the table in his State Department office, said he received signals that Hua was continuing China's tilt toward the United States.

Short-term, I wasn't alarmed by the implications of Chinese domestic political turbulence for United States-China relations, but longer term, meaning when Mao would no longer be there, much was uncertain. I suggested to Habib three levels to the importance of United States-China relations: a joint global anti-Soviet stance; specific bilateral benefits; and the impact for peace in Asia.

Xie Qimei at the PRC office asked about rising Democratic presidential candidate Jimmy Carter. "We Chinese are amazed, this man has sprung out of nowhere," the diplomat said. "And maybe he's going to be the next president of the U.S.!"

"Counselor Xie," I said, "many Americans were equally astonished at the sudden emergence of Hua Guofeng from obscurity to be China's Premier." Xie, who would later become undersecretary at the UN, had the grace to laugh.

A few months later, when Xie came to see me at Harvard, and Carter was drawing close to the presidency, I asked, "Why didn't you invite Carter to China last year!"

"Frankly," replied Xie, "last year we had never heard of Jimmy Carter."

Testifying before a Congressional committee on China policy on March 10, 1976, together with Michel Oksenberg, an academic Sinologist and later China advisor to Carter, I was impatient with some House members' suspicion of Beijing. "Depressing to see how short a distance these House guys have moved since the dark days of Containment," I wrote in my diary. "The attachment to Chiang [Kaishek]'s Taiwan is still a tug."

After the hearing, Oksenberg and I took a taxi together to Washington airport and enjoyed a drink awaiting our planes, his to Detroit, mine to Boston. In 1975–76, Oksenberg had been consulting with NBC and we had friendly banter about NBC's rivalry with CBS, where I had a connection.

When Hua was appointed acting premier in February, 1976, Oksenberg was in the NBC building showing relatives around the studios. He ran into John Chancellor, anchor of the NBC Evening News. "I've got a coup for tonight, Mike," said Chancellor, "come and have a look." Chancellor showed Oksenberg a group photo from Ford's visit to China in December, 1975. "There's me at a banquet standing next to this Hua Guofeng!" said the anchor. Hua's face was circled, ready for the Evening News. However, the face was not Hua! It was a lesser figure, Huang Zhen, of the Liaison Office in Washington. Oksenberg was stunned.

Chancellor was in a fix, as the news began in twenty minutes and the blown-up photo could not be changed. He had planned to say he'd dined with the well-known Chinese leader Hua Guofeng in Beijing two months before. Instead, he began the broadcast, "Hua Guofeng is truly an obscure figure.

During President Ford's visit, this photo was taken of all the leading Chinese officials at a welcoming banquet. Hua's face was *not to be found*!"

During Ford's trip to China, Oksenberg, appearing on NBC's "Today Show," made another alarming discovery. NBC had invited Peng Mingmin as a fellow guest and had prepared a set with three huge flags as backdrop, the PRC flag, the KMT flag for Taiwan, and the flag of Peng's Taiwan independence movement! Such was television "news." Such was excessive sensitivity over "One China."

In December 1976, a large meeting in Washington urged normalization with China. Chinese-Americans organized the gathering of several hundred people under the banner, "The Time Has Come," My key-note speech said there was little danger Beijing would attack Taiwan and Washington should move to normal diplomatic relations. Andrew Nathan at Columbia University wrote a letter disagreeing. "You have created a stylistic atmosphere of sweet reason which makes very plausible the basic reassurance that China will not attack Taiwan. I don't think it is at all plausible."

Van Long, long resident in Washington, introduced me to Chinese- American friends. Van was a masterful person, like his father, gregarious and energetic. The Long family, not Han race but Ni, was in diaspora among the PRC, Taiwan and the U.S. Van had childhood memories of his father with Deng Xiaoping. Chiang Kai-shek turned against his father during the 1940s, leading Long Yun to join Mao's government in 1949. In Van's home, I slept in a bedroom with walls showing photos of Zhou Enlai, General Stilwell, and Long Yun.

For a lunch in Arlington, Van Long brought a Congressional staffer friend, of Russian origin, a descendent of Stolypin, a major figure in the Russian revolution. I brought my lover, Phannarong Salirathavibhaga from Thailand. I happened to wear a brilliant tie. As we took our seats, Van burst out, "I like your tie!" Glancing sideways to my handsome friend, "I responded, "I like my Thai too."

Van as a youth in New York was friendly with Ji Chaozhu, then a student at Harvard, and Tang Mingchao, who ran a Chinese newspaper in New York. "Once I received $10,000 from my family," Van told me, "and I immediately gave It to Tang's newspaper. I thought it was a good paper. In those days, I didn't know what was Communist and what was not.

"Maybe, later, that gift was why Beijing considered me 'the really good one' in the Long family." In the early 1970s while Van was visiting Shanghai, Zhou Enlai phoned to invite him to lunch. He quickly flew up to Beijing. "Zhou said to me, 'Maybe I shouldn't say this, but probably your father died at the right time [1956]. He could not have stood the excesses of the Cultural Revolution.'"

After returning to Boston I received a letter from Van; "I wish I could find appropriate English words to express my appreciation for your coming down to speak and assist us. I was touched by your generous enthusiasm and support. This feeling is strongly felt by all our Chinese friends."

I went to see Shen Ruoyun in April 1976 at the Chinese Liaison Office, where the staff grew ever larger. She said Chinese foreign policy would not change because of the departure of Deng. "Everything he did in foreign relations was laid down by Chairman Mao," she said. Nevertheless, I found it hard to believe a "class enemy" could conduct China's foreign relations without error.

When I raised the "political setback" in Australia, with the fall of social democrat Whitlam and the coming of conservative Fraser, Shen was silent, her face a mask. Later in the year, Zhou Nan, at a lunch in New York, praised Fraser to the skies. Clearly, Prime Minister Fraser's anti-Soviet Union stance was welcome to the Chinese government. Little else mattered.

Miss Shen lit up when we dropped Chinese politics and talked of her hometown, Wuxi, and its lakeside mulberry blossoms. She spoke of Wuxi people's liking for sweet dishes and the delights of Lake Tai. As I left, Shen asked where I was going. I said to Channel 7, for the "Panorama Show." She said she would watch. In the taxi, her words made me uncomfortable, for the questions would be about "power struggles" in China, not ordinary Chinese people's lives.

Overall, on relations between China and USA, I saw the outlines of a hopeful outcome on the Taiwan issue. I wrote in *New Republic*, "Once Taipei ceases to pose as the government of China, or is no longer acknowledged as such by Washington, and once Taiwan is no more the site of foreign planes and joint war-games between U.S. and Taiwan forces, the question of Taiwan as a separated province may not be as urgent to Beijing as many people now assume."[4] So it would prove, for a number of years.

I wrote a column about Hua Guofeng in *Boston Globe*, saying, "Deng has enemies and black marks on his record, and Hua's career is too slim for him to have either." I said Hua was more likely to be an interim compromise, or a sign of Mao's wavering between Deng and Gang of Four, than a signal of the final eclipse of Deng.[5] Fairbank wrote me a note in his ever-larger handwriting, "You are my favorite 'expert.' The Hua article is very neat and illuminating."[6] Note "expert" with quote marks; John was shrewd, as well as brilliant. He knew none of us was truly an expert.

A lecture at the University of Chicago brought welcome contact with another Chinese-American, Tang Tsou, a leading scholar of Chinese politics.

Born in Guangzhou to a KMT family, Tang Tsou received a bachelor's degree in 1940 in Kunming. He arrived at the University of Chicago as a student in 1941 and remained there almost half a century. I had sent students to study under him.

"Since my trip to China last year," Tang Tsou said as we lunched in a Greek restaurant, "I am more pro-Beijing. For an overseas Chinese like me, it is different than for you, We Overseas Chinese are either against the PRC or for It." When Tang Tsou spoke with admiration of the traditions of the CCP in the 1930s and 1940s, I asked if he was tempted to join the party at that time. He quickly shook his head. "They wouldn't have people like me. Wrong class, wrong family." Not a worker, not a peasant.

This small, cheerful man had an air of nobility, perhaps lent by his family background. Yet Tang Tsou expressed resentment that Fairbank and other Sinology leaders did not treat him as an equal. "I am surprised that you as an Australian citizen," he said, "can testify at Congress and have access to confidential information in Washington." He had not been invited to join Sinological committees or testify at Congress. "I've had none of that."

"I have not been aggressive enough in America," he declared. "Otherwise I could have gone much further." I pointed out he was a professor of political science at the University of Chicago and one of the most respected figures in China studies. "But I am not known beyond my field," he lamented. As he generously drove me to the airport, Tang Tsou enlarged, "Jewish scholars in particular are not friendly to Chinese scholars." For all his years in America, he said, "I cannot quite feel at home as I do in China."

Tang Tsou had a convincing explanation for a paradox over Taiwan that was bothering me with Chinese officials. "Beijing doesn't push for something it feels it cannot get," he explained. "That is the position at the Liaison Office with the remaining steps to normalization.

I did not agree with Tang Tsou's view that Mao had decided in the spring of 1976, "Deng could serve no further useful purpose." Nor share his faith in Hua Guofeng. In 1978, I attended a sports event in Beijing at which Hua appeared. A chorus of tiny children sang a song about the merits of Chairman Hua Guofeng. I wrote in my diary, "How can five-year olds make such political judgments? How can Hua sit there and listen?"

One of history's most deadly earthquakes hit the sleeping city of Tangshan on July 28, 1976. Tens of thousands died in a flash. For the first time since 1949, the U.S. offered assistance to China, to cope with the terrible aftermath, but physical help was declined. Beijing also refused aid offers from Taiwan, even impeding balloons with supplies quickly sent across the Taiwan Strait. For rural folk, the earthquake was a portent. With the world still in the dark about the situation in Tangshan, the death toll climbed to 250,000. Former Australian Prime Minister Whitlam was in nearby Tianjin that night, but avoided injury.

A clever but tasteless cartoon appeared in the Australian press about Gough and Margaret Whitlam in Tianjin during the earthquake. They wake up startled in a huge bed. Margaret says to her husband, "Did the earth move for you too last night, Darling?"

The new Australian Prime Minister, Malcolm Fraser, made his first China visit in summer 1976. Fortunately, for China-Australia relations, Fraser carried on Whitlam's positive approach to China, even strengthening it, by his deep distrust of the Soviet Union's activities in the Indian Ocean and elsewhere.

Visiting me at my Harvard office, Xie Qimei warmly praised Fraser. I told Xie I simply did not trust conservatives. He asked why.

"Because they lack roots among the people," I replied.

"But [Western] liberals seldom have roots among the people either."

Of course, folk like myself, who worked for years to achieve a social democratic government in Australia, were terribly disappointed that the Whitlam era ended after less than three years. However, Fraser's anti-Soviet Union stance was clearly welcome to China.

Animosity between Whitlam and Prime Minister Fraser was intense. Simply because the Whitlam government had donated one million dollars to Harvard for Australian studies, to celebrate the American Bicentennial of 1776, Fraser fired potshots at the gift. He sniffed, "Whitlam tried to set up a memorial to his own so-called achievements in China policy." When Fraser came to Harvard to present the money, I led him into the office of Harvard President Derek Bok and introduced the pair.[7]

It was a wet and humid day and Fraser glanced at his watch several times. A staff member whispered that the prime minister, having finished his talks with President Ford in Washington, was impatient to leave for trout fishing in Canada the next day. During the reception, I introduced Fraser to several professors. Samuel Huntington mentioned Fraser's recent visit to China and the Tangshan earthquake. I remarked that Whitlam had narrowly escaped harm the night of the tragedy. Fraser straightened his shoulders and said to Huntington, "Had I been there, no earthquake would have occurred." Professors were startled; Australian humor missed its mark.

Some weeks later in August 1976, Wilenski wrote from Canberra, "I was at a dinner at the weekend where Fraser spoke and made sarcastic remarks about Harvard being so impoverished that it needed the Australian government to subsidize a new Chair on the campus."[8] Soon after the Australian Chair began, I initiated an invitation to Whitlam to give lectures on "Australia and Asia" at Harvard. This did not endear me to Fraser. The Dean of Harvard asked me to draft supporting points for an invitation to Whitlam.

During a dinner party at Rupert Murdoch's home on Fifth Avenue in New York, I saw Fraser again and asked him about Moscow and the Indian Ocean. "I now see the Russian problem in a wider context than I did earlier," he said, more mellow than he was in Cambridge. Fraser told me he tried to persuade President Carter to "take the Chinese more seriously." The Australian leader spoke highly of Hua Guofeng. "You could get him off the ideology stuff, and then he was fine."

When military chief Zhu De died on July 6, a year of unsettling events in China gathered momentum. With tensions high, local cadres were told not to leave their provinces for Beijing to attend Zhu De's funeral. A jumpy mood gripped the land.

On vacation in Morocco with a Thai friend, Phannarong Salirathavibhaga, while walking on an ocean beach south of Casablanca, two young men dressed in jelibahs greeted us. "Excuse me sir," one Moroccan said to the Thai in French, "we are very sorry your president has died." Phannarong and I were puzzled.

Then it dawned on us: Moroccans, unused to distinctions among Asians, took my Thai friend for a Chinese. To Africans, Asians were just Asians. However, one Asian was known by name in Africa as on all other continents. In the small beach town of El Jadida, when they heard Mao Zedong was dead, the Moroccans expressed regret to the first Asian they encountered.

I was far from Casablanca airport—from any airport—and I had to accept my isolation from a major world news event. After I returned from Morocco, I read a letter from the secretary of the East Asia Center at Harvard, Anna Laura Rosow: "Some of us may never forgive you for being out of the country when Mao died. The major networks and newspapers have been desperate to find you and all I could tell them was that you were somewhere in Morocco. Most of them are totally uninterested in speaking with anyone other than you or Fairbank. Sally [another secretary] finally screwed up the courage to ask why media didn't want XX, YYY, ZZ etc and was told that you and Fairbank are household words. Ross, how does it feel to be a household word?"[9]

On a Moroccan beach, I wrote in my diary on September 10, 1976, "Was Mao a great man of China alone, or can parts of Mao transfer elsewhere? Some aspects, I think. His early idea of rooting thought in observed reality. Of a leader keeping his compass on ordinary people's needs. Of taking the long view. Of holding to a poet's whimsy amidst grinding struggle." Of course, it was a day for positive thoughts.

146Chapter Eleven

When de Gaulle died six years earlier, in 1970, I wrote, "The era of World Wars has passed, and now de Gaulle, so evocative of it, has gone too. The next batch of political titans, unlike Churchill, de Gaulle and Roosevelt, will not be figures of the Atlantic world, but of the East. Mao is already a bridge from the titans of the first half of the 20th century to those of the late 20th century."

Now Mao was gone. Perhaps it was true that any ensuing titans would be of the East. However, looking back from 2019, I am surprised that in 1970 I did not doubt there would be more titans. I did not foresee that people would come to prefer no titans at all.

It happened I had written an article at the request of *New Republic* before leaving for Morocco. It was sent to the editor in Washington ten days before Mao's death and published in the issue dated September 25, under the title, "China without Mao." I said the ultra-left was doomed. I predicted that Deng would come back, and that his dictum, "In real life, not everything is class struggle" would be embraced. "Mao didn't die in time to save Deng [from being purged in April, 1976]," I wrote. "But Deng still may be back." I went on, "The left will probably lose strength. Jiang Qing in particular will be in a threatened position. Her attacks against 'pragmatists' will cease, without Mao to pass the ammunition. . . ."

With a broader prediction, I ended the *New Republic* article, "Younger Chinese leaders will not continue to see imperialism as the overriding world trait. Nor can they go on forever viewing their own formidable land as victim, as valiant David pitted against the Goliath of the superpowers."

John Service, just back from three months in China, wrote from the University of California at Berkeley, "Congratulations on your piece in *TNR*. Especially glad to see this realistic good sense after the magazine's incredible editorial two weeks earlier ('rape of Tibet' and such nonsense)."[10] Bette Bao Lord, author of *Spring Moon* and other books and wife of Winston Lord, later ambassador to China, wrote me. "After all the chop suey that journalists and experts have been dishing out lately, how I appreciated the substantial meal you prepared for *New Republic*." She added in a reference to her husband, who was then Director of Policy Planning at the State Department, "I plan to put it at the top of Winston's reading list when he returns from Africa."[11]

A few weeks later, after Gang of Four were arrested on October 6, I wrote in the Sunday *Washington Post* on October 17, "Last week's shock looks like the end of a leftist influence artificially prolonged by Jiang Qing's privileged position as [Mao's wife], rather than the start of new uncertainty." These predictions in September and October 1976 stood the test of time.

For Washington there was anxiety and hope during September 1976. President Ford wrote a letter to Mao's widow, of which he later gave me a copy.

"Mrs. Ford joins me in extending to you our deepest sympathy on the death of Chairman Mao Tse-tung. . ." The letter was addressed, "Madame Mao Tse-tung, Beijing, PRC."[12] From Australia, Prime Minister Fraser said in Parliament on September 10, "I express to the people of China profound regret and tender deep sympathy to [Mao's] family in its bereavement."

Concerned about whether China would open up or remain attached to autarchic policies, I wrote an article, "China and the World: Self-Reliance or Interdependence?" in *Foreign Affairs,* January 1977. I expected China's self-reliance to be "severely modified economically and politically, though not militarily." I suggested, "The principle of self-reliance is in large part a self-protecting mechanism for the relatively weak—and China is ceasing to be weak even in economic terms."

I predicted a quick reversal of verdicts on Deng: "If Deng is not vindicated in 1977, his policies probably will be," I wrote. I also expected a reduction of hostility between China and the Soviet Union: "Within five years at most," I said in this January 1977 essay, "there will probably be a degree of détente between China and Russia."

John Fairbank wrote me in his large, square handwriting, "Congrats. on a superb article in *Foreign Affairs*! It puts conditions and events into a mid-level framework that USA can understand." John's mid-winter letter continued on a personal note: "I phoned just now and hear you are in Puerto Rico. What a fine idea! [it was freezing in Boston]. Wilma and I are going to Honolulu and then Guatemala with no complaints."[13]

Fairbank's remark about my "mid-level" article reflected his own vocation as a China specialist. His passion was to make China understandable to Americans. In this enterprise, he was sometimes torn between the purity of scholarship and the compromises involved in effective communication. He often searched for "mid-level frameworks" with great success, as in his famous volume *The United States and China*, published in 1948 and in print for decades afterward. I hoped to learn from his example.

At Harvard, historian Benjamin Schwartz, always reflective, sometimes elusive, had a quizzical angle on Mao's passing. "Now that Mao has gone, how will we explain what is happening in China?" I suggested, "China's politics will be duller for us [Sinologists] than under Mao, but less nerve-racking for the Chinese people. China will be less tense, more predictable."

At our communal lunch, Schwartz pondered Mao in terms of global history, "Great traditions resemble each other in their complexity and their constant flux. Mao may find some of his answers in Rousseau. We may find some of ours in Lao Zi. Mao hated his father and loved his mother. Oedipus may have been more ambivalent—even filially pious. It's all part of the human experience."

Fairbank wrote "On the Death of Mao" in *New York Review of Books*. "The attack on China's outworn social structure has been Mao's province from the beginning," he said, "ever since his heterodox report of 1927 on the peasantry as the real vanguard of revolution."[14] But Fairbank underestimated the degree to which the late Mao perpetuated the one-man rule of dynastic China's "outworn structure."

Fairbank criticized the American media for seeing power struggle behind every bush in China. "Ford versus Carter is a more naked power struggle than anything going on in Beijing," he asserted. Well, no. True, there were vital policy issues between Gang of Four and Deng. Yet, within days of the publication of Fairbank's essay, power struggle was exactly what occurred in Beijing, as Ye Jianying and other leaders locked up the Gang of Four.

Writing in 1976, Fairbank felt very uncertain about China's political future. "Mao and Zhou Enlai with all their faults may look better and better as time goes on," he said. Fairbank never quite accepted the pathology of Mao as a leader who set himself above the Communist Party and condescended to the Chinese people.

Influenced by his years in Chongqing in the 1940s, John saw the passing of the first generation of CCP leaders as undermining the U.S.'s valuable historical connection with the Chinese left. "Now the generation that knew U.S. has departed," he lamented. He did not seem to foresee that Beijing's ditching of Maoism in favor of markets would provide a firmer foundation for America-PRC understanding than the thin bonding of pre-Liberation U.S. China Hands with Zhou Enlai and others.

Optimism understandably reigned among Overseas Chinese at the accession of Hua to top posts, much of it based on confidence following the fall of Gang of Four. The president of the Hong Kong Federation of Students wrote asking me to be Overseas Advisor to its "Fifth China Week" in Hong Kong late in 1977. The splendid motto of his 18,000-member organization was "Keep the World in Mind, Understand our Motherland, Be Concerned with Society."[15] The letter reflected excitement more than I felt at the task of pursuing the Four Modernizations under Hua as new leader.

As the 1970s wore on, I felt myself becoming an American, though still an Australian citizen. With a bunch of friends, I attended the annual concert and fireworks display on July 4, 1976 at the Esplanade in Boston. It was a special occasion, being the 200th birthday of the USA, celebrating 1776. 400,000 people gathered joyfully on the banks of the Charles River. Under the baton of conductor Arthur Fiedler, middlebrow bits and pieces beloved of New Englanders soared into the night. When the fireworks began, the crowd clapped each explosion as if applauding a living creature. Emotion gripped people as they sang "Happy Birthday, Dear America." Afterwards we picked our way from the Esplanade through beer cans and bread rolls from hot dogs.

America that loved instant foods was also an instant America. One could not expect the U.S. to stage a neat Bicentennial. President Ford made a wooden speech in Philadelphia. Sailors jerked off high on the masts of their ships on the Hudson River in New York. In Florida, the oldest citizen of the land celebrated his 134th birthday by recalling to visitors that he came to the USA on a slave ship from Liberia, sold on an auction block in New Orleans at age 12. America, I realized, was the sum of its instant, sparring, contradictory parts.

"What cannot be overlooked tonight," I wrote in my diary after leaving the bank of the Charles River, "is how quickly Vietnam has vanished from the national mind. Such resiliency! Yet such a lack of historical sense! The rootless, here-we-go spirit of America scares me a bit."

Coming to Harvard to begin graduate studies in 1965, I traveled from Melbourne via Vietnam to Boston. The "mindless aggression" of U.S. forces in Vietnam, and President Johnson's military encirclement of China, were the dark aspects of what was, from another angle, the "restless buoyancy" of America on display that evening of July 4, 1976. Ten years before, on July 4, 1966, I wrote of American society as "friendly, immense, human, but unwittingly brutal."

This dual spirit chipped away at beliefs of my Australian upbringing. "In the USA you start again, as generations of immigrants have done and had to do," I told my diary. "America is a kick-off point where pre-conceived notions are merely the stuff for jokes. On the shores of this continent, where waves crash without respite, I am losing my social democracy and my Christianity."

Had I been a sculptor or a taxi driver, I might have remained an Australian citizen even after living in Boston for many years. However, being a commentator on American policy toward China, I felt uncomfortable with my outsider's classification. At Congressional hearings, I felt awkward saying "you Americans" should do this or that in relation to Beijing. Yet I could not say "we Americans."[16]

In 1979, I took the step. My two witnesses at the citizenship hearing were Robert Manning, chief editor of *Atlantic Monthly* and publisher of my *800,000,000*, and James Thomson, the scholar-official and China specialist. Each was solemnly asked if I had been guilty of adultery. Each supported me on every question. At a ceremony in historic Faneuil Hall in Boston, I became an American citizen. I was no longer a guest who made suggestions, but a voter and a taxpayer.

Reflecting on the occasion, I wrote in my diary, "In the USA, you simply jump on board and find you have signed on for the duration, with a crew whose great virtue is lack of complacency. The U.S. always believes a better idea may turn up; a bright vista will lie round the next corner. Americans give the new thing, the new arrival, space to blossom." I swore allegiance to the United States and renounced "all other powers and principalities," but kept my Australian passport until its expiration a few months away.

The State Department sent me, as a newly minted U.S. citizen on a four-month tour to lecture on the U.S., China, and Asia.

In a Kyoto hotel, I wrote in my diary, "My room is larger than the one in Tokyo—perhaps three inches longer and two inches wider. The waste paper bin is the size of a large apple." After a week or so with the Japanese, I myself became tidy, passive, tranquil, and neat in my dress. I also grew accustomed to crouching in agony in Japanese restaurants, in the cross-legged position, as beer bottles came in succession from the kitchen and sake was poured by beautiful women.

Sapporo looked like a city of the U.S.'s Pacific Northwest, with wide tree-lined streets and outdoor living. I wrote in my diary, "Why do Japanese get drunk far more than Chinese? Maybe because Chinese express their feelings more readily during the day than Japanese, so in the evening Japanese feel more need to loosen up with alcohol."

"How to be secure?" my Japanese audiences constantly wondered. I asked the U.S. ambassador to Japan, former Senator Mike Mansfield, if protecting one's standard of living was a sufficient goal for a nation's foreign policy. "It is for Japan," he replied, "but it cannot be for the U.S."

I asked myself if Japan would defend its economic interests in, say, Indonesia, should political change bring a threat to those Japanese interests; and whether Tokyo and Beijing would find themselves in opposition on such an issue. I wrote in my diary at Kyoto, "America projects itself around the world then fights to protect those projected interests. But Japan, since it's poor in resources, must fight to protect its day to day life." Will war become necessary for some nations, I wondered, or will war "gradually become unthinkable?"

A few in my audiences spoke of China-Japan-USA cooperation to counter the Soviet Union. However, I felt these three mutually friendly powers were still apple, banana, and peach; they had different interests and values and could not line up as a formation. A dinner gathering of young journalists asked me, "Japanese feel guilt toward China. Why don't Americans?"

Young journalists seemed happy with Japan projecting military capacity overseas. "We felt we had to do it in 1939," one said, "We could feel the same way again." Said another; "If the U.S. was intervening somewhere, Japan

may well join in that." What young Japanese really found unacceptable looking back on WW2 was that Japan's interventions were made under the banner
of loyalty to the emperor. Youth now had a different political psychology.
However, they might still favor Japanese international intervention to protect
their affluent way of life.

Mi Guojun at the Chinese Embassy in Tokyo railed against the Soviet
Union. I asked him to explain why war was inevitable. "The gap between
WW1 and WW2 has now been exceeded by the period since WW2," Mi
replied. "Can WW3 be far away?" The reasoning seemed shaky. I asked if
Japan could become a superpower. Mi's answer owed nothing to Lenin's
theory of imperialism. "Politically they are weak," he said of the Japanese,
"and militarily they are not so strong either."

Did not Lenin teach that the economic system was the key to hegemony?
Answered Mi, "Yes, but the resistance of the Japanese people, and other
peoples in Southeast Asia, can prevent Japan becoming a superpower."

I suggested to Mi that China's preaching to Americans against detente
was not likely to change U.S. policy and that if Americans soured on détente
with the Soviet Union, they might also sour on détente with China. "I would
think," I said to diplomat Mi, "that the best possible relations with both the
U.S. and Japan would be the strongest way for China to resist dangers from
the Soviet Union."

Mi expressed astonishment at Japan as a place to work. "How complex is
their party system!" he burst out. "So many groups want to come and press
their views on China!" Mi said before he came to live in Japan he did not
believe in the term "economic animal." But he changed his mind. "Now, I
agree, Japan certainly is an economic animal."

While I was in Osaka, President Park Chung Hee of South Korea was assassinated. He was killed in a "shooting accident" at a dinner party, attended
by South Korean leaders, said the government news agency. I wrote in my
diary, "Six people shot dead at the table. One was the President. Some accident. Some dinner party. Some political system."

In Beijing, I stayed in the empty residence of the Australian ambassador, who
was away in Yunnan Province. Chinese were speaking quite freely, but they
had doubts and complaints. I asked Zhao Fusan to dine with me in the Australian residence. He never mentioned religion as in our previous conversations.
However, he spoke up for the continuing role of Marxism. I wrote tartly in my
diary, "He seems to be an ex-Christian. I suppose he doesn't want to be called
also an ex-Marxist." Zhao saw "some wildness" among youth. The week we
met, I noticed in *People's Daily* an article "Everything Starts with Me" (*Cong
wo zuo qi*).[17] It was almost the Horatio Alger philosophy of the U.S.

Beijing jumped with reports of remarks by reformer Hu Yaobang, about Mao, to a visiting Yugoslav leader. "There has certainly been a personality cult in China," Hu said. "A feudalistic monarchical system was adopted, with one man [Mao] unchallengeable. This lasted essentially for thirty years." These assertions were explosive news as China prepared for the trial of the Gang of Four and the Lin Biao group in the coming winter.

"Mao's death did not bring body-blows to China as some expected," I wrote in my diary. "No civil war, break–up of the nation, or return of the KMT. More remarkable than any consequences of Mao's absence is his post-death presence. In America, electoral loss takes a leader off his pedestal. Even death does not quite do that in China."

Charles Freeman, deputy chief of mission at the American Embassy, remarked as Ambassador Hummel and I lunched with him, "China will probably overlay Confucianism on top of a sagging communism, just as Taiwan has overlaid Confucianism on top of a sagging Three Principles of the People." For China-watchers, I said the intellectual allure of China might lesson as Deng began to pursue goals more common in the world than Mao's goals.

Editor Wang Xi told me how moved she was at Hu Yaobang's visit to Tai Shan. "Walking slowly step by step, as he did, was meant to symbolize the arduous climb for China to modernize," she remarked. "It was impressive. Putting equipment there to whisk people up in a moment would undermine the whole idea of a pilgrimage to Tai Shan."

Reaching Calcutta during the State Department tour, I wrote in my diary, "Ordinary Indians are subservient, unlike ordinary Chinese, who treat you as an equal. Calcutta is a city of non-stop words; Beijing people say less." At my lecture in the American University Center, I had an easy evening, because each time an Indian opened his mouth with a question, he or she gave a monologue, round and around in circles, with recapitulations, two sections, four more parts. . . .

Secretary-general of the Indian Chamber of Commerce, C. S. Pande, took me to lunch at the Calcutta Club. At first, he talked like an automatic rifle, but later we conversed. The Chinese trade minister had recently visited India and Pande met him at Calcutta Airport. Pande asked his wife, a scholar of Japan, what he should wear and she insisted on a simple safari suit with open collar. "Out came the Chinese trade minister from the plane," Pande related, "in a beautifully tailored Western suit from Hong Kong, with a Swiss silk tie, and a European watch. When we sat down, he pulled out American cigarettes and a Dunhill lighter. The Chinese go to extremes. . ."

West Bengal had a Marxist government and a dinner party gathered Marxist ministers from the state government who had visited China in the sunny days of the 1950s, before China and India clashed. They sounded very British. They insisted China and the Soviet Union would soon become close again. One Communist remarked that for any Indian, religion would always outweigh Marxism.

Viewed from the top of a tall building, Calcutta resembled Shanghai, but at street level, the similarity disappeared. These British-looking buildings contained people who were still quite British, speaking fast English, looking up to London. China had less destitution than India, and a public morality that India lacked. Yet India had resources of religion that lay deep in every soul.

In Delhi, I dined with Nayantara Sahgal, a daughter of Mrs. Pandit, who went to Wellesley College near Boston and was brought up close to Indira Ghandi, now prime minister. She "hated" her cousin. "It's a case of imperial glory or drinking water," she declared of Mrs. Ghandi's choice of policy line. Sahgal distrusted the Soviet Union and Libya's influence on the Indian government.

"In the 1940s," she recalled, "When I wanted to go to America, I saw my brother [Prime Minister Jawaharlal Nehru]." He fixed it, but told her, "When you're in America don't say anything against us in public."

Years later, during Prime Minister Ghandi's Emergency," Sahgal wanted to re-visit the USA, but her passport had been taken away. She went to see the prime minister. "We have our political differences," she said to Mrs. Ghandi, "but we have family ties too. I see my passport on your desk. Can I have it please to go to America?" The prime minister agreed, but said, "If you criticize us while you're in America, you will never set foot in India again."

The former foreign minister, Vajpayee, spoke about his 1979 trip to China. Foreign Minister Huang Hua offered a welcoming toast, "The Chinese government has always stood for the settlement of all disputes through negotiations on the basis of the Five Principles of Peaceful Coexistence. However, in the negotiations, the Indian, a lively and knowledgeable man, had a difficult time with Deng Xiaoping. "Deng said to me, Pakistan is afraid of you, you are big," Vajpayee recalled. "I replied that China was very big indeed, but we aren't afraid of you."

Deng said the border question could be set aside and cited a Chinese saying supporting that approach. Vajpayee responded with an Indian saying, "What is good should be done today." The pair sparred with proposal and counterproposal and made little progress. In passing, Deng mentioned Vietnamese aggressiveness, but he also said it was "China's hope that no world war would break out again within this century."

Vajpayee was packed to return to India, when his counterpart Huang Hua called to say the Chinese government had prepared a delightful regional trip for him to visit lakeside Hangzhou as the mayor's guest. While he was in the south, Vajpayee received a phone call from an Indian journalist in Bombay informing him that Chinese troops had entered Vietnam.

Vajpayee shouted at Huang Hua, "What if you were visiting India, we attacked Pakistan during your visit, and you learned about it from a journalist phoning from Shanghai? " Vajpayee felt starting a war with an Asian neighbor while he was in China was hardly the way to trigger revived China-India friendship.

"Chinese say to me in private," Chief Editor of *The Hindu* related, "'We understand how your view of the Soviet Union can differ from ours.'" The editor, from a wealthy family, with a leftist past and a British wife, wanted to see India equidistant from China and the Soviet Union. "Not allied with either, not hostile to either—that would take away China's motivation to play the Pakistan card against India."

For Jakarta, China was a major issue, but shadowy compared with China's sharpness for Japan and India. Foreign Minister Mochtar, relaxed in sandals at his home, pointed out Indonesia was already involved with China despite the continued break in diplomatic relations since the crisis of 1965.

"Twenty per cent of our consumer products come from China," Mochtar said. "Other ministers urge me to re-establish the formal tie, but I ask them, what's gained? Sometimes in life the engagement period is happier than the marriage." Cunning as a fox, he added, "We get more out of the Chinese by keeping diplomatic relations as a lever to use when necessary."

Like many Asian leaders, the foreign minister fretted about Indochina questions. He envisioned an eventual balance with Indonesia, Thailand and Vietnam together providing stability for Southeast Asia. "These are the three that count," he said bluntly. Mochtar conceded that Vietnam made a mistake in expelling Chinese people, and he considered the conflict between Vietnamese and Cambodian Communists "beyond reason." Still, he was wary of China, largely because of the complication of Chinese people living in Indonesia, Malaysia, and Singapore. Yet he summed up, "All the Chinese want is acceptance of them as the big neighbor. They don't have a tradition of dominating others."

Indonesia was at once relaxed and prickly. It felt safely removed from most major world conflicts ("Only the fall of Thailand would be a major issue for us," said Mochtar). Yet it was a proud country that did not like to see China and Japan get constant attention and Indonesia little attention. It still rankled that Zhou Enlai had once phoned Subandrio, foreign minister at the time, at 2 am to confront him with some niggling Chinese position.

The USIA tour continued in Thailand, Malaysia, and Burma. In the charming, hilly town of Chiangmai, the mayor said over a fiery lunch, "Any rice-eater is not really Chinese, but basically Thai. We are the pioneers of rice cultivation. Chinese eat other grains as well as rice." I asked if he meant all the people living south of the Yangzi were Thai.

"I do," he replied. This same mayor a few minutes earlier said in a worried tone that Beijing may harbor hegemonic ambitions over areas of Asia they once dominated.

Flying from Chiangmai to Hong Kong, we crossed Laos in six minutes and Vietnam in eleven. Yet these tiny strips have seen millions die violently, involved nations from far away, and been the focus of world politics.

In Penang, the American USIA chief gave a dinner party, inviting a Muslim political scientist and a member of parliament of Chinese race. I asked the Chinese if Malaysia might move in the direction of the religious-political situation in Iran. "I am not pessimistic," he replied, "and I am not optimistic." During the previous election, in campaigning he used the Malay form of greeting and was rebuked by Muslims for using "their" term. However, the Chinese politician asked me, "What if all the Chinese people became Muslim, could we use that form of greeting then?"

The Chinese community in Penang sought to build a statue to Guanyin, their Goddess of Mercy. The Malay authorities said the planned structure was too tall. A leader from Kuala Lumpur arrived and asked if a portico could be built to make it less prominent. The Chinese legislator said with a frown, "Chinese civilization and Buddhist religion are prepared to be eclectic. They are open. Islam is not."

In Burma, the people seemed childlike, as Thais could be, but without the touch of steel in many Thai. Burma resembled Tibet, with its economic backwardness and all-pervasive religion. "Nothing goes on here," I wrote in my diary at Pagan. "It's a museum, a fascinating one, to be sure." Pagan airport terminal was a tiny wooden cottage, covered with bougainvillea. The town had four thousand people and three thousand pagodas.

My guide said when he received a PRC delegation, after seeing two pagodas, the Chinese said, 'Fine, they're interesting, but that's enough; let's go back to our hotel.'" There was no newspaper in Pagan, none in Mandalay, none in all Burma outside Rangoon. A Mandalay man who sold me a sapphire was wearing a green silk *longyi* and an American baseball cap. On his wrist was a Japanese watch. At the town's Museum, a notice on exhibits said, "Touch Me Not."

The lecture on China saw a gathering at the American Center in Mandalay that included five representatives from the ruling political party. They sat in the front row, quiet and courteous. At the end, the leader of the group came up, touched my shoulder, then my back, and said, "An exchange of views is not possible, but please know we appreciated your lecture and learned from it. We wrote much down, and we will make use of it and pass it on." With that, the five tidied their *longyi* and were gone.

I flew from Rangoon to Australia, where a postcard dated December 3, 1979 awaited me at ANU from Wilma Fairbank. "John is in hospital after suffering a heart attack." Full of anxiety, her note nevertheless went on, "His basic health and strength seems destined to win out versus his overburdened (workaholic?) heart." She was correct. John went on strongly for years.

Reaching Bucharest, near the end of the USIA tour, I lunched with the American ambassador and two Romanian intellectuals. "These are charming, straightforward people," I noted rashly, "a change after a month in India, where verbiage exceeds thought." The vice-president of the Romanian Academy of Social Science observed, "China, after having been exotic, known for art and culture, now means two different things in Romania. Excellent consumer goods in our shops, giving people great respect for the Chinese. Second, of course, China means weight against Russia."

Romania presented an extraordinary contrast to China on birth control. As Beijing was paying folk to keep to a one or two child limit, Bucharest paid a cash bonus for extra children. Birth control pills were hard to obtain and abortion was virtually impossible. "More people will make Romania less vulnerable," said a literature professor at the Ambassador's lunch.

Seeing dark streets, I asked if a power breakdown had occurred in Bucharest. No, things were normal. This meant virtually no streetlights on at night; an atmosphere in the center of the city like a village. One evening I stopped at a cake and sweet shop with a lavish display in the window, all unlit. People crouched before the window to get a glimpse of the strawberry tarts and chocolate cakes barely visible in the shadows.

My years full-time on the Harvard faculty ended. Henceforth I would devote most of my time to writing. It was touching that many people made suggestions to make me "more secure"! Family members begged me to return to Australia. Opportunities did arise in Australia, but I felt I now belonged in the American orbit. I felt frightened at my independence, yet exhilarated at my freedom.

Franz Schurmann, a distinguished professor at the University of California, author of *Ideology and Power in Communist China,* wrote, "You are too good a writer and thinker to do nothing but China writing when the subject is getting duller by the day."[18] I did write on non-China topics, before and after Schurmann's suggestion, including British socialism and Australia, but I did not agree that China was getting duller by the day. Having done a biography of R. H.Tawney in 1973, I tackled the life and career of Mao Zedong.

The first Chinese publishers' delegation to the U.S. arrived in the early summer of 1980. My own publisher, Harper & Row, was host in New York, and I attended a delightful evening with the visitors at a ballet in Lincoln Center. Next morning, host and guests browsed in the Harper & Row bookshop. The head of Harper & Row presented the leader of the Chinese delegation with one of the first copies off the press of my *Mao*. They handled it like a hand grenade.

Later the Chinese publishers sent Harper and Row several books, including Encyclopedias we had not seen before.

The reception of *Mao* in the U.S. was pleasing and the book was translated within its first year into German, Hebrew, and Spanish. The magazine *Asia*

Figure 11.1. Author with Chinese publishing officials gingerly handling the first English edition of the author's *Mao*, Harper & Row bookshop, New York, 1980. Author's photo.

Mail, a rising publication in Washington, chose the book as one of "Ten Best books on Asia published in the United States during 1980." More than eighty publications in the U.S. reviewed the volume. A life like Mao's makes for an interesting book, especially when the backdrop is a momentous revolution.

A letter arrived on my desk from Daniel Bell in Harvard's Sociology Department; he had opened my 1974 letter of prediction on what trends to be expected four years after Mao's death. "Not bad," the famous scholar said on reading the five points in my letter.

"No one will have replaced Mao in any sense worthy of the phrase," I wrote in March 1974. "The country will not be on the verge of break-up," ran my second point, "comparable to the warlord period and fragmentation in various periods of Chinese history." On both these points, Bell gave me credit for being correct.

He did not like my third point. "Beijing will not be as deeply hostile to the Soviet Union as it was during the 1960s and 1970s," I predicted. However, I believe I was only a little ahead of the clock. Ideology had faded in China's foreign policy, competing with Moscow in aid for Africa was costly, and achieving concrete strategic action between China and the USA was not easy.

A few months after Bell opened my letter, September 23, 1980, I testified at the H of R: "The mood in China is pragmatic, economically-minded, domestically-oriented, and revisionist as to Marxist doctrine, all of which works to undermine the priority of anti-Sovietism."

As a sociologist, Bell liked my fourth prediction, "An ideological crisis shapes up as some formulations of Chinese communism, such as class determining all aspects of culture, are not credible to rising generations." However, he quibbled about my final point. I said in 1974 that some of Mao's socialism would endure because the centrality of agriculture, the necessity of self-reliance, and the imperative of bridging city and village were all rooted in China's realities. Bell said this expectation contradicted my fourth one. My fifth prediction indeed was my weakest.[19]

Shortly after Bell opened my letter, I wrote of China in the *Boston Globe,* "A certain autonomy has been ceded to economics as a science and respect for the market is in vogue. Capitalism may have more appeal to Chinese minds right now than it does to most American minds."[20]

Research for *Mao* brought adventures. In Indonesia I visited Sukarno's widow, a charming lady sitting in silk, surrounded by mementoes of her rich life; Mononutu, who was Indonesian ambassador in Beijing in the 1950s; and Ganis Harsono, a former aide to Sukarno. Ambassador Mononutu, a polite Muslim, felt tongue-tied in Mao's presence. "I felt I shouldn't ask him any questions. He was like a god." Harsono was standing beside President

Sukarno as Mao greeted him in 1956. "They hugged each other as if they'd been friends for years," he recalled of Sukarno's enthusiasm. "I just could not communicate with Mao," Harsono confessed. "With Zhou Enlai—but not with Mao—there was discussion, you knew where you stood."

Harsono later gave me papers, pictures, and letters relating to his China experiences. He quoted a Dutch saying, *"Wie niet weet, die niet deert'* ("Ignorance is happiness" or literally, "To not know is to care not"). "I knew not one stroke of written Chinese," he explained. "By holding on to these articles and letters, I would still be left in blissful ignorance, however good or bad was what the newspapers said about me."

I think Harsono, who by 1979 had the air of a world-weary philosopher, looked upon me as an earnest Western idealist. "Americans have a great attachment to China, from past missionary work there," he wrote in a later letter. "On the other hand, since the days of Kublai Khan, Indonesia's relation with China has not always been a happy one."[21]

At the Jakarta think tank CSIS, a leading figure stood up at question time, "My nightmare for Indonesia is that Japan and China will get together," In the audience was a diplomat who served in the Indonesia embassy in Beijing in the mid-1950s. He was in charge of protocol during President Sukarno's 1956 trip to China. "Chinese could not always distinguish one Indonesian from another," he recalled. "When we went to see Mao, the Chinese protocol officer confused me with President Sukarno. I froze when he suddenly introduced me to Mao, AS SUKARNO.

Mao said, "How do you do?" in English. The one-time diplomat was tongue-tied and made no response. He turned around and edged away.

At the National Library in Beijing, I browsed in the papers of leftist icon Anna Louise Strong. After checking her spicy interviews with Mao, I found the transcript of a meeting between Mao and the American black activist, Dubois, in March 1959. The American black asked what Mao would like to do if he visited the USA. "I would not talk any politics," Mao replied. "I would just swim the Mississippi River. Then if time permits, I would watch President Eisenhower play golf. Then perhaps visit Mr. Dulles in the hospital."

Mao explained to Dubois that Dulles and such rightist folk were useful to the world, because "Dulles sticks to his principles," and teaches a lesson. "The longer the U.S. Seventh Fleet is nearby China, the more it educates the Chinese people and the world's people."

Amusingly, looking back, I talked unsuccessfully with publishers in Singapore about a possible Chinese-language edition of "Mao." We all assumed the book could not be published in the PRC. "I would like a Chinese translation and Singapore seems the place," I told an editor at a Singapore newspaper. "I am thinking of the book, through links among Overseas Chinese, finding its way, not only to Hong Kong, but even possibly into China." Much later, *Mao* indeed was published in the PRC in Chinese and, to the surprise of author, publisher, and a nervous but cooperative Chinese government, by 2019 had sold 1.4 million copies.

NOTES

1. *Boston Globe*, January 9, 1976.
2. Terrill, *China in Our Time*, New York, Simon & Schuster, 1984, 41.
3. Wang Ruoshui to the author, Beijing, 1984. Wang and the author conversed many times over the years, in Beijing and later in Cambridge MA until his death in 2002.
4. *New Republic*, November 1, 1975.
5. *Boston Globe*, February 8, 1976.
6. Fairbank, letter to author, February 8, 1976.
7. Prime Minister's Visit, July 30, 1976; *Harvard Crimson*, July 31, 1976.
8. Wilenski, letter to author, August 11, 1976.
9. Anna Laura Rosow, letter to author, September 9, 1976.
10. Service, letter to author, October 5, 1976.
11. Bette Bao Lord, letter to author, October 22, 1976.
12. President Ford, letter to Jiang Qing, September 9, 1976, copy given to author.
13. Fairbank, letter to author, December 24, 1976.
14. *New York Review of Books*, October 14, 1976.
15. Chung Chi-wai, letter to author, June 30, 1977.
16. U.S Congress, House of Representatives, Hearing, August 1, 1977.
17. *Renmin ribao* (People's Daily), January 5, 1980.
18. Schurmann, letter to author, September 21, 1977.
19. Letter of author to Bell, March 18, 1974 and Bell to author, October 20, 1980.
20. *Boston Globe*, August 27, 1980.
21. Harsono, letter to author, December 1, 1979.

Chapter Twelve

Not Quite Normal

Throughout 1977, frustration mounted in China-Watching circles and in Washington at the prospects for U.S. normalization with the PRC. "What is the purpose of these House of Representatives Hearings?" I wrote in my diary in August. "They seem ill-timed—Vance and Carter are not going to do anything on China until Panama is tied up. The United States Government is such a sprawling monster that it may be unrealistic to expect overall coherence; maybe Lester Wolf [head of the Subcommittee concerned] is just thinking of his re-election race next year." Nevertheless, Wolf went ahead with his Hearing.

I sent Leonard Woodcock, chief of the Liaison Office in Beijing, a copy of testimony I gave at Congressman Wolf's Hearing.[1] In reply, Woodcock said: "I cannot say I am optimistic at the moment, but who knows what twists 1978 will bring in the world scene." Woodcock added that Beijing takes note of "our present difficulties" and went on cautiously: "Given a successful conclusion to Panama [Canal issue] and SALT, it will be interesting to see if Beijing still understands our 'present difficulties.'"[2]

In mid-1978, I wrote in *Los Angeles Times*: "Some American doves want to cut Taiwan loose so we can normalize with Beijing. Hawks want to send aid to China to antagonize the Soviet Union. But no one wants to do both—so Washington does neither." But, taking the view that Beijing cared about relations with America for reasons beyond Taiwan, I felt sure "normalization" was imminent—especially after conversations with Assistant Foreign Minister Wang Hairong in Beijing and Dick Holbrooke in Thailand.

Wang revealed a Chinese desire to normalize for strategic reasons well beyond Taiwan. Holbrooke said the American side believed it could normalize without sacrificing much in Taiwan's concrete situation. Putting these positions together, I was convinced the Taiwan issue would be finessed and normalization would soon come.

During a speaking engagement on "Prospects for Normalization" at Dominican College in California, I wrote to an Australian friend, Rachel Faggetter, who had taught English in Beijing: "I think Australian media overstate Washington's interest in 'independence' for Taiwan. The U.S. stress is on how to assure a supply of arms to a de-recognized ROC. If this can be done. Carter will concede the three key points [derecognition of Taiwan, withdrawal of American troops from the island, ending the U.S.-ROC security treaty] during 1978. In that case, I doubt China will make a fuss over weapons supplies to Taiwan. 'Men over weapons, after all,' you remember that in Beijing, Rachel? What will happen is Taiwan will lose its international links, yet lead a separate life for years. Especially if Taipei is shrewd and drops its hostility to the PRC. But 'declaring independence' has nothing to do with any of this. . ."

At a Williamsburg seminar organized by John D. Rockefeller 4th, Holbrooke said as we gazed across the blue water of the Gulf of Thailand, "There are fifty senators with whom we have difficulties, especially over the security treaty with Taiwan," and "the Taiwan issue may not be resolvable fully." However, Dick said firmly, "We have made up our mind to normalize with China. We are just waiting for the signal from Carter." Holbrooke said some in Washington had argued for normalization with Vietnam first, others with China first, but this had "now been resolved." It would be China first.

Carter soon made his decision. Normalization with the PRC had not occurred in Mao's lifetime or during Ford's administration. Now, a different pair of leaders sealed the deal: newly energized veteran, Deng Xiaoping, for China; upstart southerner, Jimmy Carter, for the USA.

My *The Future of China*, written in 1977, predicted China and America would establish full diplomatic relations before the end of 1978. Prediction became reality in December 1978 with simultaneous announcements In Beijing and Washington.

Next day, the phone rang in my office at the Contemporary China Center of Australian National University, where I was a visiting fellow. CBS in New York was on the line. Soon Walter Cronkite himself said, "Come to New York on the next plane! I'm doing a Special on the normalization with China." CBS, for all their resources, did not realize Canberra's distance from New York. I could not reach New York in time for Cronkite's Special. Within a minute, they decided to fly me to Hong Kong and hook-up from there.

I nearly failed to get to Hong Kong in time, thanks to Australian fog, a notorious problem at Canberra airport. My flight to Sydney, to connect with a Cathay Pacific international flight, could not leave Canberra. Desperate, I hired a taxi to take me 180 miles to Sydney. The local Canberra driver, reaching the outskirts of Sydney, said he did not know where the airport was. "This is my first time in Sydney," he drawled. CBS had booked me first class, so Cathay Pacific held the plane for ten minutes for me.

Cronkite began his Special with a quotation from *The Future of China*: "The four-year lull in relations between the U.S. and China will probably come to an end in 1978."[3] His chair swiveled toward me. "I'm going to ask Ross Terrill, waiting in a studio in Hong Kong, how he foresaw the Carter-Deng move on normalization so precisely?" I said it was luck. Still, I was able to quote the recent words to me of Wang Hairong and Dick Holbrooke.

As it happened, Stanley Karnow, reviewing *The Future of China* in the *New York Times*, had ridiculed my prediction as "'extravagant speculation." Later, the Paperback Talk column in the *New York Times* was gracious enough to comment: "When Dell published Ross Terrill's *The Future of China* last July, a critic or two [sic] took exception to the Harvard professor's thesis that 'the four-year lull in relations between the United States and China will probably end in 1978.' The author and publisher may soon be having the last laugh. Mr. Terrill is expected back from China this weekend and the principal television networks are vying for appearances that will promote his book."[4]

Before flying back to Sydney, I made a diary note about Hong Kong: "The smell of air-conditioning, quickness in the Cantonese step, foreign tourists bent on shopping and eating, look of commercial anticipation in almost every face. One admires the improvement in Shanghai's and Beijing's post-Mao standard of life, but Hong Kong is still years ahead of both."

The 1980s promised to be more prosperous for Chinese than the 1970s and they began well. Still, the mental attitudes needed in a modern economy lagged. At Chengdu airport, my assistant went to a well-stocked counter to buy a packet of cigarettes. "Sorry, we don't have the key to the counters," said one of six girls standing by. In Beijing's Eastern Market restaurant, a Chinese friend ordered iced beer. "No cold beer," a server said like a robot. My friend whispered something rapidly to the young woman. Soon two iced bottles of Qingdao sat before us. "All after, you have a foreign guest today," the woman said brightly. In a quick hiss to my friend, she added, "My number is 66." Later, my companion wrote in the Comment Book attached to our table, "Number 66 showed a splendid attitude of service."

Many shops withered in bureaucratic passivity, with limited hours to serve the public. "*Mei you*" (Don't Have It) was the automatic response to a request for a product. Default mode was not that service areas should be open; rather, they were closed unless aroused to action by an insistent customer. All this had to change.

Zhang Wenjin told me of his delight that hotels in Shanghai were starting to compete with each other for business. "They hire away the best chefs from another hotel," he related, smiling, "in order to serve their customers better."

Wang Xi at *Beijing Review* said circulation of her magazine abroad was down. "The would-be Maoists in the West are disenchanted with China," she said with a frown. A French friend had brought a copy of one of my works with a bookmark to pages that quoted Wang Xi. "I was uneasy to see my name," she said. Really, I think she was pleased.

"See some plays," Wang Xi suggested as I rose to leave. "Conclusions have not yet been made by the party leadership on some questions of the recent past. But the plays will give you clues." She urged "Power and Law" and "The Future is Calling," and a TV play, "Save Her." I said, give me advice on what I should tell my readers about China." She thought for a moment and replied, "Tell them China's modernization will not be rapid."

"I *hope* we'll grow closer together," my journalist friend Li Yanning of Xinhua said of China and America when we lunched during Defense Secretary Harold Brown's path-breaking visit to Beijing, "but I don't know how close it can be." In fact, despite strategic convergence, Chinese and Americans had only begun to assess each other morally and concretely.

On the thirtieth anniversary of the 1949 Liberation, I wrote in *Washington Star*: "The present moment in China is one of trembling, knife-edge hope." I pointed out, "economically, China is already in the front rank of nations in terms of GDP, but per capita GNP won't for decades reach even half U.S. levels." On American-Chinese relations, nearly one year after normalization, I was optimistic: "The PRC-U.S. tie is more satisfactory than it has ever been. Danger of war between the two has gone. The compatibility of the two peoples and economies gets a chance to express itself."[5]

The struggle to destroy Gang of Four had left China sobered. I reported in *Boston Globe*: "People are warier, now, of what the government says. The chastened authorities have to offer more concrete explanations of policies than in the late Mao period."

Robert Oxnam, historian and head of the Asia Society's China division, asked me to edit a book. The Asia Society felt that after the dust settled from the "ping-pong era," shortcomings of mutual perceptions still plagued U.S.-China relations. "How different are the Chinese" was a never-ending question from East Coast to West Coast, said Oxnam. In the American tradition, the China Council of the Asia society felt it should prepare Americans to deal with China. The old notion from the 1950s, that China should change first before the U.S. would accept dealings, had gone.

Our book, *The China Difference,* was written when normalization still lay ahead, but came out only in 1980. I wrote in my Introduction, "It is no good looking at our own cherished values, then asking if the Chinese are human enough to adhere to such 'universal values.'"

I set out a path for give-and-take with China: "Evaluation of China cannot be detached from a hope for common ground with the Chinese. . . We are evaluating a moving target with which we hope to share the planet creatively."[6]

Our book forewarned that modernization would take varied forms. "One nation's modernity may not be recognizable when put alongside another's. If Mao, Henry Ford, and the rulers of Meiji Japan were all modernizers, then the term 'modernization' may not predict much about society."

Widespread reviews were unusual for an essay collection by academics. *Chicago* magazine called *China Difference* "timely, well-conceived, and informative." The magazine of the American Bar Association said in February 1980: "Ross Terrill has done a masterly job of bringing together not only good scholars but good writers as well."

China Difference had the fluke of reviews in the two leading newspapers by Owen Lattimore, the Inner Asia authority, in *Washington Post* and by his son, David Lattimore, a China literary specialist at Brown University, in *New York Times*. Owen wrote, "Those who planned and contributed to this book are lucky to have Terrill as editor." David, aware of my dual background, liked "the Australian ring of realism" in the editing, blended with "orderly American expertise with which he marshals and parades his contributors."

The Council of Religion and International Affairs, headquartered in New York, approached me about a "values" aspect of China. Its president, Robert Myers, wrote, "The relationship between the PRC and the U.S. has been 'normalized.' Commercial exchange is expanding. However, is something not being overlooked? What about fundamental worldviews?" It was a good idea, but I was not ready for a second collective project.

That the U.S. and other Western media soured on China gave point to the values projects of the Asia Society and the Council of Religion and International Affairs. The skepticism of the first resident American journalists in Beijing puzzled the Chinese. How could Americans criticize so much now, when in prior years they praised so much, although things were worse? It was a reasonable question.

I called the leeriness the "French Syndrome," writing in my diary: "When the public grows keen about China, as the French public did in the early 1970s, the intellectuals like to 'move on' and strike a different posture, as occurred in France in the mid-1970s." By 1980, for French, Americans and others, there was also the residency factor. Western journalists now based in China saw realities close-up.

Furthermore, the Chinese government's own exposes of Jiang Qing and late Mao leftism shocked Western media. If such terrible things happened under recent CCP rule, perhaps journalists should be skeptical about what official press releases now told them of the post-Mao situation?

In Shanghai in 1980, Lin Yongyu, a great-great-grandson of Commissioner Lin Zexu of Opium War days, took a Sichuan lunch with me in Huaihai Boulevard. Lin Yongyu, who worked at the Shanghai Academy of Social Science, told me the academy had decided to translate and publish the Shanghai portion of *Flowers on an Iron Tree*. He said this quarter of my book had much interest for the local history project at the academy, especially the passages about the period immediately after Liberation.

Scholarly pursuits and Christian influence ran in the Lin family for generations. What are China's biggest problems, I asked Lin Yongyu. "Bureaucracy" he replied. "A tough nut to crack. Second, the center controls too much. Third, we are a land without law."

I told Lin that after *Flowers,* I had done a biography of Mao. "Better to leave the restaurant to talk about that," he said. "Mao is under discussion now in the centers of power in China. The question of good and bad in him is still not decided." Lin was surprised to hear my favorable report on our "Scholarly Delegation to Investigate the Problems of the Chinese Revolution" during the recent summer.

Lin Yongyu was politically "rehabilitated" after the Cultural Revolution, but not economically so. Superiors told him Gang of Four did not really have anything personal against him, and that the oft-repeated charge of being a CIA agent was without foundation. Also, that the confessions he made in prison were done under pressure. "They took the stack of paper containing my confessions and burnt it in a stove before my eyes," he said with a smile. "Was it a tense occasion?" I asked Lin.

"No, no, a cheerful occasion. I thanked them afterwards!"

Lin and I had a rich correspondence and he was among my eyes and ears in Shanghai for some time. I tried to arrange for him to do research in the USA on his project of Christianity in China, but the American side were mainly interested in scholars younger than middle-aged Lin.

As China and Australia grew closer, the results changed Australian society. In my schooldays in the 1950s, Darwin, the capital of the Northern Territory, had separate sections of its pubs and hospitals for whites and nonwhites. Yet when I returned to the northern city on assignment for *National Geographic* in 1987, Darwin had a Chinese-Australian mayor.

Mayor Alec Fong Lim, was born in the small town of Katherine and came to Darwin at age 7. His father worked in a pub and was a bookmaker on the side. "If you're going to talk of the past," Mayor Lim said with a thick Australian accent, as we lunched in Darwin, "no race was more discriminated against than the Chinese. I remember Tiger Brennan [a Northern Territory politician] decades ago, in the pub where they all used to drink, saying to me, "You know, Alec, you can't serve on a jury.""

"That's good. Tiger," I said to him, "that means I don't have to waste my time."

"No Alec, it's not good enough. You're an Australian and you should have that right, and I'm going to fix that." Alec Lim looked up from his plate of water melon. "And Tiger Brennan as a member of parliament did get that law changed."

"I've seen a transformation," said Charles See Kee, who came to Australia from Guangzhou 59 years ago and, after some setbacks, became the Northern Territory's first public servant of Chinese origin. "When I arrived in Darwin there were three groups in the city—Chinese, blacks, and what we called Europeans [whites]. Later, when Italians and Greeks arrived, Australians got a shock. Who were the Europeans? Were the Australians Europeans? What was an Australian? Surely lots of Chinese were Australians." So it proved.

The very young in Australia began to take racial diversity for granted. In 1987, with a Chinese friend from Hong Kong, I attended an international cricket Test Match in Melbourne. When the game ended with a win for the West Indies over Australia, youths rushed onto the field, searching for a souvenir, trying to touch or talk with a player. "The kids are blind to race," said my Chinese friend; being from Hong Kong, he was used to cricket. "Look at how those Australian kids are mobbing the West Indian stars—they don't care who is black and who is white." One day, I thought, some Chinese natives may be playing cricket for Australia in that same Melbourne stadium.

In international relations, success often means avoiding failure. Things that do not happen—especially wars—measure achievement in foreign policy making. The aim is a calm atmosphere in which Australians and Chinese can go about their business and enjoy travel and mutual advantage with each other. Of course, such success is a mirage. Subsequent wanderers on the same road of history will see nothing remarkable; they benefit from the absence of catastrophes and fights that could have happened, but did not.

I visited Bob Hawke, the prime minister and Mrs. Hazel Hawke in their residence one afternoon in 1987. Mrs. Hawke had just finished reading

White-Boned Demon. "What an extraordinary character Jiang Qing must have been," she exclaimed. I responded to the Australian first lady, "Well, it's nice there are first ladies less vicious than Jiang Qing!"

Looking healthy and tanned at 58 years, shoulders and neck thrust forward as if in determination, Hawke had just won his third election. "One reason we have a very significant relationship with China," he said, "is that it's is a personal thing. The Beijing leaders trust us, they don't feel stress with us—as they do with Russia, U.S., Japan."

From the Chinese point of view, Shen Chunyi and many other Chinese students in Australia, thought well of Hawke's interest in China issues and concern for the welfare of Chinese on Australian campuses.

I mentioned to the Hawkes that our conversation would be used in a *National Geographic* article.[7] Mrs. Hawke spoke with awe of the impact of this American magazine in Australia; what was the world-wide circulation, she inquired. "40 million," I replied. Mrs. Hawke gasped. Her husband, putting his jacket back on, said, "Gee, Hazel, 40 million. We'd better have a couple more pictures for this!"

Hawke's hope for a special relationship with China based on personal links worked in two respects. As an architect of the regional group APEC, Hawke helped persuade Beijing to play a key role in this multilateral form for the U.S. and China, together with other countries, to assess regional problems. Soon the APEC leaders' summit was a major event on the annual Asia-Pacific calendar, with Chinese and American leaders always in attendance.

At the time of our conversation, mining giant BHP and China had reached an impasse over a steel deal. "Yeah," said Hawke, "they're having trouble over prices. The concept is right, though." Hawke went on to sketch a picture of the economic promise between China and Australia. "Iron and steel are recognized by both sides as being important. Changes we're making here will help that area. Then there's metals, wool, textiles—there'll be enormous trade back and forth between us." He was correct.

For Americans, China resembled a suitcase quickly opened. Its contents, previously a tightly bound unity, fell out in a tumble on the rug. China was a kaleidoscope: a market huge in potential, but difficult to crack; a place of historical and natural wonders; a welcome counterweight to Russia (though a firm supporter of the murderous Khmer Rouge in Cambodia). The Chinese themselves opened the "suitcase" by being more candid than before about failures and unfinished tasks within their society.

In January 1979, Deng Xiaoping came to dine at the White House, wear a cowboy hat at a Texas barbecue, and talk about technology in Seattle. The atmosphere was a mixture of high hopes from American business and academia, yet anxiety among Chinese and American foreign policy elites about Soviet expansionism.

Van Long, the effervescent Washington restaurateur and son of the major Warlord, Long Yun, invited me to a dinner in honor of Deng sponsored by Chinese-Americans at the Hilton Hotel. The Chinese leader was sniffling with a cold, but his smile was appealing. His words against Moscow were fiery.

During Carter's state dinner at the White House, actress Shirley MacLaine said to unpretentious, grandfatherly Deng that a scientist in Beijing told her his years of caring for pigs during the Cultural Revolution were "the best years of my life." The Chinese leader responded to leftist MacLaine: "The man was lying."[8]

The shadow of Vietnam fell over the Carter-Deng talks, but, unlike in the day of LBJ and Nixon, it was China, not the U.S., which talked tough about teaching Hanoi a "necessary lesson."

Normalization and Deng's new "Opening and Reform" policies brought more business and cultural exchanges with the U.S. The excitement on the American side healed some divisions within the U.S. about the PRC. Deng as a cuddly capitalist on the cover of *Time* magazine implicitly suggested a solution, via economics, to American oscillation between demonizing China and romanticizing China. If the Communists became capitalists, some felt, Americans and Chinese could together supervise Asia.

Would-be Maoists, not right-wingers, made noisy demonstrations against Deng in Washington, The Chinese talked like capitalists in the White House; American youths shouted Communist slogans at them from the park outside. It was confusing. However, Deng surely preferred to be attacked from the left in America, rather than from the right.

Deng's two themes were ill-assorted. Like an Andrew Carnegie, his eyes gleamed at the prospect of modernization for still-poor China. Yet like a crusader of the Middle Ages, he preached against the perfidy of Moscow. Supreme irony, pragmatist Deng's worry about America's "strategic retreat" was flavored by a lifetime of Marxist belief that "imperialism is doomed." This made it hard for the CCP, even Deng, to believe in America's resilience just when they desired it.

Some pundits wondered whether Deng and Carter had really come to grips with many of the issues between China and the US. At least the Chinese leader had come to DC. Had he gone instead to Moscow, where no Chinese leader had been for 15 years, we would know what real anxiety means.

After "normalization", China policy took its welcome place within over-all American foreign policy. A dimension of reality now attached to CCP leadership for Americans who saw Deng kiss children, get tired and sniffle with a cold, wear a Stetson, and wield a knife and fork in the White House. Gone was the passion that years of isolation and ideology on both sides had given it. Modified were abstractions like American efforts to make a China in its own image, and Chinese efforts to "export revolution."

In Beijing in the winter of 1979–80, while staying in the residence of Australian ambassador Gary Woodard—as he sought sunshine down south—I asked Zhang Wenjin to explain the difference between 50,000 American troops in Korea, which China no longer criticized, and 50,000 Russian troops in Afghanistan, which China vociferously criticized.

The dapper minister replied as we lunched at Xin Qiao Hotel: "Really, the American role in Korea is an isolated phenomenon, while the Russian role in Afghanistan is part of something larger, and expanding." In Chinese eyes, America was no longer expansionist, while Russia was increasingly so.

During January 1980, Carter's secretary of defense, Harold Brown came to Beijing on a first visit by a defense secretary to the PRC. I was shopping in the Friendship Store for gloves when in strolled a member of Brown's party. Michael Armacost, with whom I spoke at Lewis and Clark College and other campuses, told me: "When I came here with Brzezinski [Carter's national security adviser] in the spring of 1978, I certainly did not expect the secretary of defense to visit this soon." I remarked that U.S.-China cooperation on Indochina had not amounted to anything much. "Yes," responded Armacost, "but without the Beijing-Washington relation, Vietnam troops may well have been in Thailand by now."

Moscow's move into Kabul put further sparkle into Sino-American relations and China's friendship with the West. The United States and China became tacit allies in supporting the precarious position of Pakistan, Thailand, and others against Soviet power, which seemed reinforced by Moscow's grabbing of Afghanistan.

Soon after Deng visited Carter, conflict broke out on China's 650-mile border with Vietnam. Two socialist nations once "as close as lips and teeth," were at war. "We are going to teach Vietnam a lesson," Deng said. "Vietnam won't listen to us," assistant foreign minister Wang Hairong complained to me at the foreign ministry. But the performance of China's armies did not match China's high pride. China lost thousands dead and tens of thousands wounded. Chinese pride took a fall.

When Carter's presidency wound down in the winter of 1980–81, the bilateral relationship between Beijing and Washington was thickening, although beset by arguments over textile imports from China, civil aviation and other specifics. The relationship as a deterrent to Soviet adventurism and a force for stability in Asia and Oceania showed promise. I felt years of struggle for U.S.-China and China-Australia relations had been worth it.

Western foreign policy circles widely believed the U.S. was in decline, especially in Asia with the unification of Vietnam under Hanoi. *Time* magazine after the fall of Saigon in 1975 spoke of various countries "still trying to adjust to a world no longer dominated by the U.S." This drumbeat of decline was an old story, but no truer in the late 1970s and early 1980s, than it had been before or would be again.

The U.S. was undoubtedly in retreat from Indochina. During it, President Nixon spoke of the world as "five stars," with the U.S. sharing prominence with the Soviet Union, West Europe, Japan, India, and China. This looked like a startling change from the messianism of the U.S. for two decades after 1946, peaking with President Johnson. Still, Nixon's rhetoric, from the Guam Doctrine of 1969 to the opening to China in 1972, was a tactical maneuver. It was not a declaration of abdication of the U.S. from Number One. As it turned out, an Age of Economics fueled by American investment and markets was beginning across East Asia. This was a boon for both East Asia and the U.S.

I felt relieved that peace or war was no longer an issue between the United States and the Chinese party-state. Finished was the long struggle for change in the West's China policy, which I joined as a youth in Melbourne.

Still, I did not expect China with its bicycles and America with its automobiles to embrace each other. I was not sure China and America could find practical joint methods of opposing Soviet expansion. In testimony at the House of Representatives in 1980, I said to the Congress-folk, "Ending an abnormality yields strangely few clues as to what the ensuing normality will be like."

At the same hearing, I pointed to substantial benefits from normalization even after less than two years. I recalled a House hearing in 1977 when I reminded Congressmen of the frustrations of pre-Normalization: "There can be no direct banking facilities, or Chinese trade exhibitions in the U.S., or Chinese ships or aircraft calling at American ports. U.S. news media cannot establish bureaus in Beijing or Shanghai. Chinese and American students cannot study in each other's countries. Beijing leaders will not visit Washington." In my 1980 remarks, I pointed out: "All of these issues have been advanced."

At its 35th birthday in 1984, the PRC, seemed quite well governed. Deng, coming after Mao, was performing a tricky balancing act, but he was popular in the way that one who pulls the veil off a myth becomes popular. New policies produced economic progress, rising expectations, inequalities, personal mobility, and contacts with Chinese who were coming in increasing numbers

to New York Melbourne, Tokyo and other cities. "I think China is generally a positive force," Australian leader Hawke said. "I mean it's going to
do silly things at times too." Later, while still prime minister, Hawke would
indeed have a major disappointment with Beijing that left him weeping on
national TV.

NOTES

1. U.S. Congress, House of Representatives, Hearing, August 1, 1977.
2. Woodcock, letter to author, January 17, 1978.
3. Ross Terrill, *The Future of China*, New York, Delacorte, 1977, 189.
4. *New York Times*, Book Review, January 28, 1979, page 10.
5. *Washington Star*, November 18, 1979.
6. Ross Terrill, ed. *The China Difference*, New York, Harper & Row, 1979, 7–8.
7. Ross Terrill, "Australia at 200," *National Geographic*, February 1988.
8. Fairbank, who was present at the dinner, to the author, 1979.

Chapter Thirteen

Mao and His Wife under the Lens

In Bangkok, former Prime Minister Kukrit recalled his 1975 meeting with old, sick Mao. In his living room of wood panels and silk cushions, the Thai leader said, "China's a very big country, right on top of our head. It didn't make sense to pretend China didn't exist."

It was "about eleven in the morning," when the Thai PM walked into Mao's study. "This big man dressed in gray faced me. He looked like a sea elephant, very broad and splendid."[1]

"Mao said Chiang Kai-shek and Western countries had called him bandit, criminal, murderer," Kukrit related. "Wasn't I afraid of him? I said certainly not. I'm not all that good myself."

But Mao continued in gloomy terms, saying to Kukrit, everyone who came to see him soon fell: Nixon, Heath, Tanaka, Whitlam. Kukrit said he was willing to risk that. Still, Mao went on to say he was soon going to die. "I said to him," Kukrit recalled, "that couldn't be, because the world could not afford to lose the Number One bad man like you. He laughed, banged the arms of his chair, jumped up, and shook hands with everyone in the room."

Fascinating to hear Kukrit say Mao lacked interest in the Thai Communist Party. "It can't be important," Mao told the Thai leader firmly, "because in thirty years as chairman of the CCP, I haven't met anyone from it." Kukrit told Mao he would send four Thai Communists tomorrow, "if the chairman would like to see some."

The Chinese leader spoke warmly of Nixon and asked Kukrit, who knew Nixon, to convey Mao's high regards to him. On returning to Bangkok, the Thai prime minister wrote Nixon with Mao's best wishes. "I believe," Kukrit told me, "this explained why China sent a special plane to bring Nixon for his visit to China in March 1976."

171

Mao, a Communist for 50 years, advised Kukrit how to deal with Communists. "First, don't make propaganda war against them; they're thick-skinned and they won't feel anything. Second, don't kill some off, because they think to be killed in action is heroic. Third, don't send troops against them in the jungle, because they'll run away and you can't keep your own troops in the jungle forever. And when you do withdraw, the Communists will come again. Fourth, see that your own people are fed, clothed and happy; then the Communists can't do anything." A pity Chiang Kai-shek did not get this advice before facing Mao in civil war from the 1920s.

Kukrit said Nancy Tang (Tang Wensheng) laughed and joked with the Chairman. Mao said, "She's an American daughter and you can't trust her." Tang bantered back, "The chairman makes up stories." However, according to the Thai leader, Deng Xiaoping sat "prim and proper" in a corner and said nothing throughout the session.

Kukrit did not believe the Mao he met in late 1975 was strong enough to purge Deng six months later, which he did. "I think somebody else did it in his name," the Thai prime minister said. "When I saw him, he absolutely had all his mental faculties, but if something were done outside his room, he would not necessarily know what happened.

The Vietnam leader Pham Van Dong met old Mao, who said to him, "We have a Chinese saying that if there's a spider in the closet and your broom is too short to reach it, you have to leave the spider there. Maybe Taiwan is our spider, and maybe Thieu [the Saigon leader] is your spider." According to the Vietnamese, Pham Van Dong was enraged by Mao's parallel.[2] However, Mao's words about the spider were in line with his quizzical mentality.

When the CCP reversed the verdict on Liu Shaoqi, I wrote an Op-ed in *New York Times*. "Communism as an idea may be dying in Beijing," I said, "but the Communist Party is growing stronger." I cited Liu's words from years before: "Big movements aren't possible from now on. The main thing now is to concentrate energy on economic construction." I concluded: "From the grave, Liu has won his point."[3] The internal bulletin *Cankao xiaoxi* translated my essay. A foreign diplomat told me younger cadres were not happy at the criticism of Mao and rehabilitation of Liu, and that my article may have been distributed within China to strengthen the Center's case for Liu as a good and steady Party leader.

In the summer of 1980, the Chinese Academy of Social Science pleased Western Sinologists by inviting a foreign "Mao Group" for discussions. Seven scholars researching Mao Zedong, led by Edward Friedman of Wisconsin, included Stuart Schram, the premier scholar of Mao's writings, and two Chinese-American professors, Tang Tsou and Jerome Chen. Originally in correspondence with the Academy, we called our group "Chairman Mao and the Chinese Revolution," but later, in China, the title became "Scholarly Delegation to Investigate the Problems of the Chinese Revolution." Our hosts were not yet ready to state many positions on Mao's deeds and ideas.

In Beijing, we talked with Yu Guangyuan, Director of the Institute of Marxism-Leninism Mao Zedong Thought and his deputy, Liao Gailong, both leading thinkers. Sessions took place with Li Rui, former aide to Mao, and other experienced officials and scholars. At Chinese People's University each of our group gave a short lecture, and we sat down for half a day with Hu Hua of the Department of Party History All this broke new ground in international Mao-discourse.

My lecture, in Chinese, was on "China's Theory of the Three Worlds." This was a leftist scheme with the USA and the Soviet Union as (opposed) villains, and the rest, in degrees, being virtuous. I praised the tactical skill of the concept, but questioned its staying power. After my talk, Dr. Niu of Chinese People's University told me that within China some had recently criticized Three Worlds. "People in China would not accept your questioning of Lenin's imperialism," Niu said, "but some would agree with you that classifying the East European countries [part of the Second World] is complex." A few days later, I asked the senior foreign policy official Zhang Wenjin about the theory. He responded with candor and a smile: "Theory is gray, actual reality is green. Maybe we'll have to put a few footnotes to this theory." Two of Zhang's staff members present at lunch put down their chopsticks and laughed.

Our Mao group visited Changsha and Mao's birthplace, Shaoshan, in the company of local historians, a great opportunity for me. The village was losing popular appeal: 2 million visitors came in 1976; 1.1 million visitors came in 1977; 800,000 in 1978; only 500,000 in 1979. Of course, children born post-Mao would soon as young adults number in the millions, all lacking direct memory of Mao.

We were surprised at the weight of the Mao clan in Shaoshan. Some 70% of the village belonged to it in Mao Zedong's day, and still 60% did in 1980, after 30 years of Mao's egalitarian socialism. The ancestral temple of the Mao clan, built in the reign of Qian Long (1711–1799), was beautiful and well cared-for.

Best event was joining a crowd of 800 Shaoshan folk watching an American movie on a screen hoisted in trees. Chairs were carried out of the dining room of the Shaoshan Hotel to the bare earth. Incongruity came to a height when Reagan (then running for president) appeared as a character in the movie. The crowd loved the film. Such a triumph of American middle-brow culture in a Chinese village suggested that cultures are not immutable.

Figure 13.1. "Mao Delegation" at Shaoshan, 1980. Back row: Friedman, center, Meisner, second from left, Tang Tsou, third from right, Jerome Chen, second from right. Front row: Schram, second from left, McDonald, center, Terrill, second from right. Author's photo.

As we waited for the movie to start, I talked with a Hunan historian about the Hunanese writer Ding Ling, whom I was soon to interview at Wellesley College near Boston. "Ding Ling's big mistake," remarked the historian, "was that in 1956 she said, 'Just because Mao says a thing doesn't make it correct.'"

Beijing granted our group's request to go to Liu Shaoqi's boyhood home in Ningxiang County. A famous photo of Mao and Zhu De welcoming Zhou Enlai back from Moscow in November, 1964, published in newspapers and books around the world, turned out to have a fourth person in it—Liu Shaoqi. In fact, in the true photo now before us, both Zhu De and Zhou Enlai were looking at Liu, not at Mao. History had been turned into falsehood, belatedly corrected.

Were there plans to enlarge the Liu site in the style of Shaoshan? "No. Liu was not a person to seek fame or display for himself," said the curator. "When he came here in 1961, sleeping six nights in his old bedroom, he remarked that the buildings would be better used as housing for local people." The curator explained: "Liu himself said it was correct for Shaoshan to have an exhibit, because six members of Mao's family were revolutionary martyrs, whereas from his family only he himself joined the revolution."

In a Changsha bookshop, one of our group, Angus McDonald, author of *The Urban Origins of Rural Revolution* on the Hunan of Mao's day, spotted *Hunan lishi cailiao* ("Hunan Historical Materials") and took it to the cash register. It was the latest volume, new to us, in a series our libraries possessed. However, an assistant in the Xinhua store said that book was reserved for another buyer. Tang Tsou, a Chicago professor and author of *America's Failure in China*, was prevented from buying a current book on Chinese socialist economic issues. At a discussion with Hunan historians of the CCP, our Chinese colleagues shared some of our frustration about materials. They expressed their own dissatisfaction that from the Cultural Revolution until 1977, perusing material in the Central Party Archives required approval from five members of the Politburo.

In Shanghai, our group was visited by Hu Fuming, author of an influential article in 1979, "Practice Is the Sole Criterion for Testing Truth." Professor Hu, of the Philosophy Department at Nanjing University, was a jovial, loquacious man in his 40s. He said with a smile, "Now is the best moment in China for thirty years!" I asked for an illustration. "Look, today I've come from Nanjing to Shanghai to see you, just because I wanted to. I have brought a student with me. We are sitting here and talking. That's what I mean." However, Hu was not satisfied with the universities. "Nanjing University has 1700 teachers and only 4000 students," he said with a snort. "We should have 40,000 students."

Professor Hu's article criticized upholding whatever Mao said, which felled writer Ding Ling in 1956. The essay ignited a nationwide "Debate on Standards for Judging the Truth" and helped usher in the era of reform. When *Guangming Daily* first published the article, some called it "ridiculous" while others praised it as "a bomb that destroys the reactionary ideological system of the Gang of Four." More than one opinion was now allowed in China.

The great difference between China and America, Hu ventured, was China's long history and the U.S.'s short one. Friedman remarked that the bureaucracy surrounding archives in China seemed complex. "In China, bureaucracy is terrible," responded Professor Hu. "You foreigners have to put up with it only for thirty days, we Chinese have to put up with it 365 days a year!" Hu complained about older cadres: "Because they've gone through decades of revolution, they don't feel required to explain the whys and wherefores."

The "Scholarly Delegation to Investigate the Problems of the Chinese Revolution" came home with two impressions of current debate about political history. A reassessment of the relative weight of capitalism as a threat to China's socialism (reduced) and feudal influence (increased). An apparent redefinition of Marxism that put "seeking the truth from facts" near the center of Marxist analysis. I saw this as a giant step away from Marxism.

Our trip to China was judged in American Sinological circles the richest exchange to date with Chinese scholars. We learned much about Mao's upbringing in Shaoshan, the existence of early writings of Zhou Enlai of which we had been unaware, unfolding awareness of Mao's "feudal-fascism," heart-rending stories of personal travails during the Cultural Revolution, and problems in the handling of archiving material in China.

At the final banquet, Chinese hosts urged our Mao group to be patient about China's changes. Western scholars should not think "China was just like little Taiwan." One had to get inside vast China, it was substantial enough to be worth understanding, and it was a "long-term relationship that we are all building together."

The U.S. Consul-General in Shanghai, Donald Anderson, and his wife were busy settling into their elegant old residence, following full diplomatic relations between China and the U.S. When the consulate opened, Anderson was moved by visits from elderly Chinese who worked for the American consulate in Shanghai before 1949. "They wanted to resume working for us," he said. "Several in their 70s, others in their 80s. Alas, I had to turn them down—our Chinese have to be hired through the Foreign Affairs Bureau of Shanghai."

Still, Anderson invited the veterans to a ceremony opening the consulate. "They all arrived dressed to the nines," he said with a smile. "[Ambassador Leonard] Woodcock came down from Beijing for the occasion. We posed for a group photo with the former Chinese staff members on the lovely steps at the front of the residence."

I received a phone call in my Harvard office from a Chinese journalist, Zhang Suchu, in New York. "I have something to give you," she said. I knew of Zhang, who was a daughter of Zhang Zhidong, a famous general who left the KMT after 1949 to become a minister in Mao's government. As a child, Suchu remembers Mao's visit to Chongqing in 1945 to negotiate with Chiang Kai-shek, since Mao stayed in her father's house.

I invited Ms. Zhang to visit me at Harvard. She handed me a Chinese paperback volume with no colors and no real cover. "It is the Chinese translation of your *800,000,000*," she said with a slight smile. "I am the translator." It was called *Ba Yi ren—Lai zi Zhongguo de baodao*. Zhang explained that it had taken years to contact me because I might be upset by the Preface. "I did not write the Preface," she said. The Chinese volume was the pair of *Atlantic Monthly* articles in almost total form, not the complete book *800,000,000*.

I appreciated Zhang's gift and enjoyed her visit. She and her husband Jiang Jinglun, son of a Protestant theologian, became my friends. In the Chinese volume she wrote: "To our friend Ross—from Suchu and Jinglun."

I marveled at the secrecy of this *neibu* (secret) publication. Though 40,000 copies were distributed, I had no firm knowledge of the existence of the book until Zhang phoned, seven years after the book's publication in Beijing. Read today, the Preface, which is dated September, 1972, seems quaint, but not bad for its time.

The editors said the book was "a sensation" in America and that the author was both a Harvard scholar and a foreign policy advisor to Whitlam of Australia. They explained that during his 1971 trip he had "broad contact" with many circles in China. "Terrill acknowledges the new man, new things, and new atmosphere of China," they wrote. "However, because of his world view and bourgeois stand point," he also "expresses disapproval on not a few issues." He "tries to paint a picture of China," but there is some "superficiality and half-knowledge, which introduces distortions and slanders."

The Preface explained: "We selected this book because it is representative of important strands of Western thinking" about the PRC. "In order to strengthen our propaganda work toward the outside world and advance our efforts in receiving foreign visitors, we publish this translated book, to supply various units with reference material." Such had been the China of the early 1970s.

By the late 1970s, I tired of analyzing Chinese politics by immediate reading of *People's Daily* and grass roots investigation. I felt most Chinese people were recipients, often victims, of gyrations of the party-state. The process of "reversal of verdicts" in China posed a credibility problem for a Western writer. I felt misled in 1975–76 by Chinese officials telling me Deng was a counter-revolutionary. To maintain the trust of readers, it was important for a scholar-writer to make independent judgments amidst the twists and turns of a Communist government. This concern triggered a turn to biography. I wanted to probe issues of power and personality, and the relation of Communist ideology and Chinese culture. First result was the original edition of my *Mao*. After Deng vindicated my feelings about personality, by his public criticism of Mao's errors, I turned to the story of Jiang Qing.

Throughout our Mao trip led by Professor Friedman, the name of Mao's wife was hardly mentioned, even in passing. To anyone who lived through the Cultural Revolution, or later analyzed it, this was astonishing. Jiang Qing was second only to her husband at the apex of power. As she herself put it, denigrating herself yet hinting at her immense influence, "I was Mao's dog. What he said to bite, I bit."

Officials in Beijing and Chinese ambassadors abroad discouraged me from writing about Mao's fallen widow. "We have explained that she is a bad woman," one said. "Why are you interested in a bad woman? Write about a good woman!" Another ambassador offered as an objection to both my Mao and Jiang Qing biographies: "Personalities don't count in our political life, only policies."

"It is all water under the bridge," reasoned my friend Zhang Wenjin when I broached the Jiang Qing project over lunch at Xin Qiao Hotel. "Now all we're interested in is economic development." However, I wasn't sure the judgment pronounced at the trial of the Gang of Four would stand unchanged in the light of history. "I can't encourage you," Assistant Foreign Minister Zhang said. "But I won't discourage you. Knowing you, I suppose you'll go ahead anyway."

I did go ahead. I knew Jiang Qing was not a politically serious person, nor a feminist hero as some Western women believed. Yet, I felt her role in Chinese politics and her relation to feudal residues in China could not be ignored. Important problems in the relation of art and politics were involved. I believed an objective view of Jiang Qing, describing her opportunism and subjectivism, but also the world she had to deal with as a woman high in the CCP, would be worthwhile.

I wrote a letter to Deng Xiaoping: "Without investigations in China, my book on Jiang Qing would have to rely on materials from outside China, which would be a pity. I know from your own record that you favor sincere enquiry, seeking the truth from facts. This is my goal too."[4] Deng had already made up his mind about Jiang Qing. The Italian writer Fallaci asked him, "What score would you give her?" Deng replied: "Below zero. A thousand points below zero."[5]

Three friends in Beijing publishing, all alumni of the same labor camp during the Cultural Revolution, expressed ambivalence about a book on Jiang Qing. "Western writers are too interested in the personal aspect of politics," said Percy Fang, who himself wrote a biography of Zhou Enlai, as we lunched at Fangshan restaurant, "and Chinese writers are too little interested." I said that would change as the reform era progressed. All three agreed that Jiang had been central to the Cultural Revolution and that the Mao-Jiang marriage was inseparable from the issue of the Gang of Four. Yet none felt able to help me in my search for materials. I understood that and we agreed to differ.

Li Yanning of Xinhua News raised a persuasive point against my project. "Deng and the others suffered terribly in the late Mao period," he said simply. I realized some in Beijing would be irritated by my book and I respected that. "But I just don't believe political struggle is a past issue," I said to Li. "I think Deng is still concerned with the past because the legitimacy of the present depends upon an interpretation of the past, including the trial of Gang of Four." Li surprised and pleased me by lighting a cigarette and saying quietly, "I agree with you."

Stuart Schram, the premier Western scholar of Mao's writings, wrote to me after he read the draft of the book: "I do not share your perverse fascination for this woman, but it is plain you have discovered a great deal of interesting information which will be of much value to scholars."[6]

Born a concubine's daughter in Shandong Province in 1914, Jiang Qing lacked a comfortable upbringing. Her father was violent; her mother struggled against high odds. By the age of 19, following a spell in a roving theater troupe, Jiang Qing (a name later given her by Mao) had wrapped up two marriages. One to a young businessman (1930), speedily divorced, the second to an upperclass radical who introduced her to Marxism.

In Shanghai from 1933 she rose as an actress in socially committed plays and movies; Nora in Ibsen's "A Doll's House" was her star role. A third marriage to a theater writer gripped the Shanghai entertainment world. Soon this stylish man tried to kill himself in despair at Jiang's independence of spirit.

Her character was strikingly willful and individualistic. Given to struggle, open to fantasy, and possessed of vengefulness, she expressed these traits in a career in the arts and eventually in China's so-called Cultural Revolution.

After Japan attacked China in 1937, wrecking the Shanghai arts, Jiang went north to Yanan to join the Communists. Mao, whose previous marriage was just breaking down, fell for her.

At first a quiet, modest housewife and mother, and during the 1950s often ill and in Russia, Jiang in the 1960s sprang back to prominence. Her cervical cancer cured, and her talents at last needed by Mao at loggerheads with his colleagues, she became the most powerful woman the Communist world has ever seen.

The passion she once brought to the theater, later to her love for Mao, she poured into politics. Jiang buoyed Mao and marshalled a coterie of youth and Bohemians to struggle against everything in the arts that she and Mao did not like. For Jiang Qing, class struggle meant revenge, and communism meant power.

"He [Mao] came to trust women far more than men," said Mao's doctor, in a remark that tied together Mao's personal and political mood. "He craved affection and acclaim. As criticism of him rose within the party, so did his hunger for approval."[7] An excellent way to get it was from the adoring lips of innocent girls.

There was a certain dignity to Jiang Qing's indirect references to Mao's womanizing. "In the matter of political struggle," she remarked, "none of the Chinese and Soviet leaders can beat him. In the matter of his personal conduct, nobody can keep him in check either."[8]

When Mao died, she felt the top job was hers almost by right. Had not Empress Wu Zetian proved 1300 years ago that a woman could rule China?

However, the succession crisis in 1976 found Jiang wanting. She lacked a national political organization and could not surmount a creeping anti-Mao mood. She discovered that what the Chairman had done cast a shadow on her. Arrested as a "counterrevolutionary," she faced a trial.

The day Jiang Qing's sentence was announced, I chatted with Joyce Chen at the annual Garden Party of John Kenneth Galbraith on the afternoon of Harvard Commencement. Joyce, the most successful Chinese restauranteur in Boston, was from a family spread among the Mainland, Taiwan and the USA. At the 1980 party, she crossed the lawn to say hello. "When they sentenced Jiang Qing," she said with a frown, "I was so mad they didn't pronounce a death sentence, all day I was in a furious mood. I made mistakes in the dining room, I got angry with people."

As the Deng era rose to its peak, the imprisoned Jiang Qing, afflicted with cancer, lost hope for herself and China alike. In May 1991, she wrote: "Chairman, your student and co-fighter is coming to see you now." Next day she hanged herself.

After my biography was published in 1984, two letters came from the White House. Nancy Reagan, wife of the president, wrote to say she was reading the book ready for Reagan's April 1984 trip to China. Vice-President Bush sent a hand-written letter. "I have just finished *The White-Boned Demon*, he wrote. "Fascinating in every way." Enclosed was a slip of paper that he asked me to sign so he could stick it in the book.

"In my day," wrote the former head of the U.S. Liaison Office in Beijing, and future president, "I met Jiang Qing only once or twice. I saw Nancy Tang and Wang Hairong [granddaughter of Mao's cousin Wang Jifan] often, so the book took on special meaning for me. . . I wonder will Jiang Qing ever get out?"

I wrote back to Vice-President Bush: "I think she will remain in prison, sewing cloth dolls and writing political manifestos, as long Deng's modernization program goes along at reasonable speed."[9]

In Australia, a playwright named Therese Radic used my book extensively without permission or attribution for her play "Madam Mao," staged in Melbourne. A friend took me to see the show and I was shocked at the naked robbery. Stories available only in *White-Boned Demon* were used verbatim. I sued Radic and won a settlement in which Radic apologized, put an ad in leading newspapers stating her regret, and promised to give credit to my book in future performances of the play.

Research for *White-Boned Demon* brought fascinating encounters. In Jakarta, President Sukarno's widow gave me a photo of herself together with Mao and Jiang Qing in 1962, the first public appearance with a foreign dignitary of Mao and Jiang Qing together in the PRC. In Switzerland, the widow of Edgar Snow, Lois, offered photos of Ed and Jiang Qing from Yanan years and other materials from Ed's files.[10]

In 1983, Zhu Zhongli, widow of senior Mao colleague, Wang Jiaxiang, in her elegant mansion recalled Jiang Qing's appearance.[11] "She was not slim and not fat." Zhu patted her own stomach. "Fatter than me." When Jiang Qing reached Yanan, where Zhu Zhongli knew her well and was one of her doctors, "she had good eyebrows, nose and eyes. She was a very good-looking young woman. She always looked fine in a *balujun* [Eighth Route Army uniform] Later, in the Cultural Revolution, her voice grew shrill, really just like Donald Duck." Zhu Zhongli said Jiang Qing's feet were bound, "so she didn't walk well, but later, higher heels disguised her walking problem. One tooth, though, was always bad."[12] And her right foot had six toes.[13]

Zhu Zhongli, a physician-turned-writer, kept in touch with Mao's eldest daughter, Li Min. "There's a family resemblance, but she's grown fatter." Zhu said the government was no longer rigid about political prisoners. "Li Na [the other Mao daughter] sometimes visits her mother in prison."

In Paris in 1982, I met Tang Na, former Shanghai literary journalist and husband of Jiang Qing in the 1930s. He ran a restaurant, *Pont Du Ciel*, and invited me to dine there. His wife, Chen Renqiong, daughter of Chiang Kai-shek's one-time foreign minister, was also present.

I wrote a letter to Tang Na requesting a talk about Jiang Qing. He wrote back negatively: "I am definitely unwilling to talk about my private life," the one-time literary Journalist for *Da qonqbao* wrote. "However, if you come to Paris for reasons [additional to] meeting me, I would be very happy to see you."

Despite many years in France, Tang Na still resembled a Shanghai Bohemian, in white suit, with hair slicked down, cigarette at the mouth, and arms gesticulating. Born in Tianjin, he was brought up by an aunt after his father, a railway clerk, died young through drinking a medicine meant for external application.

At a delicious Chinese dinner from the *Pont du Ciel* kitchen, Jiang Qing was not mentioned. However, as Tang Na said good-night, he asked, "Are you busy tomorrow evening?" I wasn't. "Come again."

Next evening Tang Na's wife was not present. Tang Na and I ate double-cooked pork, dry-cooked duck, sweet shrimp, and hot and sour soup. Evidently, I had passed Chen Renqiong's test, for Tang Na talked for four hours about Jiang Qing, her acting, her marriage with him, and its collapse.

When he first met her on the street in the French Concession of Shanghai, Jiang Qing knew of him for his warm review in *Da Gongbao* of her role in Ibsen's "Doll's House." She said, "I'm a revolutionary, you know!" Next evening, after some French red wine Tang Na recalled that startling moment 47 years before: "It was enormously exciting to me that this new actress from Shandong, right there on Huaihai Boulevard, said she was a committed revolutionary."

"I think Lan Ping (her stage name) did to me what she later did with Mao," Tang Na said. "She was attractive and she presented herself as a revolutionary—that hooked a man." Tang Na said Jiang Qing had grievances and prejudices. "Everything was personal with Lan Ping," Tang Na said. "The person she hated most was [director] Xia Yan, and that was because he gave the leading role in the production of the historical romance 'Sai Jinhua' to Wang Ying, not to her."

Just after midnight, as we arose, I asked Tang Na if he was free the following evening. He agreed, and I took him for a French dinner not far from *Pont Du Ciel.*

Over goose liver pate and *coq au vin,* Tang Na criticized Mao: "In Yanan, Mao made mistakes on art and literature. And he married Lan Ping [Jiang Qing], which wronged me." Tang Na, who in those years was on the left, raised his voice slightly: "If Mao breaks wind should everyone say that's a beautiful perfume?" His hand gripped a thin Cuban cigar as his arm sliced the air. "WE fought against Japan too. WE stood up to imperialists. In the Cultural Revolution people were given the impression Mao did it all. He was a fine leader, but he could not have succeeded without wonderful support."

I asked him about a dramatic moment in 1945 when he was at the same reception as both Mao and Chiang Kai-shek, together in Chongqing for negotiations. A line of guests inched forward to shake hands with the two leaders. When Tang Na was next in line to shake Mao's hand, he abruptly turned and left the party. I asked, "Why did you get so close to Jiang Qing's next husband, but then depart. He replied, "I didn't want a picture taken and a documentary record of Mao and myself together to exist."

Tang Na's wife popped in leave a package. After giving it to Tang Na, she disappeared into the kitchen. I showed Tang Na a letter of Lan Ping's to him that accused him of leaving the writing of his theater reviews until the last moment. He laughed. Chen suddenly arrived from the kitchen and cried, "It's true, that's his way." Tang Na riposted: "I was slow, in order to polish my sentences."

When this fourth dinner ended, after midnight, Tang Na said, "We haven't finished yet, come back to eat with me tomorrow." Once more at *Pont Du*

Ciel, the memories and opinions continued. Tang Na missed Shanghai but could not regret leaving China in 1949. "In 1956–57 I would have been arrested, and in 1966 I probably would have been killed."

When I said I felt torn between two countries, Australia and the U.S., Tang Na said, "What about me? Three countries. I'm not that comfortable in Taiwan, because they think I'm a leftist, but I can't go [back] to the Mainland. Here we are in France."

As midnight came again, Tang Na said with feeling, "I see you're not a hack for some daily news rag, but a scholar who can sort out black and white. I used to have monthly meetings here with leading French Sinologues to discuss China," Tang Na went on, "including [General] Jacques Guillermaz and [journalist] Robert Guillain. With none of them did I talk about my private life—somehow you have become an exception."

Near 3 am in the warm gloom of Paris's 16e arrondisement, Tang Na bid me farewell. I suggested his influence on Lan Ping probably made her better than she would otherwise have been. Tang Na looked me straight in the eye and said in English, "Thank you."

In San Francisco, I met another literary journalist from 1930s Shanghai, Cui Wanqiu, who remembers Jiang Qing only as "Lan Ping," her stage-name in Shanghai. Cui, literary editor of *Da Gongbao* in the 1930s, was the father of Jill Cheng who owned a Boston Chinese book store. Jill persuaded him to reminisce about "Lan Ping." A fellow Shandong native, Cui was introduced to Jiang Qing by the producer Hong Shen during rehearsals for "Doll's House."

"After the play is over," Lan Ping said when Cui met her, "I would like to come and visit Mr. Cui, to learn from you and chat about our native places." Lan Ping wrote a few articles for Cui's literary pages in *Da Wanbao*." I paid her three yuan per thousand words," Cui recalled as we talked in the Cui family home near San Francisco. "The stars like writer Guo Moruo and director Xia Yan got ten yuan per thousand words."

A member of the China Youth Party, Cui did not share Lan Ping's left political views (or Tang Na's). "We discussed the relative merits of Hu Die and Yuan Lingyu," said Cui of the two best-known Chinese actresses of the time. "Lan Ping said Hu Die was a 'wooden beauty, just like a statue.' She preferred Yuan Lingyu," a spirited young woman who killed herself when depressed about being treated as a plaything. Lan Ping hated the portrayal of women in Mei Lanfang operas like "Heavenly Maidens Scattering Flowers." They were "sentimental women," Lan Ping complained to Cui, "so delicate a wind could blow them down."

Like Tang Na, Cui was careful not to irritate his wife in talking to me about Jiang Qing, as both women saw—or thought they saw—a sparkle in the eye of their husband when Mao's wife was recalled. But Cui, like his daughter, was a charmer, and a fine raconteur on Lan Ping and the Shanghai theater world.

In Australia came a welcome discovery. The Australian Broadcasting Corporation had an office in Shanghai before 1949 and kept good records. The head of the Chinese service of Radio Australia in Melbourne tracked down a sound recording of Lan Ping (Jiang Qing) singing a song in the harrowing movie "Old Bachelor Wang" (*Wang Lao Wu)* from 1936.[14] I played the recording at many talks around the world and still possess it.

One summer morning in Taipei, I visited 86-year old Yu Dawei, former defense minister in Chiang Kai-shek's government during the 1930s. He was the uncle of the upper-class radical whom Jiang Qing fell for in Qingdao. Yu Qiwei married her and turned her into a leftist before she went to Shanghai. The uncle, a grand gentleman, dressed in suit and tie for our morning talk, graduated from Harvard in 1919. He won the top traveling scholarship for an undergraduate that year. The president of Harvard said as he presented the award: "You are the first Chinese student to win this highest Harvard scholarship."

After Chiang Kai-shek's arrest of Yu Qiwei in 1932 as a leftist, his uncle, one of Chiang Kai-shek's ministers, quietly worked for his nephew's release. "These young leftists were really just eager patriots, opposed to foreign bullying of China," Yu Dawei told me. "I didn't feel they belonged in prison." After Liberation, Yu (Huang Jing) lost touch with Jiang Qing, married the journalist Fan Jin and became mayor of Zhangjiakou.

None of my books had better reviews than *White-Boned Demon.* "A magnificent display of investigative reporting, research and reconstruction," said Harrison Salisbury, long-time writer on China and Russia for *New York Times.* (*Newsday*) "Reads like a ticking time bomb" said *Publisher's Weekly,* (12/23/83) "Sweeping and sensational," wrote *New York Times.* (3/4/84) With insight, *Wichitan* in America's heartland commented: "A chilling, disquieting story about a petty tyrant who confused independence with power, gaining ever more of the latter but never experiencing the former." (*Wichitan,* monthly May 1984) Dozens more reviews followed.

Esther Shapiro, a producer in Hollywood known for her TV series, "Dynasty" and "East of Eden," optioned *White-Boned Demon* for a TV miniseries or feature film. Great excitement and press coverage followed until the producer saw a casting dilemma.

I wrote a postcard from China in July 1984 to Esther, suggesting Faye Dunaway for the role of Jiang Qing.[15] Dunaway had won awards for her performances in *Network* (1976), *Bonnie and Clyde* (1967), *Chinatown* (1974) and other films. Esther took up the idea and made a preliminary contract with the star.

The plan was to adjust Dunaway's face to look a little Chinese! But it proved too complicated. Most people in the film would be Chinese, but box office pressure required an American star. Until leading Chinese-American actresses emerged (as Joan Chen and others did in the 1990s) a film about Jiang Qing, done in the U.S. was out of reach.

In Chinese affairs the wheel sometimes turns full circle if you wait. Although Zhang Wenjin advised me not to tackle the project, later, toward the end of his term as ambassador in Washington, he drew me aside at a lunch in the Colonnade Hotel in Boston and whispered, "By the way, I'm glad you wrote that book about Jiang Qing."

I was glad, too, that I wrote *White Boned Demon*. Still, some Chinese critics were correct. Had I been Chinese, I could not have calmly written the book. As Owen Lattimore said, the historian or social scientist from afar can never be part of the drama of another culture; his "truth" can only be partial. I remained outside the "emotional truth" of Jiang Qing's impact on China. Still, I hoped that, being outside, I had the advantage of seeing "Gang of Four" as shorthand for issues relating to Mao and the political system. The past, even its difficult periods, has always mattered to Chinese.

The volume was published in Chinese by *Shijie zhishi chubanshe* in Beijing, a house linked with the Chinese Foreign Ministry. The book in yellow and black cover, terribly censored, was quietly on sale in bookstores of China, though even its author was not permitted to buy a copy! It was a restricted edition containing a prefatory note saying the work was controversial but important.

Later the book was published in Hebei in a better edition with comparatively few changes from my English. However, it was still *neibu faxing* (internal distribution) and reached few readers.

In complex Chinese characters, 7000 words of the book was published in Taiwan by the journal *Chinese Communist Affairs Weekly*, for followers of Mainland history and politics.[16]

From Argentina came a letter: "I have found an incredible parallel between Madame Mao and Eva Peron." The Latin professor pointed out personality traits and the limited political knowledge of both Jiang Qing and the former president of Argentina, wife of the previous president Juan Peron. "Especially interesting is that both women started as an actress."

Scholarly praise of the book pleased me. "Terrill's best work on China . . . should be read by those not only interested in Madame Mao, but by students of Chairman Mao as well" wrote Professor Michel Oksenberg of University of Michigan, formerly Carter's China advisor. "*White-Boned Demon* must be one of the most relentlessly absorbing works of nonfiction to appear in recent years—on China or any other subject," said historian Professor Eric Widmer of Brown University. "A strength of this biography is that it draws attention to the role of family, kin and other personal networks, wrote Professor Elisabeth Croll in *Times Literary Supplement* of London. Dr. Elizabeth Wright gave *White-Boned Demon* a boost by writing in the main Sinology journal, *China Quarterly* of London: "The book is interesting for many reasons . . . it adds to our knowledge of both contemporary Chinese politics and the extraordinary woman who played such an important and catastrophic role in them." The influential *Journal of Asian Studies* called the book "the definitive study in any language of the life and times of Jiang Qing."

"Terrill has made this unattractive personality interesting, even comprehensible," summed up overseas Chinese historian Professor Wang Gungwu in my hometown Melbourne's *Age*. Wrote Professor Richard Solomon, formerly Kissinger's aide on China, to the publisher: "This study will be a basic reference for those seeking to understand the inner workings of the Chinese Communist Movement." Privately Solomon sent me a hand written note: "It's a terrific book. You have enough distance from the subject and grasp of CCP politics to do what Roxane Witke could not accomplish. And if some day Jiang Qing is rehabilitated, you'll be one of China's ten Most Wanted foreign devil intellectuals."

Could Mao's revolution go on without Mao and Jiang Qing? Most of my Harvard colleagues saw China after Mao as likely to resemble the Soviet Union after Stalin. Yet I felt East Asia was changing and Beijing knew it. The Vietnam War was over and East Asian capitalist economies were soaring. Chinese leaders, I believed, realized China was lagging economically compared with countries around it. I expected Mao's passing to bring drastic new thinking in Beijing. The jailing of Jiang Qing and her Gang of Four seemed to prove it.

Two world views had been shot down in the space of a century. The imperial mentality was attacked during and after the fall of the Qing Dynasty in 1911. Now, Maoist utopianism, sold to the Chinese people as the "new" that replaced the imperial "old," was likely to be rejected.

Mao's greatest achievement was to consolidate the unity of the Chinese realm, to restore "one China." But the China that Mao left was still searching for a just and stable political form to replace the Confucian monarchy that fell in 1911. Chiang Kai-shek's regime from 1928 was crippled within a decade by the assault from Japan. In 1949, the totalism and autocracy of pre-1911 were largely revived.

Mao is a witness to the Communist Party's fundamental evolution back toward Chinese autocratic tradition after 1949. "For the past four thousand years," he observed when 30 years old, "Chinese politics has always opted for grand outlines of large-scale projects with big methods. The result has been a country outwardly strong but inwardly weak; solid at the top but hollow at the bottom." He later blamed all China's weaknesses on Western imperialism: But this wasn't true. Mao could never agree with a one-time German Communist's remark: "The problem with capitalism is capitalists; the problem with socialism is socialism."

By 1976, political gymnastics had exhausted the people; campaigns and "fights to the end" lost their capacity to seduce. Meanwhile, the East Asian region off economically in the 1970s, making China look like a laggard.

Contemplating China's twentieth-century quest for a new political forum, Owen Lattimore asked in *Inner Asian Frontiers of China*: "How much of the ancient fabric will have to be destroyed? How stable a modern structure can be set up on the ancient foundations?" This question was still in process of being answered. More than Japan's co-prosperity dreams in the 1930s and 1940s or Soviet-style communism thereafter, felt Lattimore, "it is the Westernizing of China's own ancient civilization that will in fact be decisive." Yet never in Chinese history has the political outcome of Chinese-foreign synergy been as expected. The post-Mao leaders cannot know where the market is taking them. Still less do foreigners know.

As for Jiang Qing, post-Mao she faired badly. Her policies were often harsh and bizarre. Still, her story is replete with horrors of the Communist system no less than with horrors she herself wrought. She was a mirror to some traits of the CCP. In shutting Jiang up from 1976, Deng acted out of revenge as well as higher motives.

NOTES

1. Kukrit's words, spoken to the author, Bangkok, November 10, 1979.

2. Seymour Hersh, spoken to author, Cambridge, January 17, 1982.

3. Ross Terrill, "In China, 'Liuism' Is Back, But Not Capitalism," *New York Times*, May, 16, 1980.

4. Author, letter to Deng, May, 25, 1982.

5. Fallaci, cited in *Guardian*, September 17, 2006.

6. Schram, letter to author, September 23, 1983.

7. Li Zhisui, *The Private Life of Chairman Mao*, New York, Random House, 1994, cited in *Los Angeles Times*, March 8, 1998.

8. Li Zhisui, Ibid, xx.

9. Vice-President Bush, letter to author, "Easter, 1984"; Reply, author to Bush, May 14, 1984.

10. Lois Snow, letters to the author, June 23, 1983, July 28, 1983; author to Lois Snow, July 15, 1983, August, 22, 1983.

11. Dr. Dong in Shanghai said to me of his relative's mansion: "Not everyone goes to her house. It's a special house. It's beautiful, furnished in the Russian style, and every night there are dancing parties where young people, many of them the offspring of the privileged elite, dance to advanced music which Ms. Zhu imports from Hong Kong. She herself dances. She has long hair done in a permanent wave."

12. Visit to Zhu Zhongli, October, 30, 1983.

13. Li Zhisui, Ibid. 175.

14. John Dudley, letter to author, June, 29, 1983; author reply to Dudley, July 15, 1983.

15. Author card from Beijing to Esther Shapiro, July 2, 1984.

16. *Chinese Communist Affairs Weekly*, Issue No 141, Taipei.

17. *New York Review of Books*, October 14, 1976.

Chapter Fourteen

Deng and Reagan

In US-China relations, the 1980s were the decade of Ronald Reagan and Deng Xiaoping. A long climb up for the movie actor; a stunning recovery for the chain-smoking Cultural Revolution victim.

Voting for the first time in the U.S., in the November 1980 presidential election, I walked to a voting station at a high school near Harvard. It was almost automatic for Harvard folk to vote Democratic. But I decided to vote Republican. Absurd inflation with interest rates of nearly 20% shook me, as did Carter's failure to recover hostages from Iran. Telling no one, I went alone to the high school. In the booth, my hand trembling, I pulled the lever for Reagan. Still a registered Democrat, I was a ripple in the tide of "Reagan Democrats."

A month after Reagan took office, William Buckley invited guests who had appeared on his TV show "Firing Line" to a 20th anniversary extravaganza at the New York Yacht Club. Kissinger, a Republican and Senator Moynihan, a Democrat, were among the evening's sponsors. Governor Brown of California, also a former guest on "Firing Line," talked about China and his plans for a visit there. After the event I wrote to him, trying to answer his sharp questions."[1]

Stephen Solarz, the Democrat head of the House Foreign Affairs Committee, said he wanted to hold hearings on China policy during the spring. I urged him to think twice. Shouldn't we wait until the administration made its mind up on a few points? Stephen said he wanted to help them make up their minds. "This time I'd like to get some people with impeccable conservative credentials," he added. I said it wouldn't be easy in the China field.

Former president Nixon sent me a copy of his 1982 book *Leaders,* with vivid portraits of Mao, Zhou Enlai, Churchill, de Gaulle and others. Ceaucescu of Romania, whom Nixon knew well, was not included. The book

Figure 14.1. Deng Xiaoping, exiled during the Cultural Revolution, returned to public life in 1977 and began his climb toward the summit of power. Here, in 1978, he listens to sustained applause from the Chinese People's Political Consultative Conference, of which he was elected chairman. Chinese People's University Press, courtesy Tracy Liu and Sara Wang.

showed skill in blending reminiscence, biography and estimates of the ingredients of leadership. Nixon cited my *Mao*. Soon, I sent him a copy of my next book, *The White-Boned Demon*.

In *Leaders*. Nixon said little of Jiang Qing and nothing about her as a leader. "I found her tough, humorless, totally unfeminine," he wrote after sitting next to her at the theater. "I have never met a more cold, graceless person."

Two years later, Nixon wrote again sending me a copy of his *No More Vietnams*. "Dear Ross," he began, "April 30 [1985] will mark the tenth anniversary of the fall of Saigon." I agreed with Nixon's judgment: "Our defeat in Vietnam was only a temporary setback after a series of victories."

For a period after Reagan's victory, Reagan's circle wavered between an ideological approach to China and a national interest approach. In Congressional testimony and in several newspaper columns I favored a national interest policy.[2] In Beijing in 1980, when Assistant Foreign Minister Zhang Wenjin expressed alarm about Reagan, I responded: "If Reagan is elected, his strategic anti-Russian point of view will prevail, when it comes to China policy, over his moral pro-Taiwan point of view."[3]

Nearer to the election, I wrote to Zhang: "I would not worry too much about Mr. Reagan. . . There is very little he can do about Taiwan."[4] I told the *Boston Globe* on September 5, 1980 "There's not much wrong with China-Taiwan relations, and I don't think we should try to fix them. Derecognition [of Taiwan by the U.S.] has worked." So it all proved, luckily for me. Reagan continued the approach to China of Nixon, Ford and Carter.

In Orange County, which looked like Sydney, with its eucalyptus trees, wide open spaces, glare of sunlight, and people's cheery faces, I wrote in my diary: "A different atmosphere in my audience tonight as compared with today's lunchtime speech in LA. Orange County is full of right-wing Republicans. Dinner began with the Pledge of the Allegiance to the Flag (fortunately I was not facing the audience—I turned to face the flag—so they probably did not notice I fumbled the pledge's words)."

Instead of being asked, as in San Francisco, how much better things might have been between America and China if Truman had reined in General Macarthur in Korea in 1950, "I was asked whether we shouldn't have gone across the Yalu River and knocked the Chinese out while they were still a baby in the cradle."

Campus liberals lamented Reagan's election and predicted disasters. A female professor at the University of Oregon managed a mixed view. "The Reagan victory is worrisome," she wrote in an invitation to lecture. "Perhaps the fact that he is closer in age to the Chinese leaders will ameliorate his heretofore atrocious attitudes." She saw two more redeeming factors. "All those [Carter] Georgians can go home to peanut farming at Plains and I can stop killing myself trying to learn Mandarin."[5]

In San Francisco, a questioner asked, "Won't Reagan's attitude to the Third World upset the Chinese?" She, like many Americans, was unaware that China, since its split with Russia, had been at least as conservative in its attitude toward the Third World, for example Chile, as Reagan could possibly be.

As the Reagan era unfolded, China's foreign policy grew modest and cost-conscious. Deng told China "We should bide our time." Zhang Wenjin said, "We won't be able to donate military assistance as in the past. You know, lots of countries didn't pay bills to China and other countries for foreign aid." The minister laughed. "Egypt didn't pay Russia, and we actually encouraged Cairo not to pay Moscow. But in the future," Zhang went on, "all our military and economic assistance will be approached like tailoring a suit. We'll take the measurements, look at the stature of the one seeking the suit, consider the price, and do the garment if it's worth it."

During the mid-1970s, Zhang Wenjin had praised turmoil and talked about "international class struggle." However, after lunch with him in 1981, I noted, "He sounded today like a blend of Bismarck and an overseas Chinese businessman." Just as Chinese domestic policy grew bold, Chinese foreign policy grew measured. Just as domestic policy favored rapid change, foreign policy chose stability.

The days of Mao's China "punishing" American Express because it did business in Taiwan, and telling the *New York Times* it couldn't have a bureau in Beijing if it published advertisements from Taiwan, gave way to more comfortable days. Under Deng, China weighed the balance of power, counted its foreign aid pennies, and tackled the unmodernized condition of its own armies. China was buying time, coping cleverly with the gap between ambitions and capacity. Its top priority was economic development at home.

As we lunched at Xin Qiao Hotel, I told Zhang Wenjin I liked the absence of any big political campaign in China at the present. "We like it too," he responded with a smile. In 1981, Zhang Wenjin was extremely helpful in smoothing the path for an Australian TV program, "Sixty Minutes," to film in various parts of China, including inside a PLA unit near Nanjing. I was adviser to the project as it filmed in Beijing, Shanghai and Nanjing. The "Sixty Minutes" episodes were widely viewed throughout Australia in 1982 and helped China's image.

Flying out of Shanghai after the "Sixty Minutes" program, I picked up a copy of *Barron*'s as the Pan Am plane fronted the Pacific Ocean. Everything the American financial weekly said about business seemed to apply to politics in China. "Trust this man," said an ad for a stock broking advisor. "Can you do without this man?" It was the same appeal made in the name of political leadership to the people of China.

The front page of *Barron*'s carried a piece analyzing how and why economists and advisors—including the financial weekly's own journalists had erred in foreseeing recent trends in the American economy. It reminded me of Chinese postmortems on mistakes of the Gang of Four. In both cases, there was a granite confidence that the present line of advice was fine. We understand the past—perhaps!—but how about the present?

Even in two cultures as different as Chinese and American, I reflected, people need myths to embrace. They want to believe they know the road, even though experience may suggest that no one can know it. As the Pan Am plane climbed higher, I shook my mind away from the comparison. The stock market in America was a voluntary activity, whereas politics in China was compulsory—or used to be.

Chinese foreign policy became more nationalistic. During 1982, Zhang Wen-jin was snappy on America. "China suffered from the 1950s to the 1970s when there was no link with America," he said over lunch in his favorite room at Xin Qiao Hotel, "but America suffered more." The minister offered two Chinese proverbs for my edification. "The best shop keeper doesn't hang all his fine goods outside the window," he remarked when I mentioned doubts within the United States as to China's weight in world affairs, "but keeps them stored behind the counter." He delivered another swipe at America: "It's better not to have a big name, and be able to live up to it, than the other way around."

"American people are pretty unconcerned about international affairs," Zhang complained. "Their own way of life is the great thing for them. And your politicians just think in 'four-year boxes,' looking at the next election." Washington seems to "look down on China," he said. "Yet many of our friends now accuse us of being pro-American." I observed that China, too, was looking more to its internal life, less concerned to push socialism upon the world. "In the end," I observed, "Americans are simply pro-American and Chinese are pro-Chinese." We ate our lunch and changed the subject.

My British friend David Wilson, who had given me advice on churches had temples in Beijing in 1964, now Governor of Hong Kong, looked back on the anti-Americanism of the China he knew in the 1960s. "Someone I know predicted that one day soon Americans would be assisting China with the development of the waters of the Yangzi," Wilson said. "I thought this was the wildest fantasy."

Sir David commented on the new outlook of post-Mao Chinese, "The new Chinese attitude was not so much pro-Americanism, as a wish to be part of the world." Surely correct.

Soon, the Reagan administration, under the influence of Secretary of State Schultz, reduced its belief in China as a counter-weight to the Soviet Union. In parallel, Beijing reduced its hostility to Moscow. At this time both

Washington and Beijing were nervous about what the other may be doing with Moscow. Edgar Snow's widow, actress Lois, exchanged letters with me on these traits of American policy. In one reply, I wrote to her in Switzerland, "As you may know, American policy under Reagan is trying to de-emphasize China. Reagan's decision to go to Japan, Korea, and Indonesia, and not to China, on his forthcoming trip fits in with this. What they now say in Washington is that China is a regional power, not a power of global reach."[6]

Talking with my old friend Zhou Nan, I probed China-Soviet Union exchanges and trade. The vice foreign minister responded with agitation: "Why shouldn't we trade? You Americans trade with Russia. Our trade there is only one-sixth of yours. We have just arranged for ten students to study in Moscow. You have many more than that." I countered that at Brezhnev's funeral, Huang Hua called him "an outstanding statesman." Zhou Nan said, "That's just politeness on the occasion of a funeral."

Fairbank, in dialogue with Qiao Guanhua tried to justify the U.S. security treaty with Nationalist China by saying if the Americans abruptly left, Japan might jump in. "If you were China," objected the foreign minister, "could you tolerate occupation by one foreign power done in order to prevent occupation by another?"

Shen Chunyi told me of a demonstration in Beijing the night the Chinese women's volleyball team defeated the United States in New Jersey in April 1982. After the game, young people left their TV sets for the streets, lit brooms to make torches, and paraded across the city, chanting in delight. Foreigners were insulted, some hit, and when a large crowd reached the gates of the American Embassy, the young demonstrators cried, "We shall certainly beat the Yankees!"

Shen watched the demonstration, but did not join it. "Nearly everyone in that mob would visit the West if they got the chance," he said. "Yet they were gripped by frenzied patriotism." I suggested they jeered at something admired, but beyond reach. Shen added, "Whereas people who mix too much with foreigners are punished, these anti-foreign hooligans weren't." I thought of a curious remark by Bo Yang, the eminent Taiwan writer: "You could say that the Chinese are the most patriotic people in the world, but also the most anxious to become foreigners."

Shen, with his stubborn drive for self-fulfillment, wanted to leave China again. He grumbled that I wasn't helping him enough to go to the USA. "A fat man can't understand the hunger of a thin man," he chastised me at the Temple of Heaven. However, I could not flick a switch and get the college of his choice. On the other hand, I knew Shen's will was strong and that he would achieve his goals. He was too bright to be patient. He was a patriot, but his drive for self-fulfillment was in tension with his love for China.

Happily, when Premier Zhao Ziyang arrived in Washington to visit Reagan in 1984, ideology and hyper-nationalism took a back seat in United States China relations. Zhao was born to a landlord family in 1919 and when I saw him at the Chinese Embassy, he still possessed the son of a landlord's mien, immaculate in a gray Western suit and red tie, with a prosperous air and receding hairline. "The danger and the glamour have both gone from the China issue," remarked Donald Anderson, just returned from being consul general in Shanghai, as we chatted at the Chinese party, watching Zhao at close range. "Zhao's main purpose is to sell China economically to the United States government and the private sector."

Leonard Woodcock, American ambassador in Beijing, told me the previous evening's White House dinner was "a most gracious affair. But they didn't ask Carter," he added with a frown. Reagan invited Nixon and Ford, but not the ex-president who finalized normalization. Later, the Chinese phoned Carter and suggested he meet Zhao in New York. Perhaps Beijing realized that within 12 months, the White House could be occupied by Walter Mondale, Carter's vice-president, who was a leading candidate for the Democratic nomination. However, Carter, miffed, declined the invitation.

When Zhang Wenjin became ambassador in Washington in 1983, I wrote a welcoming letter. "We all know what a strong and helpful role you have played for many years in China's relations with the West," I said, "and you have come here at a very important time." Zhang wrote back recalling our talks going back to 1973 and saying he looked forward to contacts at Harvard and in Washington with an "old friend" such as myself.[7]

Zhang skillfully handled the period in which Reagan settled down and ultimately followed a successful policy toward China. I met Zhang several times in Washington and Boston. When *China Daily* began its North American edition in 1983, Jiang Muyue, publisher of the newspaper, held a party in New York to celebrate the occasion, with Ambassador Zhang as honored guest. I was delighted at this development since a newspaper of my home city, Melbourne's *Age*, had been the pioneering partner with Beijing in setting up *China Daily*.

One place where ideology lived on was Taipei. *Zhong yang ribao* put a negative spin on any report by me on China. It said I found mainland youth "unhappy with the extent of privilege" and that was true in part. However, the newspaper exaggerated the extent I expected Beijing would cancel the legacy of Mao, and expected American influence would fill the vacuum offered by a retreat from one-man rule. It was difficult for the KMT elite to see that China could evolve, that no system remains fixed in place.[8]

After the state-enforced honesty of the Mao era, some Americans were surprised to find Chinese people standing up for their interests and being assertive. One day in Shanghai, I ran into the Washington lawyer Eugene Theroux, who often worked on China cases. He was representing a U.S. client in the establishment of a production plant in the northeastern city of Shenyang. "The Chinese side quoted a price, which allowing for the cost of materials, equaled a labor cost of 35 yuan per hour per worker," Theroux said. "I walked away from it. The Chinese came back. A few days ago, I concluded an agreement at a price which works out to the Chinese workers receiving 7 yuan per hour." Theroux chuckled wearily. "Of course, the Chinese workers will never as individuals get most of that 7 yuan."

"We're still being ripped off," the attorney summed up, "but we're going ahead." That night in my Shanghai hotel room I wrote in my diary: "China, shrewd, proud, and still quite poor; but China does not expect to remain poor for long."

A former student of mine from Japan, now a diplomat in his country's embassy in Beijing, spoke of an experience his ambassador had while flying on CAAC, the Beijing state airline. A good speaker of Chinese, the envoy during a flight from Pakistan to Beijing asked the hostess in the first-class cabin in Mandarin for a drink. "She was apathetic to the point of being rude," the young diplomat said. "The Japanese ambassador asked again for the drink in English, and the hostess was all smiles and quickly fetched it."

A mix of assertiveness and self-doubt in the Chinese grew stronger as the 1980s wore on. My former student told me Japanese businessmen visiting Shanghai found themselves giving away more gifts than before. "One man from Tokyo presented a calculator to his Chinese host," he related, "and the Chinese said it was fine, except that he would prefer an alternative brand, with a larger size battery, which would be more convenient."

A young Chinese friend arrived in the US and declared: "I had been trying for so long to get to USA—four years—that the actual departure from Shanghai airport left me feeling nothing." He said, "In Boston the sky seemed so beautifully blue! In China I had never seen a sky like that!"

He continued with a tumble of impressions and emotions. "I prefer American people to Chinese people. They are open, they say what they feel." When my friend extended this admiration to American women, I asked why he wanted to bring his wife and baby daughter here.

"It is my duty."

"But your wife may think you now prefer American women to Chinese?"

"I would tell her! I mean, this is freedom. This is not China. You can speak your mind here."

Later he gave another reason for wanting to bring his family to the US: "I just don't want my daughter to be shaped by the narrow Chinese cultural world." His viewpoint made me think of May Fourth era Westernizers like Chen Duxiu, who thought the West's ideas would rescue China. A few years before, *chong yang* (worship the foreign) was a pejorative term. but now many Chinese students "worshipped the foreign." They had gone too far.

Admission to Harvard arrived for Wu Zhenzhou, who as a student in Tianjin had translated from English the first Chinese edition of *Mao*. Wu's father, when given the news, wrote to him, "To study abroad is exactly what a fine husband should do!" An uncle wrote, "The news of your admission is what I have been waiting for. As a Christian who studied theology in America for three years before 1949, I will pray for you with a sincere heart."

A young diplomat Meng (not his real name) arrived in Washington as chief aide to Ambassador Han Xu, who replaced Zhang Wenjin. In 1986, Meng visited Australia and found it a "marvelous country," he related as we reunited in Boston. On Chinese internal developments, Meng was fairly optimistic. "In the Boston area at present are concentrated some of the best minds of a new Chinese generation," he remarked of the city where he once studied. "They cannot fail to have a big impact on our nation's future." He says the biggest problem is the bureaucracy. "Haven't we heard that before?" I said with a smile.

Meng was more confident of Hong Kong's future than I was. "The Chinese government has gone about as far as it can go," he said. "I believe our present leaders are prepared to leave Hong Kong alone." I wondered.

Meng took the view that Hu Yaobang and Zhao Ziyang were a little different on the Soviet Union from Deng because they did not have Deng's bitter personal experience with the Russians. "Deng's passing will produce more openness to the Soviets."

Chinese people were flexing their muscles, whether at home or abroad. Many were not sure how free they could feel or how confident they could be about the future. It became a matter of an individual's past experience, or of her temperament, whether she smiled upon the new or frowned at the passing of the old. The state was beckoning normal social life into existence, but still under political supervision.

By the mid-1980s, U.S. and China dealt with each across a vast array of spheres. It was typical of the "normal" mood when the China Institute in America, based in New York, mounted a "1984 Chinese Film Festival." Held at the splendid Carnegie Cinema, it featured twenty-odd outstanding films from China, together with symposia on Chinese movies. I was pleased to serve on the Scholarly Advisory Board for the festival.[9]

A reader of *Flowers* who supplies strings for violins wrote about his worldwide quest for fine horsehair. "It is for use in violin bows," he explained. "I

must take note of climate and variations of hair from breed to breed of horse."
He had scoured Mongolia and Siberia and now wished my help in searching
western Sichuan and Tibet for suitable horses. Could I provide hair samples
from a dozen varied Sichuan horses? "The hair must be white, or nearly
white," he insisted.[10]

A reader named Jere Van Dyk wrote from New York about "mounting an
expedition to retrace the Silk Road route of Marco Polo across China." He
once worked for Senator Henry Jackson who pushed his proposal with Han
Xu, as did I when I got his letter. Van Dyk realized some of the difficulties
facing his plan. "I believe the Soviet invasion of Afghanistan is a factor
in the delay, along with natural Chinese reluctance to let foreigners travel
through their western reaches." However, American enthusiasm knew few
bounds. The New York adventurer spent three years trying to arrange his
repeat of Marco Polo's travels. He wrote presciently in a letter to me about
the complexity of the maneuvers involved: "Nothing, however is certain for
my project yet. But is it ever?"[11]

Dominican College in California, where I was a Council member, made
efforts to internationalize its energetic Catholic campus. Dean of the College
wrote in excitement in fall 1984. "Last Friday at 10.45 am Pan American
flight 12 from Beijing touched ground in San Francisco bringing Wu Xiao-
xin." Mr. Wu was the pioneer teacher of Chinese at Dominican College,
under the Exchange Visitor Program. "It was your thoughtfulness," wrote the
Dean generously to me, "that led to this connection." She said Mr. Wu had
only been at the college five days, "but it feels as though he's been one of us
for years, because we are a friendly place and his English is excellent."

The Dean gave an extra reason for her excitement: "I was a tiny child
of two or three years when my father was stationed in China on the U.S.S
Augusta. . .Tales of China were part of our household tradition. Mr. Wu is
bringing alive for me part of my heritage."[12]

Inevitably, academic China specialists became less influential in the assessment of China. As Americans once more lived in China, a lawyer residing
in Beijing, a newspaper correspondent writing human interest stories from
Shanghai, an Ohio businessman in a joint venture with a county government
in Sichuan Province, an artist on loan to a Chinese museum in Xian—all
might evaluate China no less competently than diplomats or professors of
Chinese studies at U.S. universities. The Western "China expert," disliked by
Beijing, was probably on the wane.

Joan Kennedy, divorced wife of Senator Kennedy, made a trip to China in
the spring of 1984, and on her return, I gave a dinner party with Fairbank,
his wife Wilma, the China journalist Fox Butterfield and some writer friends.

Joan recalled that in 1975 she had traveled to China with Ted, "and everything was formal." I had dined with the couple to brief them prior to that trip. However, in this 1984 trip, there was no Senator Kennedy, Joan was in charge, and music was the topic. She interviewed Chinese musicians, attended concerts, and learned about *pi-pa*, *er-hu*, and other age-old instruments.

As Joan bubbled over with impressions, Fairbank nodded gently at her points, not projecting his own views. Alas, at the end of the evening, the Fairbank's car had disappeared from beside my apartment. It took three days to get it back.

At a Harvard dinner, former defense secretary McNamara was chief guest to speak on "China's Way." The elegant dinner was essentially a fund-raiser with fat cats from business expected to open their wallets for Harvard. Physically a little shrunken from my first sight of him in the 1960s, McNamara was nevertheless sharp and confident. Before dinner I recalled to him the day during the Vietnam War when, as Secretary of Defense, he came to speak at Harvard and students jumped on his car shouting at him angrily. "We all learned something from it," he said uneasily.

After dinner of seafood bisque, swordfish, fruit pie with whipped cream, and champagne, McNamara rose to praise China's self-reliant policies. At question time, he was asked if a quarter of mankind could really hold back from interdependence, and if the world's problems could be alleviated should China stay in its shell. However, the comment was lost in the consensus that self-reliance was the greatest thing since sliced bread.

I felt McNamara condescended to the Chinese, as many Americans still did. He praised China for the material progress of gadgets in the kitchen. Yet the Chinese, like ourselves, possessed values, and loved freedom. Cassette recorders and fridges did not sum up life for them any more than for us. Surely, I felt, the future of China would hinge in part on how much internationalism tomorrow's China displayed.

Some of the fat cats told me during dinner they had read various of my books. Wealthy New York women, visiting Cambridge, tried not to look wealthy, but rather like ageing students; some carried green cloth book bags during the day. I suppose Harvard invited me—no longer a faculty member—to the fund-raiser because I was a draw card to affluent outsiders, not true of all current East Asian faculty.

Deng's China outdated McNamara's understanding. Although Deng matured in an era of civil and international war, he developed excellent instincts on economic development. He embraced the law of comparative advantage, a huge change in Beijing's economic policy. China must selectively use its strengths to export goods the world needed, he insisted, in exchange for foreign goods China needed. Chinese leaders learned this lesson as they traveled to Europe, the U.S., and Japan, observing the importance of international trade for developed countries. Autarchy would only hold China back, Deng and his lieutenants believed.

Deng also released the arts from their previous anti-intellectual straitjacket. During the Cultural Revolution, I wrote cynically in my diary at Dalian, after a visit to a theater and middle school, "One goes to the theater for political education, and one goes to a school for song and dance performances." Deng had a similar skepticism about Jiang Qing's theater pieces, saying, "The model operas nowadays are no more than gong-and-drum shows. Go to a theater and you find yourself on a battle-field." All this was laughed off in the 1980s.

Tragic as the Cultural Revolution was for China, it became a springboard for Deng to leap without qualms toward fresh thinking. As his premier put it: "We had missed many opportunities. We could not throw away another chance!"[13] Lee Kuan Yew told me that Deng, visiting Singapore early in the reform era, expressed rejection of China's 1960s ways and absolute commitment to bury them. "Marxism has failed in China," Deng told the Singapore leader.

Mao devised communism for China. Deng Xiaoping tried to save communism with one hand and bury it with the other. He built a China economically minded at home and nationalistic abroad. His way was to achieve a desired result without regard to image, theory, or elegance of method. He never was a diligent reader or given to philosophizing, but he displayed a knack for knowing what to do and what not to say. He once described his political style: "I cross the river by touching my feet against the stones, this one and that one, to keep my balance and get to the other side."

NOTES

1. Governor Brown, letter to author February 26, 1981; reply to Brown, March 1, 1981.

2. House of Representatives, Washington, September 23, 1980.

3. Author letter to Zhang Wenjin, August 22, 1980.

4. Author letter to Zhang Wenjin, October 3, 1980.

5. Prof Deanna Murray, letter to author, November 5, 1980.

6. Author letter to Lois Snow, July 15, 1983.

7. Author letter to Zhang Wenjin, April 18, 1983; Zhang Wenjin, letter to author, May 7, 1983.

8. *Zhong yang ribao*, Taipei, October 22, 1980.

9. Janet Yang, letter to author, September 21, 1983.
10. Stan Thurber, letter to the author, May 16, 1984.
11. Van Dyk, letter to the author, July, 29, 1981.
12. Dean Nimitz, letter to the author, September 19, 1984.
13. Zhao Ziyang, *Prisoner of the State*, New York, Simon & Schuster, 2009, 151.

Chapter Fifteen

Beyond the Mountains

Sichuan Province brought home the liveliness of grass roots Chinese society and showed that Beijing politics was not the totality of life in China. I wrote in my diary at Chengdu, the capital of the province, "Basic-level Chinese life will never lose its fascination: Endless ingenuity, unfussy rationality, a contrarian strain below the surface." The lush countryside with its blend of green (bamboo and other foliage), black (roofs and beams of the houses) and white (walls of the houses).

Sichuan was a "Texas of China," far from the nation's capital, pragmatic, artistic, good-humored, commercially-minded. I found in Sichuan an independence of spirit that issued in a-politicism, bluntness, and informality. At a welcoming dinner in Xichang, one of China's space centers, I mentioned that in my native Australia there were more sheep than people. "In Sichuan," rejoined my host, quick as a flash, "there are more pigs than people."

I visited more than half the counties of the province, leading to articles in *National Geographic*. Said the head of the province tourism authority at a dinner following the publication of one 1985 essay: "Those forty pages in *National Geographic* really helped us here in Sichuan!" This article was "Sichuan—China Changes Course." It was published in Chinese translation by the Sichuan Social Science Academy.[1]

On one trip in 1984, I set off for Sichuan from Beijing train station and shared a compartment with a military commander, born in the northeast but now serving in the southwest. I asked which of the four modernizations was the most important. "The economic one," he replied. I suggested defense seemed basic. "No," said the commander, "the purpose of defense is to defend China's economic development. Without economic results, there's nothing to protect."

In its vastness, Sichuan, like Texas, was a universe. From nature's wonders in Aba, to teeming Chongqing, to the religious mountains of Omei and Qing Shan, to Chengdu with its oil painting artists, to the hanging coffins of the Bo minority high above the Yangzi River. In Zigong, home of the salt industry, the dishes tasted salty; in Neijiang, a sugar-producing area, everything was sweet. In Mianyang, lunch was chicken's stomach; in western Sichuan, bear's paws.

One night at a banquet in Chengdu, I said to my host, "It's difficult for a foreign writer to understand China." She rejoined with a sigh, "Sometimes it's difficult for the rest of China to understand Sichuan." I soon learned that by "the rest of China" she had in mind Beijing and Guangdong.

In 1985, Minister Ji Zhaozhu in Washington complained that I was "hostile to China." I explained I was an independent intellectual who had to seek the facts as available. "I am sure you realize that a captive intellectual is a worthless item," I wrote to Ji. The cooperation within Sichuan was much greater than in Washington. It was appreciated in the province, that President Reagan chose to present Premier Zhao Ziyang with bound volumes of *National Geographic* during his visit to China in April 1984.[2]

I asked an official at the valley of grottos in Dazu which impact was greater, that of Buddhism or Marxism. "Old people believe in Buddhism," he replied. "Some young people in Marxism, many young people believe in nothing."

"Can people go on believing nothing for a long time?" I asked.

"Yes, I think so."

Stunning Tibetan tapestries distinguished the Sichuan Museum. The curator himself brought them down from Beijing to Chengdu. "Found in the province, they should be preserved within the province," he declared. Of course, Tibetans might feel that the wonderful artifacts, found in Aba, should find a home in Tibet.

"We used to think bronze making was from central China during the Shang Dynasty and the Zhou Dynasty," said the curator, "but now it looks as if it was mostly in Sichuan." As we walked by superb jade and a walking stick inlaid with gold leaf, he remarked, "These things go further back than the five religions of the world. Even Japan sent reporters to look."

The curator summed up: "Now we know Chinese civilization is not just one group, that at a certain time, we can call Han." A special role certainly belonged to Sichuan.

Amidst the Buddhist world of Omei Mountain, one enters an all-encompassing religious community. On both Omei and Qing Shan mountains, one Buddhist and one Daoist, you find great areas essentially appropriated by private religious organizations. The local travel director tried to counter my surprise:

"Myself, I was amazed that so many New Yorkers turned out to see the Pope on his visit to the USA."

On Qing Shan, I met a sixty-four-year-old Daoist named Wang. A fountain of maxims, he taught Daoist doctrine. Also, Chinese classical literature, which he said was "necessary to understand the Daoist sutras."

I asked Wang about the effect of the reforms on Daoism. "It has brought prosperity to the monks and the monasteries," he replied, puffing on a cigarette. "As the farmers prosper, we do too." Classes are financed by small tea and wine factories, restaurants, and tourist fees at the mountain.

"Many people exaggerate *qi gong*'s power," Wang said candidly of China's famous breathing and stretching regimen. "It can't change objective rules of the universe, but it can adjust your inner organs according to nature. My case is clear. Yesterday I had a check-up and they said I have the body of a 50-year old. I climb Qing Shan without difficulty."

I asked Wang about Marxism. "I have learned from Hegel's philosophy and from Marx on political economy," he replied, "but the utopian aspects, such as Engels on family and property, I have not yet grasped."

"Who has grasped these?" I asked.

"Maybe our leaders have." I wondered if Wang felt Marxism was for the leaders to figure out and Daoism was correct for the people.

"I favor direction from the leaders," he said evenly, "but independent thinking by the people."

Were any CCP leaders influenced by Daoism? "Central Committee Secretariat leader, Xu Zhongxun, said Daoism is one of China's finest traditions," Wang responded. "In Mao's four volumes of essays, there are seven citing's of Lao Zi."

When we ate lunch Wang said, "Don't stand on ceremony, be comfortable." He took off his jacket and poured himself a beer. "I visited Japan and the ceremony nearly killed me. At the banquets I couldn't eat, so uptight I was with the nodding, bowing, and ritual words." He talked on as we munched leaves and drank tea. He laughed. "My director said to me, 'No more foreign guests for you, you talk too much.'"

I asked Wang if Daoism is an international religion. "As long as a person is happy, and makes others happy," he responded, "there is no boundary among states."

"Happiness is the best medicine," Wang declared. "Better than exercise, better than *qi gong*. Being happy, I never get sick," he said as we strolled after lunch. We talked about sex; Wang said, "The East has too little, the West too much. We should find a middle ground."

He recalled the Cultural Revolution: "I was framed as a useless person, but it didn't make me gloomy. Many people died of gloominess at that time."

In those years, the only books Wang had access to were on herbs and Mao's writings. Which were the most valuable? "Mao's you couldn't neglect—anyway, Mao didn't write all those by himself. We called his works *xiong da*, so great and wonderful—we were being sarcastic." In a play on the word *xiong*, Wang went on: "You have to get back to wife and kids to attain balance." (*xiong* and *nan*)

What exactly did Lao Zi mean, I inquired, with his remark about how to cook a small fish? The founder of Daoism said ruling a large kingdom should be like cooking a small fish. "Not too much stirring, as you'd do for a soup," Wang said. "A small fish cannot take turbulence. All this goes for ruling society too. And for the needs of the body."

Wang saw death as a return to nature. "Buddhists stress a paradise after death, but Daoists pay all their attention to life before death. Being alive, living, is the stress of Chinese religion." He coughed and spluttered. "A French Daoist gave me these Western [Citane] cigarettes. I'm not used to them."

As I made ready to leave, Wang had advice. "Crying will not bring you a meal," he said. "Life is full of happiness and joy. You don't have to ask for trouble and worry." He proposed we both live to one hundred and twenty years and then greet each other again with a handshake."

"Where will we meet?"

"In my room on Qing Shan, where I'll make magic medicines. By then, I'll be a master of Daoism—we'll both become divine."

I attended mass at the Catholic cathedral in Chengdu. 400 worshippers, grand ritual, slow singing. Religion is a massage for the individual soul and a social need following doubts about Marxism. My gaze hit on two young women, kneeling in prayer, tresses of gleaming black hair slanted across the forehead. Eyes closed, brows knitted in concentration. The Catholic faith, like the Protestant, claimed more Chinese people than at any time since Liberation.

The Yi minority, strong in Yunnan and Sichuan, was pushed into barren hills by the stronger Han race centuries ago. "A horse cannot have two riders," runs a saying on these chilly slopes. Unfortunately, the slogan captures the history of Han dealings with Yi, China's fourth-largest ethnic minority. Tension long existed over territory and culture.

"Don't cry or the Yi will come and get you," Chinese traditionally said to their children in these parts. "Don't cry or the Han will chop off your ears," some Yi parents told their kids. The Yi are famous, or notorious in China for female domination over males.

In the Yi town of Zhaojue, females sparkled with embroidery on their shoes, bags, and headbands. As Vice-Mayor An strode toward me in welcome, he swished his gray pleated cape to one side. He supplied me with a heavy blue cape against the cold. Spherical shapes by rural roads turned out to be capes hiding a woman sitting with a child at her neck, or a farmer squatting at rest after the day's labor. In towns, on the pavements, a human form often resembled a coat rack.

At the town telephone office, I made a call to Hong Kong. Twenty people gathered round in fascination. "We have never had a call to Hong Kong before," whispered the charming telephonist. The term "Third World" came up in conversation. The vice-mayor said quietly, "Here we really are a Fourth World."

Young Yi like to marry within their race. Whenever possible, a young man marries the offspring of his father's sister or mother's brother. "We are fussy as to kinship," explained Vice-Mayor An. "We are not so romantic as to marry strangers." Still, An predicted that Yi culture would eventually melt away. "Some of its good customs will remain, if people want them—loyalty to friends, the language, hospitality to guests." Brightly colored capes may give way to Chinese tunics, "except on holidays." An offered me as a parting gift a boiled pig's head, hard-boiled eggs, a slab of lamb, and red and yellow wooden spoons that the Yi use instead of chopsticks.

The mood of the later 1980s was vivid across Sichuan. "Everyone Has a Responsibility" said a billboard by the road from Chongqing to Dazu, home to Buddhist rock carvings. "Settle Down and Have a Child," said an inscription at a temple in Changlin. Jeans and shirts in brilliant colors brightened small villages. "Obey the Law, Learn about the Law" was a common admonition.

At Mianyang Silk Factory, I asked the director if she approved of the idea adopted in Wuhan, according to newspapers, of having a foreign director for some enterprises. "Yes, I do," she quickly replied.

"But doesn't that reflect badly on China, to do that? Aren't Chinese just as good as foreigners?"

"Not in managerial experience."

Mao-period values lost out to Deng-period values. At the Lantern Festival in Chongqing, on an ice cream and soda stand, I found "Serve the People" redone as "We Serve You!" Nearby was a bookstand with the slogan, "Knowledge is Power," making a bridge from the impulse to study for the sake of the revolution, to study to make China and yourself successful.

A dancing fad hit Chengdu. Venues were a riot of soaring music, faces shining with excitement, and sartorial incongruity. At one dance in a one-time exhibition hall, young men with long hair wore striped ties and Texas-style hats. Women had cloth butterflies tied to the back of their hair. Musicians in three-piece suits with orange ties mounted a platform, fingers drumming and feet tapping as if they could hardly bear to wait for their first song.

Hundreds stood in line on a staircase. Some came direct from the job, in overalls or farmers' boots. Behind the bandstand, Marx, Engels, Lenin and Stalin stared down from dark frames across the dance floor.

More people came in from the staircase to occupy three rows of chairs by each wall. The room was filling by the minute. "Dancing fever," murmured my Chengdu friend "You can't delay," Xu said tersely, "they're only allowed to sell 300 tickets and hundreds of people are waiting on the staircase." Youth in army uniforms, *qipaos,* mini-skirts crowded in. We hardly had time to reach the chairs, still clutching our glasses, when tango music began and couples, about a quarter of them dancing same-sex, gathering before the dance band like ants around sugar.

"Dance with me ?" a grinning man asked me. Girls hovered noiselessly by posing the same question with their eyes. But Yang grabbed my arm. "Did you know the prettiest girls in China are from Anhui Province?" It's a well known prejudice, yes.

"What's the point?

"I have some downstairs. 10 Yuan. Or 20 Yuan for the night. OK?"

When Shen Chunyi came from Beijing, one evening in Chengdu he saw a young woman being booked by a traffic policeman at an intersection. Always inquisitive, Shen went over to listen. Before he could say anything, the cop booked him 2 yuan for walking out to the traffic island. We were ordered to the police station. Shen objected that in Beijing, even going against a red light warranted only 1 yuan. "Things are different in different places," said the cop. Shen hit back, "You're charging me a black-market price, that's what you're doing!"

Another time we dined with a former student of Shen's who worked in a bank. She liked Chengdu better than Beijing. "Vegetables are better here," she said. "And things are closer together. In Beijing I had to ride a bus two hours to work." I asked the young banker what were the main problems in the city. "Wages don't keep pace with prices," she said without a smile, "and the pressure to own something foreign is terrible."

Shen criticized Mao at the dinner table. Said the female banker, "Don't pick on a dead man." She thought Mao was a great personality. Deng was good for China, she admitted, but he was too shrewd. "Look at the way he got rid of Hua Guofeng." Later, Shen told me the banker's point of view was probably influenced by her father; he came from the same county as Hua. "You can't spend your whole life eating vegetables," Shen whispered to me.

Shen met a pretty, brightly-painted young lady who came back to his room at the Chengdu Hotel one afternoon. At dinner, Shen told me she explained

Figure 15.1. Shen Chunyi (second left) and author at Zigong Lantern Festival, Sichuan Province, 1986. Author's photo.

she was a virgin and could not do much. Shen suggested one or two things. "Why do you want me to do that?" she inquired. Said Shen as we ate, "She really didn't know much." He replied to the girl, "Well, the Americans do it that way." After they finished, she said to him, "Of course, you're in foreign languages. I suppose Chinese in foreign languages become rather open-minded."

That night Shen, a Beijinger, remarked, "Sichuan women may not be elegant, but they're straightforward and self-reliant."

In the grimy *Jin Niu* (Golden Cow) section of Chengdu, I sat in a district court, huddled in an overcoat, as Judge Tan Changhua, in a blue uniform with red epaulets, cried, "Bring in the defendant." Xiang Jiachuan, aged 25, a thin farmer in khaki pants, blue jacket, and cloth shoes, slouched to his place. Some 200 spectators jammed the gallery to hear charges of stabbing and robbery. In the center of the court chamber sat a jacket with stab holes in it, a shattered wristwatch, a bloodstained shirt, and a pork butcher's chopper.

Judge Tan, whose career prior to reform was entirely within the police force, like most judges, boomed out instructions. If Xiang didn't like his attorney, he could find another (as provided in article 27 of the Criminal

Code) . . . If Xiang thought any member of the court was prejudiced against him, he was free to bring forth proof of that prejudice (article 24) . . . The defense attorney had the right to challenge any prosecutor's accusation (article 114) . . .

Xiang had a criminal record. Back in 1981 he stole, and went to prison for three years. A few weeks after his release, before he could resume work as a farmer, he encountered a pork peddler in his home village of Gaojia. After drinking *xiang bin* (sparkling wine), he stumbled down a riverbank and dropped his bicycle into the shallow water. "I said to Yan the pork peddler," Xiang testified, "get my bike and I'll sell the pork for you while you do it." Yan said it was too cold to go into the river to fetch the bike.

"I killed a pig that day," began pork peddler Yan when he was called to the witness stand, "and took the meat to my usual selling spot by a bamboo grove. Xiang asked me to fetch his bike. When I refused, he stabbed me in the back."

The court learned that the day after Xiang's attack on the pork peddler, a police officer arrived and accused him of the assault. "I offered to pay for Yan's medical costs," Xiang told the court. "I was afraid. Being just out of prison, I thought I'd get extra punishment for this thing with Yan. So, I bought a knife."

"Why?" asked Judge Tan, gently.

"To kill myself." A muffled collective gasp rose from the spectators.

"Why didn't you do so?"

Xiang replied softly, "I didn't want to die. And I thought, I want to kill Yan before I kill myself."

A few weeks later, a Ms. Liao and a Mr. Zhou, two members of an entourage around Xiang, sat down with Xiang to talk in a teahouse on the outskirts of Gaojia. "They advised me to hide in the house of a friend," Xiang related.

The judge interrupted, "Why didn't you?"

"I told Liao and Zhou, all my friends were in jail. There was no one left to go to." After much drinking, Xiang ended up "borrowing" the watch of his companion Zhou. Soon an argument flared and Xiang became angry and took out a knife. Zhou ran away, leaving his bike, which Xiang took. Judge Tan broke in. "Did you ask for Zhou's watch, or did you borrow it, or did you steal it?"

From the defendant came a flash of candor. "Asking, borrowing, taking more or less the same." Laughter erupted across the room.

"I felt he was a nuisance so I took my knife to him," Xiang went on. More laughter broke the tension. Judge Tan asked Xiang where Zhou's watch was now. Xiang sold it in the county town Xindu. Wretched Xiang offered another flash of candor. "I'd stolen the bike—that was going to be reported to the police," he said. "I felt I might as well be killed for a sheep as a lamb and have a watch as well."

"My plan was to kill [pork peddler] Yan," Xiang continued, "but on the way to Yan's I changed my mind. My heart softened. I thought, it can't have been easy for Yan's mother to bring him up . . ." A muffled murmur rose in the gallery.

Xiang said he went to a teahouse, where he drank more than tea, then mounted Zhou's bike and headed for a nearby village. He collided with another cyclist, Yang, who was on his way home from shift work at a cement factory. Both Yang and Xiang fell to the ground. Xiang asked Yang to pick up his bike, holding a flashlight to his face with one hand and a long knife in the other.

According to the prosecutor, Yang, in tears, picked up Xiang's bike. According to Xiang, Yang refused, saying, "You knocked me over, you pick it up yourself." Xiang took out a knife and stabbed Yang in the head.

The defense attorney, He Chunyi, whose salary, like Tan's, came from the law department of Jin Niu district, in no essentials differed from the judge, who in turn followed the line of the prosecutor. Attorney He told me with a shrug after the court adjourned, "Xiang was guilty of everything."

When the court reassembled, a smiling Judge Tan pulled out a prepared statement and announced that the defendant was guilty of robbery and assault. Ten years in prison, and no appeal permitted.

I sent a note in Chinese to Judge Tan asking to interview the convicted man, and soon Xiang was before me and guards took off his handcuffs. "Do you regret what you have done?" I asked. "Yes, I do," Xiang replied sadly. His father died when he was 11, he told me. He had five brothers and two sisters, a huge family for the reform era.

Over a lunch of *dan dan mian* (spicy noodles) and other dishes at Chengdu Hotel, I asked Judge Tan's opinion on why Xiang went off the rails. "Many reasons," the judge replied. "He was brought up in the Gang of Four period when schools were poor. He didn't learn a lesson from his first imprisonment. And when he got out and went back to Gaojia, people discriminated against him as an ex-prisoner, which made him bitter."

"What's the opinion of China specialists in the U.S. at present," Judge Tan asked me as we rose to leave the dining room. I replied, "Some say there's a tension between economic reforms and the political system." The judge rejoined, "No, the economic reforms take place on the basis of the socialist system." Of course, time would be needed to test this proposition.

At a lively basement cafe in Chengdu, sprawling rooms with low couches were packed with young men in black jackets with small mustaches and women with powdered faces and fancy hairdos.

"After the economic reforms," explained Li Pingfen, founder of West China Coffee House, "people's lives got richer and they needed more things to do." Early in 1984, Li raised 130,000-yuan capital, 80,000 of it from friends and organizations, 50,000 yuan from his own funds, profits from a soft drink business he started on the side. "West China" opened, a child of the reform era. By 1985 the takings had risen to 1500 yuan a day, and 10 per cent of that was profit. The coffee house, a completely private outfit, was employing 38 people.

The talk over coffee or Sichuan beer on the cafe's soft couches was about culture or private life, seldom about politics. When I mentioned this impression to Li, he looked pleased and said, "You're right. This is a pleasant, relaxing place. Who'd want to talk politics here?" "West China" had caught the spirit of the times.

In the fall of 1988, visiting Sichuan for a *National Geographic* article, I checked on the progress of Li Pengfen and his coffee house. I was surprised to find chicken bones on the floor, shabby couches, and candles sitting in mugs to assist the dim electric bulbs. "We met heavy competition," Li said with a wry smile. "Other new coffee houses put in beautiful fittings, offered live music, and kept their prices down."

Crucially, Chengdu's big tourist hotel, the nearby Jin Jiang, tried to put "West China" out of business by having it incorporated into the hotel. "How petty," said Li. "A vast hotel worrying about a small cafe! Jin Jiang Hotel relies on the state; we rely on ourselves."

Income at "West China" had plummeted from a peak of 2000 yuan a month to 600 yuan, and staff was down from 38 to 26. In a declining situation, Li in 1987 turned his attention from the coffee house to a beverage and candy enterprise owned by Guanghan County, not far from Chengdu, that was near bankruptcy.

Li and associates stepped in on contract with Guanghan County to try to turn the business around. In their first year, gross output approached 3 million yuan, and 10 per cent of that was profit for Li and his couple of helpers. He reaped nearly 300,000 yuan for his planning and management efforts.

On China's economic experience in the later 1980s, Li Pingfen had mixed views. "Yes, priority has at last been given to economic development," he said, "but the methods are flawed. The environment still isn't favorable to business. China's not giving full play to individual talents."

Li made a comparison with the United States. "In your country, fairness of the laws is very important," he said. "In the New Deal, Roosevelt stressed that competition must be equal competition." Here in China, Li saw tax dodging, backdoor deals, and undue influence. He shrugged his shoulders as he addressed the issue (I did not believe Li himself would lack ability at back door deals and using networks of influence if necessary!).

"I just don't like it," he said. "One reason for not setting up any more shops or cafes is that to make a profit you have to break two laws: price laws and tax laws. That's why I went to Guanghan." Li represented a new variety of people in China, who, from their own experience in business, had vividly learned what was wrong with old-style socialist management.

Sichuan officials spoke of problems candidly. "We just don't know what a 'planned commodity economy' will look like!" confessed Xiao Yang, mayor of Chongqing, in late 1988. He pronounced the words "planned" and "commodity" with an emphasis suggesting contradictory ideas thrust together. "In the countryside people build huge houses, but put little in them," remarked the mayor, "whereas in cities people snap up appliances but no expenditure goes on a house and rents are derisory." Under China's planned system, I wondered, could urban housing really be made a commodity, instead of a highlysubsidized freebie?

The heart of the problem of Deng's reforms, and the reason for the mixed mood, was that the revolution set in place a Leninist political system, while reform sought a commodity economy—and the two don't mix.

Xiao Yang, who had been a classmate at Qinghua University with my Washington friend, Van Lung, son of ex-warlord Long Yun, was bothered by an inflation rate above 20 per cent, a shock for people used to prices as flat as the Gobi Desert. People talked much of housing and food costs. One friend in Chengdu cursed farmers for selling so much of their produce at private markets. "It drives prices up," she lamented. Xiao Yang acknowledged with regret that dealing with inflation required delay in deregulation of prices and a cutting back of investment.

"We just have to solve the present problem, then later we'll move forward again," the mayor said. Contemplating the shift from ideology to economic development, I wrote in my diary at Chongqing: "Allocating resources can be just as exacting as catching the bright butterflies of Marxist polemic."

The next day *Chongqing ribao* (Chongqing Daily) reported, "Yesterday afternoon, Mayor Xiao Yang met the American friendly personage (*meiguo youhao renshi*) and well-known author (*zhuming zuojia*) Ross Terrill." The newspaper referred to my previous visits to Sichuan in 1984 and 1985 and my writings that introduced the foreign world to Chongqing's *gai ge* (reform) achievements.[3]

In Sichuan, some workers received a bonus in the form of shares in the capital stock of their factory. "An ownership system of shareholding is just right for our situation now," said Sichuan vice governor Pan Haiqing in Chengdu. "It reduces interference in industry by the state. It's better for the initiative of the workers." Pan, a former engineer, added a startling tribute to the role of shareholding in breaking down equality. "Though we've been trying to 'break the iron rice bowl,' in fact distribution has remained very egalitarian. The share system will bring a welcome change."[4]

After Deng commercialized the countryside, households leased land under contract and operated it like private land. "If the contract system is working so well in the countryside," I asked Wang Gaolong, an official in *Jin Ma* county near Chengdu, "why lay down that a contract can last only for 20 years?" Wang looked at once vehement and confused. He replied, "We won't stop at 20 years . . . not necessarily!"

Pressure of events led the CCP to a clever stance at its 13th congress in 1987. Party general secretary Zhao Ziyang stated that China was only at the "preliminary stage of socialism," which justified small business, family farming, and shareholding. This fancy phrase pushed socialism ahead to a vague future. It was akin to saying the preliminary stage of sleeping is being wide awake.

"Marxism isn't suitable for China," Lin Ling of the Sichuan Academy of Social Science said with agitation at the end of 1988. Perhaps wary of his own conviction, he adjusted the point: "Of course, one day it will be." I thought of the famous Christian prayer, "Lord make me chaste, but not yet."

During the early 1980s, Beijing neither banned small business nor publicized it. But in 1987 the Communist Party publicly stated, "the existence [of individual enterprise] is allowed." Clever zig-zags were the name of the game. Although China's rulers knew that communism had run dry as a fount for future policy, and in economic policy had their feet on an un-Marxist path, they were still China's rulers. They were not about to step aside for non-Leninist alternative rulers.

Journeys though Sichuan brought some of my happiest times in China. National Tourism Administration of the PRC awarded me a Certificate of Honor for writing about Deng's native province, as well as a beautiful blue silk tablecloth. The gold and red certificate hangs in pride of place on my study wall, and the silk cloth graces my dining table. The National Tourism spoke of my "contribution to the development of tourism in China and to "enhancement of understanding and friendship between the Chinese people and people of the world." China and the world had made real progress in just a decade!

NOTES

1. *National Geographic*, September 1985; *Shehui kexue yanjiu cankao zi liao*, Chengdu, July 5, 1986 and August 15, 1986.

2. Author letter to Ji, February 2, 1985.

3. *Chongqing ribao*, November 6, 1988.

4. Interview with "famous American writer," *Sichuan ribao*, October 27, 1988.

Chapter Sixteen

Agonized Years, Late 1980s

My physician friend in Shanghai, Dr. Dong, one of Zhou Enlai's doctors, remarked, "Recent years have been more encouraging than anything I remember. We have waited a long time for China to change and improve." That evening, he was preparing for a banquet with a delegation of cardiovascular surgeons from San Francisco. The cultural exchanges with the West pleased him greatly.

Dong was medical consultant to the American airline Pan Am. He was the one Chinese physician authorized by the American Federal Aviation Administration to investigate immediately should an American plane have an accident within Chinese territory. "I went through a training course at Oklahoma City," he explained. "I know just what to do. I would have the authority to employ people, to get blood tests out of surviving passengers and so on."

Dr. Dong said the post-Mao leadership in Shanghai was fairly enlightened. But in anything to do with him, they refer to Beijing, because Dong is a member of the People's Political Consultative Conference.

If he wants to go abroad, they have to refer "north" for a decision. Does he think China can maintain prosperity in Hong Kong after Britain leaves? "Yes, under the present leaders, as distinct from the ones they're getting rid of."

Of course, Dong is a doctor, not a political analyst. He's not a Party man. He's been through the mill as an intellectual, and so have his children. One of his daughters spent ten years cleaning windows, getting her hands frost bitten. All of his children, he said, lost ten years of their lives.

Dong seems to be respected across China because of the role he played in the last year of Zhou's life. People know about it, and it gives him an aura in some circles. Does he operate on any high officials? "About once a week." He looked at his watch. "I must get back soon because there's an operation in progress and I should be there to look for the last few minutes." As Dong jumped into a taxi he called out, "Come back tomorrow!"

I suppose, when you reach the top, that's the way you behave. Still, one thought of the poor person being operated on, and how any patient would want Dong there, making sure everything was right. Instead he was ready to entertain me and even take me shopping!

In Dong's bookcase was a postcard of the grand Exhibition Building in Melbourne. One day, I asked about it. "Oh, I'm sorry to say that involves a story of my former son-in-law. He turned out to be a homosexual. He married my daughter here in Shanghai and then she came to me and said she still was a virgin." It turned out the son-in-law was sleeping with a seventeen-year-old boy in Shanghai. Dr. Dong said to the daughter, just seek a divorce, which she did. The ex-son-in-law, a pianist, studied at the Music Academy at Melbourne; hence the postcard.

I asked whether in the long-term China would go the way of the West and Japan in terms of social trends. "In the long run, but it's going to be very slow, unfortunately." I had in mind corrupting forces, also. I asked if recent social trends in Taiwan and Japan might appear in China. I instanced the increase in homosexuality.

This seemed an absolute blank for him. He didn't know about homosexuality in Taiwan and Japan.

He said as we got into the taxi and drove to my Peace Hotel, "Homosexuality must be some sickness of the mind. Anyway, my daughter now has an American boyfriend and we hope they will marry."

In Cambridge at a Nieman Foundation party, I meet Liu Binyan, a prominent journalist and author, now optimistic on China's future, flecked with anxiety. His face is stately, owl-like. He holds his cigarette as a Hong Kong businessman does. "Nearly everyone in China is pessimistic, but I am not," he says. "China has two advantages compared with Russia. The Cultural Revolution scared everyone off the leftist path forever. The reforms have gone on a decade already, and much experience has been gained." I pointed out that on the other side of the ledger, economic levels in China are far below those in Russia; to the degree economic attainment precedes political change, that gives Moscow the edge.

Unscripted friendships with Chinese individuals were a bonus from reform and normalization. Chinese students at campuses in the West quickly rose to 10,000. Living quite near me in Boston were the son of Huang Hua and a daughter of Liu Shaoqi. In the other direction, Western academic and commercial units had connections in Beijing, Shanghai, Nanjing, Chengdu,

Dalian, Xian and other cities. Within China, communication between Chinese and foreigners became easier.

Yet, I noticed the frequency of the phrase, "Conditions are not there for it" (*meiyou tiaojian*). whether in China's situation or in personal life. In TV dramas, there was often a strain of fatalism. A woman was in distress because she turned thirty years old! "Privilege" (*te quan*) was criticized but in a spirit of what-can-you-do-about-it.

Writers moved away from works about correcting injustice to introspective works. Zhang Jie's successful novel *Heavy Wings* left the impression that socialist society did not necessarily make people happy. External forms of any kind were not of final importance, the novelist implied in her account of life at an auto plant in Beijing. New issues and grievances came to the fore. In *Heavy Wings*. Zheng Ziyun's daughter rebels against her tedious mother. "I didn't ask to be born," she rails when mother reminds daughter she has been fed and clothed for years. "People who want children have a duty to raise them. I don't owe you a thing!"

Another character in the novel. He Jiabin, seeks to comfort his mother who is disappointed with the world around her: "It's because we're living in a society that's neither capitalist nor socialist, neither fish nor fowl" he suggests, "where everything can be interpreted one way or the other. Nothing's ever made clear." I wrote in my review of the novel in *Washington Post*: "Zhang Jie has caught a moment of transition from a tame populace to a skeptical populace."

Still, the tame era was favored by an older worker in the novel. The ardent days of the Great Leap Forward were the happiest of his life. People "pulled together and worked as one," in that politics-as-religion period. "Every day, people as if in a military parade, crowded into Tiananmen Square, chests thrust forward, marching onward, arms swinging proudly, all united in their mission." For this old worker, "it all went downhill after that, as everyone began undermining Chairman Mao's revolutionary line."[1]

My old friend Zhou Nan, after years at the UN Mission in New York, was back in Beijing as vice foreign minister. He had filled out but in style he was unchanged.

"How are you, Ross?" he cried with a grand gesture and a broad smile. Zhou Nan knew about the Jiang Qing book and insisted I send him a copy.

"What's this notion of Secretary of State Schultz that China is just a regional country?" he asked, growing sterner. I told him Paul Wolfowitz, later to play an important role in the second Bush administration, had inspired this idea. Paul persuaded Schultz that China did not yet have the "weight" to be part of the "triangle" envisaged by Washington in the 1970s.

Little theory entered Zhou Nan's remarks. I remarked that China no longer called the Soviet Union "a revisionist country or speaks of capitalist restoration there." Replied Zhou: "We are only interested in their foreign policy—we don't like that. They are the main threat to peace."

On China's domestic situation Zhou Nan expressed satisfaction with rural reforms. "There's a new buoyancy in the villages," he said. Clearly the next challenge was reform in urban China. A few days after our talk, I ran into Jack Service, the former diplomat who had lived in pre-Liberation China. He was just back from Yunnan and other parts of the southwest. "The countryside is prosperous," he pronounced with enthusiasm, "especially the free market activity. It's like the old days!"

Zhou Nan stressed the technology transfer problem in US-China relations. Within the category of "friendly country," America had three subdivisions and Zhou Nan said China was discriminated against within this category. He said unless the offensive Taiwan Relations Act is repealed, there will be future serious crises in U.S.-China relations. I said I was more worried about Hong Kong, because in this case there's a date looming.

Zhou Nan was optimistic about Hong Kong, telling a story from a dinner in New York to buttress his belief. "Our foreign minister had dinner with [secretary of state] Vance and [secretary of defense] Schlesinger," he related. "Schlesinger said to Huang Hua that if he was in British shoes he would accept immediately the terms China was offering. Vance had the same opinion."

Zhou Nan said the sovereignty of Hong Kong was not negotiable. "We'll leave the economic system unchanged. We'll change the legal system just a little to accommodate those things—a high court appeal to London—that are part of the colonial structure." I told Zhou Nan I wasn't worried about the British, but about the five million people in Hong Kong, and the image of China in the world if these people, rightly or wrongly, let their uncertainty turn to panic. "Many may leave," I suggested.

Zhou Nan said: "If some run away there'll be plenty more to come there".

"What about the Cantonese dialect being replaced with Mandarin?"

"Look, if we can't do that in Canton (Guangzhou), we're not going to be able to do it very quickly in Hong Kong".

As the government asked less in the ideological realm, private business, personal attachments, and religion came to the fore. In urban China especially, with Western influence and commercial opportunities, the individual pushed out from political and cultural collectivism. Sun Muzhi, the student whom we met in Chapter Five, said to me after reading my articles on foreign policy in 1982 and 1983: "They were interesting. But why don't you write love stories and stories about ordinary people?"

Figure 16.1. Author with Sun Muzhi near Forbidden City, Beijing, 1989. Author's photo.

"We knew that in the West a hug leads on to sex," Shen Chunyi said of the assumptions of his upbringing. "But we regarded it as a capitalist activity." Australia had adjusted his view of capitalism. Shen told me he and a young lady spent the night in a room that belonged to a teacher friend who hardly used it. The next morning Shen said to himself: "Is it really so easy?"

Shen was a rebel at his institute. Fitzgerald, the former Australian ambassador in Beijing, wrote me in November, 1980: "Shen is in a slightly delicate position, having been warned by his institute that he must not have contact with anyone from the Australian embassy, or with myself, without first seeking approval." Fitzgerald went on, "He had one or two run-ins with the [teachers'] institute leadership on this issue, which he argues is an infringement of his rights." Shen said his boss's refusal to increase his salary was "unconstitutional." He threatened to take the institute to court![2]

Visiting Shen again in 1983, when I was traveling on the Royal Viking Star cruise ship to lecture to European and American passengers, I found teachers and students at his institute no longer had to write essays celebrating the fall of Gang of Four. "All that's gone," Shen said with a grin as he reflected on the shift from ideology.

Like other young Chinese friends, on initial return from the West, Shen was unhappy with the situation in China, but later settled down and modified his awe for the West. At first, he criticized Deng Xiaoping: "He says to cross the river by touching the stones, but we don't know the shape of the stones." But later he was more accepting of hard realities. "If we try to get rid of communism, we'll make matters worse," Shen summed up. "I think we have to hope for an evolution toward a liberalized situation." He railed against "bureaucrats," but not against the political system itself, and he spoke of "limits" to what the Chinese should hope for. "You know, Wei Jingsheng's ringing appeal for democracy probably wasn't helpful. If China voted today, Wei would lose, Deng would win."

Shen and I went shopping in Wangfujing and came upon a book store. I said I didn't want to see the politics section, "because it will all be propaganda." Shen looked at me sharply and said, "You've changed a bit." He too had changed; some of the nationalism of the Deng era had rubbed off on him.

A young friend in the foreign ministry, Meng (not his real name) had just returned from Tufts University in Boston. "I think my boss thinks I'm too pro-American," he said as we dined at the Huadu Hotel. I asked him whether the hard-core alligators are really more patriotic than he. Are they serving China better than cosmopolitan Chinese are?" Well, discussion of the new constitution was "a sheer farce," Meng grumbled. "No one says anything about what's wrong with it, only how glorious it is." But, like Shen Chunyi, Meng was doing well at work (as I write in 2019, he is a Chinese ambassador in Asia-Pacific).

I was gripped by a similar dualism as my Chinese friends. I wrote an article in *Atlantic Monthly*, "Trying to Make China Work," much reprinted, that praised the reforms yet also made complaints.[3] My foreign ministry friend Meng declared of the article: "You criticize things in 1983 that are actually better than they were before—and you didn't criticize them before! The courtesy campaign is excellent. Why are you grudging about that?"

"But please keep writing about China," Meng said. "Send a letter to Hu Yaobang. Don't make requests for this or that, like you did about research on Mao and Jiang Qing. Tell him how you see China's future. Then he's more likely to listen to you." He paused to take chicken with peanuts. "If they don't pay attention to you, who understands China and is fair to China, who would they take notice of?"

I heard on all sides that material well-being is all that matters for China now. "Is that the Number One priority?" I asked Meng. "No, of course not," he replied. "In a socialist society the most important thing is that everyone enjoys the power to exercise his rights as master of the country." He was sharp about China's current condition: "Now, I'm afraid, we have a combination of feudalism and the worst elements of communism."

Atlantic Monthly received many letters in response to "Trying to Make China Work." A Chinese-American professor in California liked my suggestion that Confucianism and nationalism were rising to fill a vacuum: "The return of Confucianism and the intensification of nationalism, I believe, are good signs that the nation is moving away from communism. It does not matter what they say so long as they are not clinging to rigid ideology and declaring it is the panacea to all China's ills."[4]

The best critical letter to the magazine was from Zhao Jingling, a journalist friend. He said I failed to appreciate that "Deng's socialism is very different from Mao's." He pointed out that "as the regime presses ahead with the reforms, no one is very certain what the irreducible core of socialism really is." Zhao correctly predicted that China "has finally achieved the kind of political stability that will allow steady economic growth to happen. America can underestimate China only at its peril."

In a wrap-up reply to all the letters I conceded: "We Americans don't have the clear-cut 'truth' about China in today's era of skepticism, any more than we had it in yesterday's era of good feelings. China remains a difficult place for foreigners to understand."

Wilma Fairbank criticized "Trying to Make China Work" from a novel point of view. I had come back from China ill with tuberculosis and spent weeks in hospital; in fact, I wrote the first draft of the *Atlantic* essay lying in bed under intravenous treatment. Wilma, at lunch in the East Asian center, said, "In my opinion, you would never have written that article if you weren't sick with TB and in hospital for weeks."

Frequently, I agreed with Chinese friends on sociopolitical issues, but disagreed where China's national emotions were involved. Typically, they felt Hong Kong's future would be rosy after 1997, Japan was cheating China, and the United States was "insincere" toward China in selling weapons to Taiwan. Rightly or wrongly, I had reservations about these positions.

Back in the 1950s nationalism was enthusiastic, as many Chinese took post-Liberation China to be the love of their life. Such patriotism did not survive the 1960s and 1970s. The nationalism of the 1980s was less altruistic. People felt strongly for their country because they didn't like the idea of its being left behind by Japan, Taiwan, and others. And they wanted progress for

China in order to have a better life as individuals. This they got. Nationalism helped leaders Hua and Deng.

Actually, Shen made good progress in Beijing, like Meng at the foreign ministry. He was a teaching assistant to a visiting professor of economics at his institute. He had been asked to teach an economics course himself. He obtained a small room in the center of Beijing to meet his girlfriends. But still he was dissatisfied. "Lazy old men are everywhere," he complained. "To get a Ph.D. in China is almost a lifetime affair. And you have to bow and scrape to people to get anywhere."

He gave up applying to one American university. "They asked for a copy of the term paper I wrote at ANU," he told me. "I explained I only had one copy; I couldn't send it. Are you putting everyone through this kind of procedure, I asked, or is this just a special demand for me?" I told Shen almost certainly, he was not being singled out. "I have had enough trouble with Chinese bureaucracy," Shen went on. "I don't want to go through the same thing with Western bureaucracy!"

Harvard graduate student Yang Bingzhang, a former Red Guard imprisoned during the Cultural Revolution for criticizing Jiang Qing (chapter 5), walked into my office at Harvard. Yang was a student of unusual distinction, combining political experience with historical knowledge. He complained that Harvard professors were "arrogant, without reason to be so." A contrarian spirit had remained with him since the Cultural Revolution, as had the virtue of political shrewdness.

Yang clashed with his chief advisor, historian Phillip Kuhn. He insisted he did nothing to hurt Kuhn "personally." But in the USA a professional hurt (graduate students have to flatter their professors!) could be just as deep as a personal hurt; he had cooked in his dorm room, against the rules. Asking my advice as to whether he should choose Kuhn or Schwartz as his advisor, Yang, who seldom took anyone's advice, said the main criterion was "I do not want to be controlled." Yang, always adventurous, wanted to go to Japan, Taiwan, and (less explicably) to Russia.

Agitated, he sprawled in a chair and spoke of a recent CBS program on China. "In the film Chinese people stared at foreigners just as animals stare," he said. "And intellectuals gave answers to the American journalist that simply were false. I don't see how modernization can succeed in China. My goodness, what was our Chairman Mao doing for thirty years!"

He spoke of a Chinese girl he met in a Cambridge apartment. "She has just arrived from Beijing and has no money, but she wants to study," he related. "I told her to get a job. She preferred to marry an American, because that way everything would be paid for. I pointed out she may not like, or be liked by the American man for long. She said, 'In America it's easy to divorce someone'!"

"I tell you," Yang went on, "most of those who came to Boston from China are interested basically in money. In the CBS documentary, you could see that when Chinese confront the foreign world, their main thought is those damned Westerners are richer than Chinese are! I tell you, Ross, the first great invasion of China by the West was with guns, now the second one is with money."

Yang added bleakly: "I can distinguish people from the PRC in the streets of Boston. Compared with people from Taiwan, they lack creativity, their gestures are all alike, they are part of a pack."

Yang had spent three years as a graduate student at Harvard, an experience which changed him and allowed him to look back on the politics and culture of his own country with a fresh eye. I recognized the power of Western society to recast the ideas of a student from China. But I resisted Yang's notion that Chinese behavior in general was at a low ebb. I thought he'd feel better once he finished his Ph.D. This indeed happened.

A person in exile was similar to a salesman. Both had to accept they are always "wrong." Dealing with a salesman, the customer can do no wrong. Compared with an exile, the local within China is always correct.

Like Yang, I felt unease at the materialist scramble in China, but in a different way. I wrote in my diary: "The budding prosperity is certainly welcome. But there is a tendency for some Chinese to trample on other Chinese. The new economic policies can encourage that. It happened in a political form— money not involved—during the Cultural Revolution."

Yang, like other male Chinese students, was having trouble with his wife. The women wanted to join their husbands in the USA. The husband could not or would assist this process. Of his wife he said: "We don't get on well. I like my child, but not my wife." He smiled. "You know, this is the Chinese way."

A Chinese voice reached me on the phone from Florida. It was Shen Chunyi, announcing his arrival in America. In Beijing, his life kept improving under the reform policies, but not enough, and the gap between Chinese frameworks limiting him and Western horizons opening to him seemed great.

Of his trip here: "I had been trying for so long to get to USA—four years— that the actual departure from Shanghai airport left me feeling nothing. In Miami the sky seemed so beautifully blue! In China I had never seen a sky like that!" He made quick judgments: "I prefer American people to Chinese people. They are open, they say what they feel."

Shen had become restless in Beijing, teaching beginners in English, which he found tedious and boring. What he'd learned in Australia seemed irrelevant to life in China."I don't reject the introduction to democracy," he said, "I merely say an authoritarian government will never allow it."

But later he gave another reason for wanting to bring her here: "I just don't want my children to be shaped by the narrow Chinese cultural world."

In America, Shen lacked the masterfulness I observed in Beijing, as he battled to balance study with part-time jobs and found American girls more assertive than Chinese. But he quickly advanced, leaving Florida for Dominican College in California, where I obtained a scholarship for him. He gravitated to the topic of international business.

One day a year or two later Shen reported exciting news. He had fallen in love with a Japanese classmate at Dominican College; they were off to Nevada to get married. Neither had met the parents of the other (her family lived in Tokyo). After graduation, both found jobs with a corporation in Minnesota, although still not American citizens or even green card holders. America ceased to be an abstraction for Shen, and as he became a self-confident individual and a father, the China-America dichotomy lost its bewitching power over him. So, probably, did the China-Japan dichotomy.

I saw a hint of Sun Yatsen's philosophy in the Communist Party's modernization policies of the 1980s. The pragmatic modernizing zeal of the Honolulu-educated revolutionary, aimed against Confucian monarchy, seemed reflected in Deng's efforts to adjust Maoism with broader ideas. Sun's blending of seeming incompatibles found an echo in the "market plus planning" policies of the 1980s. These tensions of progress were felt in the lives of individuals.

The Chinese classical scholar Hugh Dunn was Australian ambassador in Beijing 1980–84. He had previously been Australian ambassador in Taiwan, 1969–72—until Whitlam's switch of diplomatic relations—and was a keen observer of Chinese politics and economics. Dunn was deeply impressed with the unleashing of incentive in the PRC. When talking with me in Taipei in 1970, he held a bleak view of the Mainland's prospects, but in 1982 he spoke glowingly of China's modernization. "The turningpoint for me, a moment of illumination, really," Dunn said, "was when I heard Li Xiannian, on his official trip to Australia, say that equality was harmful." The rejection of equality was widespread. "During a revolution you must have egalitarianism," said Li Yanning of Xinhua, "but after the revolution egalitarianism must go or there can be no progress."

Chinese of varying ages and jobs had other views. One day I chatted with a cabbie on a drive to Qinghua University. We passed fancy new apartments and I suggested there seemed to be inequality in China. "Yes, but when we get to communism it will disappear," said the cabbie, who was a wonderful guide to the buildings of the Haidian area. "Some people feel inequality is growing at the moment," I said. "No, it's not growing," he responded, "and we will conquer it, we will get to communism."

Reform replaced Mao-period values with Deng's neo-socialist values. At an ice cream and soda stand at the Lantern Festival in Chongqing, I found "Serve the People" transmuted into "We Serve You!" Nearby was a book stall with the slogan, "Knowledge is Power," making a bridge from the impulse to study for the revolution, to study for making China and yourself successful.

Three barriers to individualism were weakening. One, the pre-Liberation norm of the individual fulfilling himself less through own impulses than by fitting in with society and especially his family. Another, the peril the Chinese nation faced from the late Qing through to the 1950s. As China felt more secure in the world by the 1980s, the imperative for demands of the nation to take priority over wishes of the individual was reduced. Third, the "Lei Feng model" in the Mao era of the loyal individual as a cog in the machine of the Party was no longer in fashion. The CCP ceased to hand down truths to citizens of Deng's PRC. *Zheng* (politics) and *jiao* (doctrine) were no more a single force. Security, knowledge, mobility, an end to awe—all these had allowed the individual to breathe more freely. Friendship was important as well as citizenship.

Back in Boston, I wrote an essay, "China Enters the 1980s," in *Foreign Affairs*. "The historical goals of the Chinese Revolution in its broad form, first stated by Sun, are reasserting themselves," I said. "To lift the Chinese masses out of backwardness, catch up with the West, and make China a great world power as befits a great civilization."

My *Foreign Affairs* essay was translated into Chinese and published in a book, *Meiguo ren kan Zhongguo* (Americans Look at China). From Tokyo, the American ambassador to Japan, former Senator Mike Mansfield, wrote me: "Your *Foreign Affairs* article is an excellent analysis of the ever-changing Chinese scene. Just as you indicate the Chinese are looking at themselves and the world with a more realistic view, I note a tendency among Japanese toward a more realistic view of China."[5]

Despite optimism based on continuity between Sun Yat-sen and Deng, I had questions. How would Deng reconcile Marxism with the nationalistic aim of seeking wealth and power for China? Would the hopes of the individual for self-realization fit together with the drive for national strength?

Fairbank had down-played individualism in Chinese history after his rediscovery trip to China in 1972: "I do not recall a very outstanding demand for individual political expression in the past," he remarked, "and there is little evidence in the countryside of anyone thinking of an alternative to the collective effort which has paid off so well." But Fairbank did make a sharp forecast: "Perhaps the assertion of political views by individuals will come only as the authority of the central father figure-new emperor begins to decline." So, it proved.

By 1989, Deng's immense prestige within the CCP meant he had become a plausible replacement for Mao. Leadership within the Party was still not institutionalized. Deng threw a long rope to both Hu Yaobang and Zhao Ziyang, and major achievements resulted, but he had political problems with both. He insisted on a tight ship politically in order to safeguard economic development. "You know China has a lot of people," Deng said to the first President Bush in spring 1989, "each of them has his or her opinion. You protest today, I protest tomorrow, and one year has 365 days. We would have protests every day. How could we continue our economic construction?"

"Marx and Engels lived and died in the last century," Deng wrote, "They were great, but we shouldn't expect them to come alive and help solve all our problems today." Deng was one of China's greatest-ever problem solvers. Philosophically, he jumped ahead from Mao to put Chinese socialism within the tradition of the 19th century self-strengtheners Zheng Guofan and Li Hongzhang.

NOTES

1. Zhang Jie, *Heavy Wings*, New York, Grove Weidenfeld, 1979, 232.
2. Fitzgerald, letter to author, November 11, 1980.
3. *Atlantic Monthly*, July 1983; Constance Jordan, Voice of America, letter to author, June 22, 1983.
4. Prof James Feng, letter to the author, June 11, 1984.
5. Senator Mansfield, letter to author, May 14, 1980.

Chapter Seventeen

China Rides a Tiger

Two young companions drove around Beijing chatting about music. Miss Song, a student of journalism in Beijing, and Mr. Zhang, a government official from Chengdu. Both liked romantic Chinese songs as well as Western disco. "It's amazing, now, to remember how we used to have to hide Deng Lijun's cassettes," said Zhang, referring to a stellar Taiwan vocalist. "Today, few care what we listen to."

"The issue used to be, what was good for China and what not good for China," explained Song with a smile. "These songs are capitalist songs, you see."

We drove past gray apartment blocks in rays of a winter sun refracted through the smog. "But the whole world is capitalist!" Zhang said. "It seems so stupid for us Chinese to be hung up over capitalism versus socialism!" For young Song and Zhang, it seemed, the individual was the meaningful unit.

"What is news," the journalism student asked. Feeling provocative, I said, not anything a government wants known. "Oh, that's the opposite of what we say," said Song. "In China, news is the tongue and throat of the party and people."

I asked Song what Liberation meant for her. "When I first heard of it as a school girl," she replied, "I thought it meant the poor will be equal to landlords and capitalists." Now, what did it mean to her in 1988? "Now I think liberation should also mean liberation of thought. We should be allowed to speak our minds."

Zhang mentioned his father-in-law in Chengdu: "He thinks democracy is awful. He's thinking of extreme democracy, I believe, and he fears disorder. Without the party leading, just a mess." Zhang smiled at me. "I said, father, you mean like a chicken running around with its head cut off? That's exactly what the old guy thinks your bourgeois democracy is."

I conclude that Modernization puts youth in a different mental and material position from their parents. China, offering more to its youth, found it enjoyed less spiritual adherence from its youth. Those without a hungry past lacked gratitude for half a loaf. Zhang Wenjin, while ambassador in Washington, complained one day: "Some young people say, hasn't capitalism done better than socialism?"

In Chinese foreign policy, "nation" replaced "revolution" as the policy's central value. China was more involved in the world by virtue of its new stress on economic development, and the world had become more complex than "imperialist superpowers" menacing a righteous "Third World." Most of the world's disputes in fact are among third world nations. As for British colonialism, Japanese imperialism and American hegemonism, big targets of Mao's worldview, their impact on the Chinese territories of Hong Kong, Taiwan and Singapore actually helped produce excellent economic results.

At Harvard in the mid-1970s, I established a course on China's foreign policy that featured Mao's theories of "imperialism," "three worlds," "contradictions," "united front" and "hegemony." One of my students was an Australian foreign service officer, Richard Broinowski, spending a year in Cambridge to recharge his batteries.

Early in the Deng era, Broinowski became Australia's ambassador in Hanoi and in the autumn of 1984, we met in Melbourne. "I still consult notes from your lectures on China's foreign policy," he said, "especially when facing a journalist. Yet, these Chinese foreign policy ideas you lectured about don't fit today's realities." Of course, Richard was correct.

The side effects of economic growth caused public debate and private turmoil. Chen Yun, second only to Deng in seniority, attacked "capitalism" for producing crime and corruption, while party secretary Hu Yaobang and Hu Qili sometimes blamed "feudalism" for the same evils.

As often happens in China, re-appraisals within high Communist Party circles produced an opportunity for students to raise their voices about political change and educational grievances. At colleges, first in Wuhan and Hefei and soon on 150 campuses in 17 cities, December 1986 saw large demonstrations.

Deng blamed Hu Yaobang for the turbulence. Hu admitted "mistakes" and resigned. Deng stabilized the situation by defining reform as a streamlining of socialism and not a transition to some unknown realm. "Democracy is far away," I wrote in the *Boston Globe* in January 1987, "yet we will hear more from Chinese students because a little reform is a dangerous thing."

Zhao Ziyang, who had led reforms in Sichuan, replaced Hu as general secretary of the party. Washington under Reagan welcomed the elevation of a known quantity.

"Consumerism is galloping along," Zhao Fusan, the former pastor at Beijing's Rice Market Church told me. "I'm glad there's a new consciousness of individualism, but that, too, could swing to an extreme." Zhao went on to criticize Western individualism as "selfishness," He saw a gulf between Chinese and Western ideas of freedom and morality. "In the West," he said, "children have the freedom even to make mistakes. In China, parents have a responsibility to make young people good."

I asked Zhao if religion could contribute to a new public philosophy for China. "Given China's culture," he said, measuring his words, "religion has never had the role it has in Europe, with Christianity, or in Southeast Asia, with Buddhism. Religion can raise issues; it can challenge people to answer the question of values. It can't direct the course of moral development in China; it can just be a conscience."

The Soviet Union under Gorbachev also began reform in the mid-1980s. Like Deng, Gorbachev opened windows to the West. However, whereas Deng's radical acts were in the villages, Gorbachev left the Soviet countryside strangled in bureaucracy. Moreover, while Deng pushed economic reform alone, Gorbachev shook up Soviet political institutions.

Gorbachev hoped the Soviet people would put freedom ahead of the pocket book, while Deng was confident the Chinese people would put the pocket book ahead of bourgeois-style freedom. The bittersweet quip in Gorbachev's Moscow as *perestroika* unfolded was, "We are shifting from driving on the left side of the road to the right side gradually."

"An agricultural nation cannot be a modern nation," burst out Xiao Yang during dinner in Chongqing in late 1988. Modernization of Chinese agriculture (as distinct from its de facto privatization) mostly meant *shrinking* agriculture as farmers entered rural industry or left village for city. In the first decade of reform, essentially the 1980s, 80 million Chinese farmers left the land.

"I almost prefer the Mao period," said a Beijing woman as she lamented rising prices for pork and children's school expenses. "In economic things, you knew where you stood under Mao." The paradox in China, as in history all over the world, was that rising material levels and increased opportunities sometimes produced not contentment, but anxiety and evergrowing appetite. The powerful leader Xiao in Chongqing complained: "People are silent when things go backward, and they're not happy when things move forward!" Today's achievement was tomorrow's challenge.

A Beijing taxi driver asked me if I'd met the writer Han Suyin, who happened to be a friend of mine. "What do you think of her views," he enquired. I said I thought she was a leftist. "A lot of Chinese used to be leftist" the driver remarked, "and now they're rightist." Politically well informed, the cabbie was driving me from the Sheraton Great Wall hotel, where the results of the American presidential election, Bush versus Dukakis, were being relayed by ABC News. "Who did you vote for?" he asked.

As the 1980s drew to an end, I reviewed the reform era with Professor Zhou Yiliang, a friend of twenty years, still teaching Buddhist and Japanese history at Beijing University. Over tea and candy in his study, Zhou expressed gloomy views. "Today it's just like pre-1949," he said. "Rotten politics and bribery everywhere. You can't get a license, a certificate, you can't do anything, without first presenting a gift. Provincial officials, to get anything done in Beijing, bring carloads of gifts for the families of officials in Beijing."

I asked if the remolding of thought during the Mao years had not been thorough after all. "In some ways," replied Zhou, "I overremolded myself!" Out of guilt at coming from an upperclass family in the face of communism, the professor had rejected, he now thought too many pre-Communist values.

Zhou regretted that Confucian ways had withered. "There is no sense of justice [*zheng yi*] in China today," he said. "The old ethics were destroyed, but little new has come." He criticized youth. "Young people don't care about education and culture." Perhaps expressing professors' perennial dissatisfaction with society beyond the campus, he added, "Knowledge has been devalued." Whether or not Confucianism was a solution for China's crisis of values, I could see the lack of a believed public philosophy was a problem.

"The power of the party lay just with one leader," Professor Zhou conceded of the late Mao period, during which he was a political advisor to Jiang Qing. "It wasn't a reflection of the interests of the working class." Said Zhou: "When I first met you in 1971, I was a firm believer in Mao's doctrine. Later I came to see words and deeds diverge. Today, I don't believe that any leader can do no wrong," Zhou said quietly. "I believe in Marxism, I don't think capitalism is eternal, but how to get from capitalism to socialism, that is tough." He sighed, then reached for pen and paper and wrote in characters. "After all, to be a scholar" (*Bijing yao dang xuezhe*).

Students saw the issue differently. "Some professors cannot bear to be ignored," observed a student of Zhou's who criticized his professor's readiness to put his pen at the service of Jiang Qing.

Zhou Yiliang had reread my *800,000,000* and he pointed to marginal notes he had made in his copy. I wrote of a conversation between Zhou Nan and two others in the car while traveling in Shaanxi. Probably assuming I was asleep, they talked of China's backwardness and how important it was for China's dignity to advance economically. Examples bubbled forth of small successes in development that excited them.

Suddenly in the car, Zhou Nan asked a colleague from Xian: "Where were you during the Cultural Revolution?" The mood changed abruptly. "The momentum of talk about steel and cotton gave way to subdued and fragmentary remarks. The conversation ceased to be open and spontaneous. Were the memories of the Cultural Revolution troubling?" In neat Chinese characters, Professor Zhou had written on the book in pencil, "After the fall of the Gang of Four [Jiang Qing's leftists], at last we could understand these men's feelings at the time you were with them."

Zhou Yiliang remarked: "When [Emperor] Tang Taizong (ruled 626–649) saw newly-appointed *jin shi* (high scholars) come to the court, he was delighted and said that all the heroes in the world were within the reach of his shooting [*Shijie shang suoyou de yingxiong dou zai ta de sheji fanwei nei*] After Gang of Four fell, I gradually realized that all the Chinese intellectuals were in such a situation with Mao."

From Professor Zhou's home at Beijing University, I visited Mao's mausoleum on Tiananmen Square. A line of people shuffled ahead to enter the lofty marble chamber. Ushers called out "*Qing jing,*" and the crowd, including quite a few military, obediently fell silent. Inside the glass sarcophagus the body of Mao lay bathed in soft light within the gloomy hall, face bright pink, corpse clad in a green army uniform.

Near the south door of the mausoleum, a sculpture of revolutionary figures clutching guns and books illustrating Mao's twin themes of war and ideology faced commerce and carnival. On sale were toy pandas propelled by a motor, and earrings to pierce through the ear on the spot. Near the vendors' stalls was a notice in neat black characters on a white board: "MAO ZEDONG, ZHOU ENLAI, LIU SHAOQI, ZHU DE, MEMORIAL HALL." Mao now shared the honor of his mausoleum with three other top revolutionaries.

Beside me stood a young man from an army family in Hubei, on his first trip to Beijing. I asked him if he admired Mao. "Yes, of course I admire him. He was our leader," he replied crisply.

Over the years, the Mao mausoleum was often open and closed on alternate days, and that seemed a symbol of the dual nature of Mao's reputation. He was admired as a strong leader, but criticized because in the end he did not bestow on citizens the prosperity they expected, when comparing China with other countries. The majority of Chinese by the late 1980s wanted more than anything a strong China and a normal life with steady material progress; they would accept any leader who smoothed the path to such a life.

Economists at many colleges asked themselves if Chinese culture hindered economic development or aided it. Internationalists said traditional culture was an obstacle to China's participation in an interdependent world. Marxists

worried that China could not be socialist until all feudal traditions were elimi-
nated. Many tasks (however "modern") were being accomplished through
connections, and corruption provoked unease with reform.

Two great issues of contemporary Chinese history, the impact of the West
and the development of a Marxist-Leninist political system, were joined by a
third issue—China's problem with itself. Some Chinese even wanted to abandon the entire cultural tradition of China behind a Great Wall that precluded
give and take with the world. All this self-flagellation was surprising, because
kai ge (Opening and Reform) seemed to be going from strength to strength,
bringing a better life to most Chinese.

The book *He Shang* ("River Elegy") and six TV programs based on it in
1988 became controversial. I carried a copy of the book (in Chinese) to a
meeting with a Chengdu academic. Fingering it, he said, "This book makes
us see many things we thought were right are actually wrong. It's quite different from our history text books." He said it had been a mistake to take the
Yellow River as the cradle of the Chinese nation. "Chinese culture is a blend.
Huang Di [Yellow Emperor] is not our only ancestor."

The young historian lamented China's sealing off from the rest of the world
for many parts of its history. "Dragon is a ridiculous symbol," he said. "We
should stop celebrating this thing! Dragon is supposed to stand for strength,
but China has been weak." The Great Wall, he insisted, "ties the Chinese
down, shuts us in." He saw the culture of the future as industrial, "while we
Chinese are still agricultural." Taking his leave at my hotel, the historian
quipped: "Lucky you bought a copy of *He Shang*. Soon it will sell out."

Cautious and older people were less happy with *He Shang*. Yuan Ming,
an international relations specialist at Beijing University said: "The book is
a stimulus against inertia, but as a scholar I can't agree with all its conclusions." I had the impression she chose to sit on the fence, out of prudence.
Some students were bolder.

At the same university, during a seminar I spoke at on the history of China's relations with the West, including the Opium Wars, a student rose and
shocked many by saying: "I don't agree with criticizing Western aggression.
I think *more* aggression would have been better for China. Our problem is not
the West, but Chinese feudalism." I sat before a class at Sichuan University
and asked what foreign books had been memorable. A young woman caught
my eye: "Lee Iacocca's [head of Chrysler] autobiography. I liked the capitalist spirit of it. As an individual he got up and did things, so different from the
traditional ways of China."

However, many people were reluctant to blame Chinese culture. Tan
Zhenzhou was a sharp-featured man of thirty from Shenyang. "I joined the
army at age 14 in the mid-1970s," he said. "I thought Russia and China were

going to fight and I wished to help." Later he became a sailor on a Chinese merchant vessel. "I went to North Korea and Somalia, both poor like China," Tan said, "then to Antwerp, just beautiful." In Gdansk, he observed the Polish Solidarity movement. However, the deepest impression from his travels came in Singapore. "I thought all Chinese people were poor," he said, a smile creeping over his face. "Under Chairman Mao, that's how we saw things. Nevertheless, in Singapore I found a Chinese community not poor!

"There was more Chinese tradition in Singapore than on the mainland," Tan continued, revealing a second fact that made him ask questions. "So, I could not believe the line that Chinese tradition was holding us back." On board ship, Tan educated himself by reading books, and at the end of the 1970s when entrance exams for college resumed after the Cultural Revolution, he gained admission (although still not a high school graduate) to Fudan University in Shanghai and did well. In theory, there is available the unique possession of Confucian culture. It is still serviceable in some respects for China's current stage of social development. It offers ethics for the maintenance of discipline in industry, society, and the family.

However, there are obstacles to reclaiming Confucian tradition. It might be a confession of intellectual bankruptcy for Communists to appeal to Confucian values of hierarchy and moderation and harmony. Youth are almost as opposed to residues of Confucianism (the requirement to "obey," to "conform") as they are to Marxism.

Still, a turn back to traditions, both religious and secular, was occurring. Unexpectedly, the issue of the role of the Chinese past in the future became live again.

Wasted and ill in his prison cell, Wei Jingsheng saw the issue, not as culture, but as politics. "Without democracy," he insisted, "modernization will not be achieved." The young electrician uttered an unpalatable truth. His reward was many years in prison.

Zhu Zhongli was a well known and bold writer, the widow of a senior Mao colleague. In her large beautiful home, she welcomed me in high-heel shoes, black slacks, and a bright red sweater. "Each morning I write," said the 73-year old, "take a nap, and then play music."[1]

She was famous for giving dance parties, with Western music acquired in Hong Kong.

The widow of Wang Jiaxiang, a right-right hand of Mao for many years, she kept busy in committees on medicine, education, and writing. On a side table sat a photo of herself with Wang Guangmei (once First Lady of China) and the widows of Peng Dehuai, He Long, and Zhang Wentian, all top leaders, taken just the year before in 1987.

The mansion had tall ceilings and a piano in one corner of the living room. The outside was stucco gray with green-painted window frames. When the phone rang, an assistant answered it, but Zhu Zhongli cocked an ear to listen, before resuming our conversation. Now and then, she barked an instruction to the assistant.

As we drank tea and ate moon cake, I asked her to explain "*ye shi*" in the title of her book *Jiang Qing yeshi*.[2] "I am Zhou Li!" she burst out in reference to the doctor in the biography. "Most of the things in the book I experienced myself, but the way of writing is that of a novel." She confessed to some ultra-leftism in the book. "At that time, the Cultural Revolution was considered 70% good and only 30% bad." I gave Zhu a copy of my book on Jiang Qing and she autographed my copy of her *Jiang Qing yeshi* (The Romantic Story of Jiang Qing).

"I've only been writing eight years," Zhu Zhongli explained. "I'm really a physician, not a writer."

We talked of foreign editions and serializations of our respective books. My *Mao* was now in eight foreign languages and Zhu Zhongli's fiction was in Burmese and Thai. "A Japanese edition is on the way," she said brightly. Nothing translated into Russian yet." Her *Jiang Qing ye shi* began as articles in *Gongren ribao* (Workers Daily) in December 1987, an article each week through to March 1988. I explained how my *800,000,000* began as articles in *Atlantic Monthly*.

Still well-connected with Mao, Zhu Zhongli, while the youthful head of a hospital in Harbin in 1946, arranged for Mao's previous wife He Zizhen to go to Harbin, and later to Shanghai, where the Central Committee arranged simple work for her. "The diagnosis of mental illness was certainly correct," Zhu said. "She had hysteria. She had lost two sons and in Moscow it was miserable for her not speaking Russian—this contributed to the hysteria."

Had Zhu Zhongli suffered as the wife of Wang Jiaxiang in various ups and downs of politics? "Wang only got what many others got," she said evenly. "Personally, I felt bad, but one looks ahead." Was she optimistic or pessimistic? "One should always be optimistic, hoping for something better. Nevertheless, you can have doubts, too. Today, there's so much more freedom to speak."

In the garden we walked by roses and persimmon. Zhu Zhongli suggested I take a persimmon with me. I reached up toward a high wall and plucked one with its garnish of leaves. "That's Guo Muoro's house," Zhu Zhongli said of the large dwelling beyond the wall where the elderly writer lived.

In 1989, awaiting the fortieth anniversary of Liberation, sweet fruits of the Deng era were enjoyed, despite unsolved issues. CCP rule was less heavy-handed on people's lives than previously. Urban young people, individualistic and cosmopolitan, saw open doors and mostly disregarded politics. Ordinary Chinese happily traveled around tourist spots of China as never before. At the Summer Palace in Beijing, domestic sightseers from out of town far outnumbered foreign and Beijing folk, and it was hard to tell farmers from workers or anyone else.

Economic progress was pursued as the top priority. Steps toward laws and rules reduced the arbitrariness of the late Mao period and seemed to make politics more predictable. With a new modesty, China was open to ideas and products, as well as loans and investment from abroad. Ideological belief shrank to a minority taste.

The threefold strength of the economy lay in decollectivized countryside, small business, and industrial enterprises that enjoyed foreign money. However, disagreement over economic policy occurred during an economic summit at the resort of Beidaihe in 1988. Pressure on the government of public alarm at inflation in the high teens was eased by the decision to postpone further deregulation of prices. However, some impatient reformers regretted the delay.

Pressure on the government of public alarm at inflation of nearly 20 per cent was eased by avoiding further deregulation of prices. However, the public's fear of impending price rises resulting from price deregulation made the challenge of further reform more difficult. Deng himself said, "A quick sharp pain is better than a prolonged pain," but Party elders successfully resisted that idea. Zhao Ziyang later admitted to "improper publicizing of price reform" that spurred panic, hoarding and bank runs.[3]

"In the long run the present complicated prices situation is untenable," economist Lin Ling said in Chengdu, a city once ahead in reform. The outcome of the debate within the party over the economy was the retention for the time being of the honeycomb of subsidies. "It would have been too much for people to bear too quickly," a planning commission official in Chengdu said of price deregulation.

However, some in Sichuan and elsewhere believed reform, which could only go ahead or go backwards, was now in the untenable position of "pause." Lin Ling observed, "Chinese people can be very reasonable if they know the difficulties being faced by this government."

My Beijing journalist friend, Li Yanning at Xinhua, discussed "half-way reform." This was a fundamental contradiction, which seemed to threaten an explosive denouement. Li had visited his home county in Jiangsu Province, where friends were active in small enterprises. "Tax is the key to their success," Li said. "They don't pay tax. A factory starts under the name of a middle school, earning money for teachers; as a school operation, it is not taxed. There is a rule that a rural enterprise gets a tax holiday for the first two years. After two years, the enterprise's name is changed and a new tax holiday begins. Local officials know all this, and wink at it." Nevertheless, people outside the charmed circle "resent the injustice of it," Li said.

Li found it inevitable that new enterprises would be corrupt in acquiring materials and in marketing. "The debate over price deregulation in 1988 raised the issue acutely," he said of Jiangsu. "To free prices would have increased inflation, which Zhao Ziyang was prepared to do. He lost out. To keep manipulated prices, with many products having two different prices, was to continue corruption."

Li Yanning explained how the web of corruption touched relations between authorities in Jiangsu and central ministries in Beijing. "Local officials just cheat," he said. "Beijing gives an order to cut back on capital construction. Locals comply on paper. Yet the construction they agree to abandon in fact had never begun. Nothing already started is ever abandoned." Li favored "commercial courts" to rule on dealings between public units with different interests. "People used to say, whether it was this government unit, or that, it's 'all out of Li Xiannian's pocket,' referring to a top finance politician. But that's not satisfactory anymore."

Li, now in his sixties, was sufficiently old-fashioned to think Deng brought a moral shock to socialist China. He disliked the crude newlyrich, and the rush to print escapist novels at publishing houses. Indeed, he criticized the materialism of his own high-flying daughter, who rose rapidly in a computer business. "Deng said it's fine for some to get rich first," Li said, "but look at what kind of people get rich first—the worst kind in China."

I asked Li to explain his disappointment with China's senior leader. "During the Cultural Revolution, I did not have that high an opinion of Deng, despite what he suffered," Li replied. "But in the mid-1970s he handled the period of Zhou Enlai's illness and death well, and he was the real alternative to the Gang of Four, whom I hated. Now, unfortunately, with political reform essential for the success of economic reform, Deng stubbornly refuses to accept the least political reform!"

A generation gap opened up between Li and his daughter, who, as a computer specialist, earned much more than her father at Xinhua and had zero interest in politics. Li felt some youth were dreamy, noisy, materialistic, without discipline, and blasé about past revolutionary struggles. He was unsettled by rock and roll, motorcycles, avant-guard art, fever to go abroad, and casualness about sex. He disliked youth's insistent cry, "I will do things my way." Of course, youth for its part tended to find older people rigid, dull, fatalistic, hung up on Chinese-ness, and too much in awe of education.

Professor of literature He Daiquan in Chongqing agreed with Li's views: "Materialism grows to excess, especially among young people. They demand from their parents more than parents can give. The strain of giving thousands of yuan at marriage time is resented by parents." Even my friend and assistant Yang Bingzhang, now in his forties, criticized the young ones. "Those in their thirties or so," he said, "don't blindly worship the West. However, the young do. They think the West is all flowers and free sex. Instead of thinking, what they might DO with themselves, given the opportunity to study in the West. They simply want to go there, to be there!"

Rewi Alley, the veteran New Zealand-born resident of Beijing, was also critical of flippant attitudes among youth. He complained about his (adopted) grandchild, who worked in the library of the Academy of Sciences. "She keeps asking me to help her go to New Zealand. I ask her what for; I ask will she return? The answers are never clear." I chatted with Su Fei, actor and wife of Ma Haide, a doctor who threw in his lot with the CCP, and mentioned my talk with Alley. Said the delightful Su Fei, "There are some Chinese who love their country, but others no longer do so, and Alley is a foreigner who does love China."

Su Fei had recently lost Ma Haide and she looked older, more fragile than a few years earlier. She left her husband's study ("very Chinese-style") just as it was on the day of his death. A picture of the two of them together with Li Peng and Zhao Ziyang, two leaders now in tension with each other over economics and politics, sat on a side table. I recalled to Su Fei that Rewi Alley had introduced me to Ma Haide. "It was Rewi's death that threw Dr. Ma off, really cast him down," said Mr. Sun, a longtime aide to the couple, as the three of us drank tea.

In April 1989, I reached Beijing on a trip as lecturer on board the beautiful Pearl of Scandinavia. The cruise ship sailed up the China coast, starting in Hong Kong with stops in Fujian, Shanghai, and Qingdao. Buses took us from Xingang near Tianjin into the capital for a hotel stay. As the flock of passengers surged out of Qian Men hotel to a row of eight buses for a trip to the Great Wall, I recalled a comment by Fairbank after his first return to China in 1972: "Every Chinese official we've met, up to the Premier, has told us China is not ready for Americans in numbers, and tourism to see sights (rather than to take the guests to factories, nurseries, communes etc.). To descend from a cruise ship in hordes for shopping is quite unimaginable." Yet what Fairbank could not imagine, happened within two decades.

My student friend Sun Muzhi, whom we met in Chapter 5, ate a simple lunch with me at Eastern Market while four hundred colleagues from the Pearl of

Scandinavia dined grandly at Mongolian Hotpot. Soon, to Tiananmen Square and the Forbidden City. I introduced Sun to China International Travel Service officials, explaining he was the relative of friends of mine in Washington. "Of course he can come; how nice to have him with us."

As the four hundred trooped through the palaces, Sun and I went into Sun Yat-sen Park. He showed me a recent poem, full of yearning as always. He had found a book on China that contained a chapter by me, bought it, and read it. He found it "quite nice" but urged me to do "love stories and stories about ordinary people."

We returned to the cruise ship. Beijing had come and gone, almost like a dream. Sun and other Chinese friends were wrestling with large issues and acute personal dilemmas. Yet all this lost meaning when the ship gangplank greeted us, "Welcome Home!" Ladies rushed to the hair salon. Men sat down at the bar. In our cozy cabins, the charm, drama, and tension of China was absent.

A Chinese-American businessman passenger from Florida who left China in 1949 said to me at dinner: "Well, progress is being made at last. However, the Communists lost opportunities. After 1949, they thought they had the support of the Chinese people and they could do anything. In fact, some of the people's feeling was just revulsion against the Chiang Kai-shek outfit, not exactly pro-Communist. But now, goodness, China is really catching up."

A San Francisco woman turned to me as the glistening white and blue ship pushed out to sea: "China's more Western than I expected. I go into China-town in San Francisco and things look more traditional than here. The gowns men wear. Funny curved roofs on the buildings. Smell of rice and soy sauce. But in Beijing, people are plain and modern, eating hamburgers, just like us!"

On the deck of Pearl of Scandinavia, I wrote in my diary, "After an hour on board with the cruise passengers, the gulf between ourselves and China remains. Sun's world and Shen Chunyi's world recede. Another world draws me in. Sometimes I feel a let-down on returning from China to the West; other times I feel pleasure." Yet the gulf was narrowing.

At the Pearl's travel office, a poster in English from China International Travel Service cried, "Do You Want to Know the Thousand-year old Civilization of China at One Glimpse? Do You Want to Travel to all the Wonderful Highlights of China in One Day? Join Our Day Trip to Splendid Shenzhen!" Relations between China and the West had steadied and brought mutual benefit. Crude as the poster and busloads of tourists may have been, they were fruits of progress and peace between the U.S. and China, and they delivered money for China and photos for Americans.

History was taking a turn. For a long time, the direction of influence was one way: the West made an impact on China. However, a new era began:

Figure 17.1. Author consults China's future in Sichuan Province, 1988. Author's photo.

China was also impinging on the West. On the high seas I wrote, "China leads me into many situations. In recent days, I have talked philosophy with young Chinese friends and learned what is happening in their country. A few weeks ago, I sat at the Sausalito waterfront near San Francisco, answering questions on China from Marin County identities after lecturing at Dominican College. A week later, I was near Osaka with Professor Ihara, the Japanese specialist on Jiang Qing; all day we talked in his office and walked on surrounding hills."

Now, Pearl of Scandinavia has thrown me together with four hundred passengers whom I would never meet in any setting chosen by them or myself. China joined me to them, to chat about Mao and the Great Wall, as they take a painless glimpse of the Middle Kingdom. A letter awaited me on the ship: My publisher asks if I have another book on China up my sleeve. Am I married to China? Sometimes, I feel China has conquered me, and taken control of my days as a would-be expert on China. Of course, that would be nothing, compared with China taking control of the West. Momentous challenges and benefits beckoned for both sides as the fateful year of 1989 unfolded. Knowing the past did not guarantee knowing China's future. Still, it was a stirring life experience for a boy from the Australian Bush.

NOTES

1. Visit to Zhu Zhongli's home, Beijing, October 29, 1983.
2. *Yeshi* (Wild Story); the title implied a semi-fictional life of Jiang Qing.
3. Zhao Ziyang, Ibid, 129, 222.

Epilogue

Returning to Beijing on the Pearl of Scandinavia in April, 1989, I met cries of youth for individual freedom.[1] At Beijing University "democracy salons" were organized by Wang Dan, a history student, and Shen Tong, a biology student. Professor Fang Lizhi, an outspoken astrophysicist, wrote a letter to Deng Xiaoping demanding the release of Wei Jingsheng, the martyr of Democracy Wall in 1979.

A middle generation of tenacious pro-democracy veterans from Democracy Wall and other past struggles, headed by Chen Ziming and Wang Juntao, were promoting a "civic culture." Their Social and Economic Research Institute (SERI), a private outfit that planned research with implications for sociopolitical change, had the ear of Communist party chief Zhao Ziyang. SERI's "correspondence colleges," attracting 200,000 students nation-wide, were at once a money-spinner and a pro-democracy tool.

On April 15, 1989, Hu Yaobang died of a heart attack. The loss of the idiosyncratic Communist who had fallen out with Deng two years before during student demonstrations spurred the cry for freedom. At Beijing University a couplet was posted on a bulletin board: "A SINCERE MAN HAS DIED, A HYPOCRITICAL MAN LIVES ON."

Hu's death brought out the anguish that a dualism of hope, yet limits to hope, had stored up in Chinese society. Deng's open-door policy enabled comparison with the non-Chinese world, and his economic reforms had brought a new stress on incentive and ambition. Meanwhile, reforms had produced the unsettling side-effects of inflation and corruption, and students and teachers felt education had suffered from a prevailing money-mindedness.

Ma Qingguo, a psychology major at Nankai University in Tianjin, a port city two hours by train from Beijing, told me of grievances on his campus: Students living eight to a room, professors earning in one month what taxi drivers earned in a few days. "Please answer this question," ran one of Ma's handbills, "How much money has Deng Pufang [Deng Xiaoping's son] spent betting at the horse races in Hong Kong? Where did this money come from?"

On April 22, the day of the memorial for Hu in the Great Hall of the People, the authorities ordered Tiananmen Square cleared for the occasion. But 200,000 students formed a defiant phalanx in the square as the aged leaders slipped in by back doors for the ceremony.

Speaking to 4000 funeral guests, Zhao Ziyang, now the hope of the students, praised Hu and glossed over his "mistakes." Incidents between Hu's widow, Li Zhao, and Marshal Nie Rongzhen and Deng showed tensions in the Politburo over Hu's softness toward "bourgeois freedom." When Nie in politeness asked widow Li Zhao if there was anything he could do, she replied crisply, "Yes, clear my husband's name."[2] Deng himself approached Li Zhao to offer his sympathy, but she waved him away.

By now "seven demands" had emerged from a student movement quickly taking on a national dimension: restore Hu's reputation; end attacks on "bourgeois freedom;" allow a free press; allow free speech; allow peaceful demonstrations; spend more money on education; punish corruption among fat cat officials.

On the day after Hu's funeral, I inspected wreaths and memorial messages in Hu's honor left in Tiananmen Square by students. Stenciled, handwritten, and photocopied manifestos respectful of Hu, critical of Deng, and extolling democracy. Many youths with pen and notebook were copying down the Chinese characters. One poster read: "Comrade Xiaoping, You realized long ago that it doesn't matter if a cat is black or white; as long as it catches mice, it's a good cat. Doesn't it show a lack of logic, then, to try to distinguish between 'red' [orthodox] freedom and 'white' [bourgeois liberal] freedom?"

Official Beijing walked a tightrope by offering praise for the dead Hu, whom Deng and many of his colleagues denounced in January 1987, while avoiding praise for the student movement that his death had triggered. "Democracy is something everyone builds gradually on a proper foundation," blared the government radio, "not something grabbed by a handful."

In my room at the Kunlun Hotel I stared almost in disbelief at two books on the coffee table. They were Chinese translations just published in China of my two biographies, *Mao* and *The White Boned Demon*, and across the table sat Liu Luxin, a young sociology teacher who was the translator of the Mao biography. Liu brought the news that the book, released only a month before, had sold 50,000 copies. One staff member at the Book Exhibition told Liu she sold 1000 copies in a single day.

How was it possible that a populace now apathetic about Marxism would want to read about Mao? Previously Mao had been a kind of religion, but the new interest in him was in Mao the man, a feature of my work, and in an objective appraisal of why he did what he did. There was also nostalgia and admiration for Mao on the part of a fresh generation that reflected disappointment with Deng and fury at today's corruption.

My biography of Mao's widow Jiang Qing, *The White Boned Demon*, had been published in Beijing by a house linked with the Chinese Foreign Ministry. The book in its yellow and black cover was on sale in the bookstores. It contained a prefatory note saying the work was controversial but important.

On the second floor of the Wang Fu Jing Bookstore I found a separate room given over to "inside" readership books, including a large pile of *The White Boned Demon*, called in Chinese "The Real Story of Jiang Qing." When I went to purchase two copies the assistant inquired, "Where's the permission from your organization to buy the book?" I confessed I did not have one. She asked for my unit identification (where I worked). I explained I was a foreigner, but was also the author of the book. She went away to check with her supervisor, but came back to say it wasn't possible to sell the book even to its author.

The incident reminded me of the twilight character of Deng's reform era. It was a society, I felt, in which the government could not but be jumpy; even a small event might trigger a large outflow of discontent. Mao had written in 1930: "All China is littered with dry wood which will soon be aflame . . . it cannot be long before a 'spark' kindles a 'prairie fire.'"[3] In those days the Communists were the spark; now they were the dry wood.

Ma Qingguo, the psychology major from Tianjin, told me of the reaction to Hu's death on his campus. He helped put up a poster that inquired: "HOW MUCH MONEY HAS BEEN EATEN UP BY BUREAUCRATS TO BUY FOREIGN CARS DURING THE PERIOD OF REFORM?" Not one word of the posters appeared in Tianjin's press. "Getting rich by using power is an awful feature of China," Ma told me, "and only when information gets out to the people can that be stopped."

The terms "political struggle" and "planned conspiracy" became rare in the Deng era, so I pricked up my ears at Beijing railroad station, heading for my train to rejoin the Pearl of Scandinavia. A radio broadcast of an editorial from People's Daily used these ugly phrases in condemning the student demonstrations and posters. The tone was hectoring; a government was warning its people about the danger of chaos.

"It is a shame that we have wasted time," Deng remarked at a meeting intended to be secret. "We need to quickly use a sharp knife to cut the tangled weeds in order to avoid even greater turmoil." The knife was ready; how would it be wielded?

Tour guides in China usually sang variations on the theme, "Everything is glorious," but in April 1989 as the Pearl of Scandinavia passengers walked on the Great Wall of China, our tour guide, a student of hotel management from Qingdao, said to his busload of foreigners, "Unless something happens, this country is doomed." That night as the Pearl sailed into the Bohai Gulf, I wrote in my diary: "The fading of communism is not the same thing as the coming of democracy."

Telling people not to join a rally planned for Tiananmen Square on April 27, the government inadvertently informed them of the demonstration. Like a huge bonus beyond their dreams, the student organizers found on their hands a tumultuous rally of one million people which made of Tiananmen a district of dissent. Citizens climbed trees to shout across the street their support for the students in a display of popular will that lasted 18 hours.

Shen Tong, the biology major who had organized seminars to discuss democracy and now was one of the student leaders, dropped by the house of his proud but anxious parents and overheard an exchange between his mother and his father, a government employee. "My friends at work were all asking me why my son is so fearless," Mr. Shen said to his wife. "And what did you say?" inquired Mrs. Shen. "I told them," said Mr. Shen, "it must be because we—the people of our generation—have been cowards for too long."[4]

Hundreds of students signed up for a hunger strike. They took a fasting pledge and put on white headbands reading, "GIVE ME FREEDOM OR GIVE ME DEATH." They operated from buses parked in the middle of Tiananmen Square, piercing tires and removing steering wheels so the government could not drive away their headquarters.

"Literary critics could be seen shouting in streets and alleys," Liu Binyan related, "famous writers ran around in a sweat, buying urinals for students."[5] "THE APRIL 26 EDITORIAL WASN'T WRITTEN BY US" cried the banner of one group of demonstrating journalists.[6] Some newspaper editors marched to the door of the Communist Party's Propaganda Department, which instructed and censored all Chinese publications, and shouted through the windows, "Don't call us anymore!" An unusually large headline was placed over a dispatch from Iran: "KHOMEINI AGED AND IN POOR HEALTH; WHO WILL SUCCEED HIM?"[7]

With exquisite historical awkwardness, the hunger strike began just two days before the arrival in China of Mikhail Gorbachev, on a long-planned visit to bury the deep antagonism between the Soviet Union and China from the days of Khrushchev and Mao. The student movement benefited from Gorbachev's arrival and from the presence of 1200 foreign journalists in China to cover it. Beijing had given permission months earlier for CBS, CNN and other news organizations to bring satellite dishes and extra journalists into China to report on the Deng-Gorbachev summit.

In Tiananmen Square, instead of the expected display of Soviet and Chinese flags, there were calls for democracy. One proclaimed in Russian, "DEMOCRACY, OUR COMMON DREAM." Another implied an aspersion upon the Beijing leadership, "WELCOME, TRUE REFORMER FROM MOSCOW," A third read, "GORBACHEV IS 58, DENG IS 85," with reverse arrows linking the two pairs of numerals.

Never in the history of the PRC had a visiting leader's Beijing schedule been mangled this way. The welcoming ceremony, planned for Tiananmen Square, had to be held at the airport. The Soviet chief's visit to the Forbidden City and the opera both were cancelled, and his press conference was at the last moment moved from the Great Hall of the People (outside of which 100,000 people were gathered to cheer the hunger strikers) to the guest house where he was staying. Copies of Gorbachev's address to the Chinese people did not reach the press as scheduled because photocopy machine repairmen were out in the streets demonstrating. A leaflet prepared by the students said, "The Communist Party's own backyard has caught fire," and it seemed to be true. By now the student movement virtually controlled parts of the city and some 60 public bus routes had stopped operation.

Zhao was not quite finished politically and he chose to use his meeting with Gorbachev to boldly turn up the heat on Deng, who was calling the shots behind the throne but silent in public. "On the most important questions, we still need Deng as the helmsman," Zhao said to Gorbachev (and the press), thus putting responsibility for the crisis on to the shoulders of the 85-year old patriarch. Zhao's belated decision to stand, even elliptically, against Deng was perilous.

There had been no such thing in the PRC as a separate business realm, intellectual activity as a free and independent vocation, an opposition political party, or a national election. Probably it was inevitable that many of the students would think in terms of "good men" rather than new structures, and act in experimental mode rather than in accord with a long-term program.

Yet if the students of 1989 had paid closer attention to the split within the party that opened in 1988 and now widened, the outcome of their passionate endeavors might have been better. They stunned China and the world because of a pure aim, yet the very abstraction of their purity made it difficult for their movement to be politically successful.

After five days of the hunger strike, with emotions soaring across Beijing, a million and a half people choked the streets on May 18, perhaps a majority

Figure E.1. A hardly believable sight: Railway ministry officials and workers protest Deng's leadership. The front banner reads, DENG XIAOPING STEP DOWN. GO AND PLAY BRIDGE. A first in 40 years of the PRC. Charles L. and Lois Smith Collection on Contemporary China, Harvard-Yenching Library, Harvard University courtesy Ma Xiaohe.

of them workers. Posters and banners sharply attacked Deng, taking a cue from Zhao's remark to Gorbachev. "XIAOPING, THANK YOU AND GOOD-BYE," said one in Beijing, and another made a play on the Communist leader's famous maxim of pragmatism: "IT DOESN'T MATTER IF THE CAT IS BLACK OR WHITE, SO LONG AS IT RESIGNS."

In the streets the police were nowhere to be seen and student leaders became heroes, signing autographs with one hand, scribbling a will with the other. Old women walked miles to bring salted eggs to the youths, food vendors donated their cakes and soda pop, and nurses volunteered their services after hours to tend the faint and the ill.

With Gorbachev gone, the Chinese government announced martial law for most of Beijing. The hunger strike was called off, but the occupation of Tiananmen Square and the propaganda activities of the movement continued.

Zhao declined to go along with the declaration of martial law and that ended his career. By late May the militant core that had emerged from the hunger strike was nakedly face to face with the army.

Just as the northern China sky in May can sharply change, so the student democracy movement did so by the end of May. The leaders inside

Figure E.2. Students at Beijing University wrote an American protest quotation, on a bedsheet grabbed from a Dorm, to add to myriad Chinese language messages calling for freedom and democracy. Charles. L. and Lois Smith Collection on Contemporary China, Harvard-Yenching Library, Harvard University, courtesy Ma Xiaohe.

Zhongnanhai were enraged when students from the Central Arts Institute erected in Tiananmen Square a huge white "Goddess of Democracy," which bore a resemblance to Guan Yin, the Chinese goddess of mercy, but also to the Statue of Liberty in New York. A factory donated 8000 yuan to pay for the Styrofoam, plaster, and wire.

When the goddess was ready to be taken to the square, a phone call came to the Arts Institute from the Police Ministry saying any truck driver who transported the statue would have his driver's license cancelled for life. The art students took the goddess to Tiananmen Square in four parts on small carts.

At Xidan market, a meeting of thieves announced a strike of ten days so that they could concentrate on impeding military vehicles. Citizens joined in the blockade and persuasion of PLA units. One woman said to a troop truck: "My grandson is among the students camped at Tiananmen Square, and if you are on your way to kill him, here am I, kill me first." Students settled accounts with their families, and made plans for escape from China or an invisible existence in the countryside.

At Harvard, some faculty wondered if the certainties about China that we taught our students were not, after all, written in stone. Ted Koppel phoned from ABC News to ask me to rush to China with him for a "Nightline" special program. Spring classes were finished, so, just one month back in Boston, I got a visa for a return to Beijing. Asked his opinion of the student democracy movement, a Chinese diplomat at the New York PRC Consulate said, "It's all over and everything is returning to normal." Three evenings later on June 3 at Beijing airport, Customs officials ignored my luggage and declaration form. My flight from Tokyo was the last international flight into Beijing for the night, next day and beyond.

Outside, there were many taxis and few passengers, yet drivers rejected my business. One cabbie with eyes averted asked an outrageous 180 yuan to take me into the city. "It's complicated and dangerous to drive into that part of Beijing," said a second driver, asking 220 yuan, after we began the trip.

Bumping down dusty ill lit lanes, we were on a checker board of trial and error as passers-by leaned toward the taxi window with advice on which streets were tractable and which not. Cream and red-painted public buses were parked in key positions to block military vehicles. Students in their red or blue head bands were speaking to the crowds about corruption and the need for democracy, and arguing to nearby troops that the army should not advance to Tiananmen.

"Don't go into the streets, in particular don't go near Tiananmen Square," said the Chinese language taxi radio as we neared the Palace Hotel. "Citizens of Beijing, stay in your homes." It was ten o'clock on the evening of June 3, 1989. I headed for the square.

"There is war!" said a pedicab driver, as he quoted a fare five times the norm to pedal me from the Palace Hotel to Tiananmen Square. "I could be arrested."

As we rolled down Beijing's leading shopping street of Wang Fu Jing, the air was turbulent with shouts and sirens. When the pedicab reached Chang An

Avenue and the beige hulk of the Beijing Hotel, my driver had to stop in the face of a huge, agitated crowd facing west toward Tiananmen.

I had come upon an extraordinary cat and mouse game between the Chinese military and a citizenry with anti-government emotions on the boil. Armies had been inching toward the city for days, but as they advanced, they were resisted by tens of thousands of people. The city was full of damaged military vehicles stopped in their progress by the cunning of the populace.

It was not yet midnight and still possible to go into Tiananmen Square in my pedicab. "Square" is hardly an adequate word for the oblong expanse, so vast that each flagstone is the size of a Chinese bedroom. Its 100 acres are like a separate district of Beijing, normally empty and monumental, a sort of abstract political district. Yet tonight the flagstones of Tiananmen had come to life as angry youth laid claim to an abstraction with their own hands.

Through rising coils of smoke I made out the giant portrait of Mao that hung at Tiananmen (the Gate itself). As I drew near it, the tall white student-erected statue of the Goddess of Democracy, its surface looking as smooth as marshmallow, loomed from the south. My pedicab whirred between Mao and the goddess. Symbols of two divergent philosophies of how to order society, a collectivist one and an individualist one.

As I moved around on foot or in my pedicab, the student radio, "Voice of the Hunger Strikers," spoke of democracy and determination to attain it. "Democracy is something everyone builds gradually on a proper foundation," rebutted the government radio from near the Great Hall of the People. "Tiananmen Square is a sacred place."

As I glided in my pedicab by the cypresses along the southeastern rim of the square, students and workers drew close on their bicycles to chat. "What do you think of our movement?" "Please take care of yourself." It was part of the camaraderie of those hours that people shared information with cheerfulness and good humor, and the foreigner was welcomed with absolute openness.

"Have you heard the one about Li Peng?" said a rakish young man in a straw hat, and I motioned my driver to speed up so I could listen. "'Premier Li,' says this citizen, 'how come we ordinary folk haven't benefitted from all the foreign money that floats around China?' And Li Peng says, 'The people have received; we've imported tear gas specially for you.'"

Soldiers were jogging into the eastern fringe of the square past the Museum of the Chinese Revolution. "Go home, we don't need you," a young man cried to a row of troops. "We are all Chinese," a girl shouted in an appeal against the use of force.

Chai Ling, a psychology graduate student who was commander-in-chief of the Tiananmen Square operation, rose from the steps to say through a bullhorn. "Please go home now." Chai meant to convey, I think, not that the confrontation in the square was none of my business, but that the danger was overwhelming.

The last voice I heard on "Voice of the Hunger Strikers" before we pedaled out of Tiananmen was Chai Ling's. "This evening people have been killed and wounded," she said, her voice at one moment shrill and the next cracking. "We say to the government, this cruel slaughter will only make us struggle harder for our goals." Strains of student voices singing "The Internationale" wafted across the square.

My driver sighed with relief as he swung into Wang Fu Jing. "Were the Martin Luther King demonstrations like that?" he asked as we found ourselves in a more normal street setting. "I suppose they were in a way," I said, groping a little.

"Did you have as many people in the streets as we saw here tonight?" he inquired.

"About the same," I replied.

He jerked his head sharply sideways to look at me. "You know, mister, we shall overcome too."

We turned into Goldfish Lane. "You know, I carried the students for free," the driver said as he pocketed his large fee for our dangerous foray. "Didn't charge them a penny." Why was that?

"Because they're doing something" he went on.

As I entered the Palace Hotel's lobby, troops marched along Goldfish Lane past our glass doors. Some, heading east, wore bandages on wounds to the head or arm; others, heading west, looked fresher. I sat down in my room to scribble notes, feeling I was no longer in Beijing, where history was being upturned two miles away at Tiananmen Square.

In the hotel lobby as I headed back toward the streets, a green-uniformed concierge said to me: "If they kill the students, I will attack them myself." A fresh pedicab driver, making good business out of danger, used the same argument to bargain with me, but with extra resonance. "It's war," he said, "war or civil war—I could be killed."

Angrier, now, were the confrontations between regular troops gathering at the square and agitated crowds backing up the students' last ditch struggle from Chang An Avenue and other streets east of the square. On all sides there were shouts, smoke, and cursing of soldiers. Rocks, bottles, and chunks of flagstone were being thrown toward the massed troops. I could not hope to enter the square again.

"Stand on the bicycle seat and you'll get a better snapshot," cried a bystander as I readied my camera to photograph wrecked buses and smoke puffing irreverently around the Mao portrait and the Goddess of Democracy.

From the west, a move or was it just a threat of one? by the soldiers who now seemed installed in Tiananmen Square sent people scurrying. "They're going to shoot," someone called out and all of us flew eastward, bumping each other as we turned and ran, my pedicab driver maneuvering his vehicle in the new direction as best he could. The flagstones beneath our feet were littered with the debris of street fighting.

T T T T T T...T T T T T T...T T T T T T. For years that sound for me in China meant firecrackers, but tonight it meant gun shots. The firing was

Figure E.3. A young Chinese man lies dead after being struck by an armoured personnel carrier as it rumbled in for the showdown in Tiananmen Square. Grieving, angry students and their supporters react to the loss. Charles L. and Lois Smith Collection on Contemporary China, Harvard-Yenching Library, Harvard University, courtesy Ma Xiaohe.

close, offensive, terrifying. Deng Xiaoping's soldiers were firing on unarmed crowds in the streets of Beijing for the first time since the revolution in 1949. "Tell the world our government has gone mad," a woman cried to me, tears running down her face.

I looked up at the Beijing Hotel and saw two banners in white Chinese characters on red cloth which seemed to have strayed upon the night from another time and place: "UPHOLD THE SOCIALIST WAY" and "STRUGGLE RESOLUTELY AGAINST BOURGEOIS FREEDOM." On the streets of dozens of China's cities, students loudly backed by millions of Chinese citizens had for six weeks been trying to tell their government, and the world, that the socialist way had run into deep trouble, and that bourgeois freedom is, well, freedom.

That night, despite the horrors, my view of the capacities of Chinese people was enhanced. The courage, humor, practicality, and sense of history of youth whom I talked with intensified my faith in the Chinese. Yet I also felt that the courage of the crowd was almost suicidal, for Communists when their grip on power is threatened have a strong tendency to behave like Communists,

A near-festival atmosphere ended as fifty meters ahead on Chang An Avenue gunfire rang out and people at the front of the crowd fell down. We surged back, turned around, and fled helter skelter to the east. Where the crowd had made contact with the troops, to the west, the Gate of Heavenly Peace had become a scene of tumult.

In Qian Men Wai Street, along the southern edge of Tiananmen Square, at each window of apartment blocks citizens leaned down to watch, wailing or shouting. Qian Men Wai Street has fewer lights than Chang An Avenue and I felt less conspicuous. On the street and sidewalks were confrontations, gutter level cursing, whistle and snap of gunfire, and fury as the crowd realized that people at the western edge of the throng were dead and wounded.

My pedicab driver and I argued. "If you stop, it's dangerous," he gasped. "You look suspicious. Let's keep moving." Hot, shocked, nervous, I objected, "But I want to talk to people!" I would instruct the driver to pedal me deeper into the crowd, keeping to the darker edges of Qian Men Wai. Then shots would crackle, cries of horror and alarm would rise from the front of the crowd, and impatiently I would him urge to turn around and flee, grabbing his waist in my eagerness to have him whip us to safety.

Incredulity spread across central Beijing like a whirlwind. Sustained crackles of gun fire close by made me retreat north along Zheng Yi (Righteousness) Street and about 4 AM I reached the Beijing Hotel. Some in the huge crowd in front of the hotel were overwrought. One woman sobbed uncontrollably, kneeling on the ground, as she told of people mown down by gunfire. "Two young people fell dead at my feet," she screamed. Holding her spectacles in her hand and looking upwards from the pavement, she begged me: "Please tell the truth about our land!"

I took an elevator to the seventeenth floor, hoping to view Chang An Avenue and Tiananmen from on high, but a white-jacketed man at the service desk stopped me from stepping onto his balcony. "There's nothing to see," he said in the familiar style of a Chinese government gatekeeper. It was the first time all night, starting with Beijing airport, that I met a hand of authority.

Picking at random a lower floor, the twelfth, I found a guest room open and peered inside. Four Hong Kong businessmen were on the balcony. They were speaking emotionally in Cantonese. I crept into the room. So preoccupied were the quartet with the scene below on Chang An Avenue that I remained unnoticed beside a bed near the window. Beneath us the front entrance of the hotel was barricaded with buses, minibuses and trucks.

"Excuse me," I said, "could I watch with you from the balcony for a moment?" One Hong Kong businessmen replied, "As long as you're not from the press." Another burst into English out of mental turmoil: "It's the last straw! China is finished!"

A military presence, vehicular and on foot, had produced shouting and clashes at the intersection of Chang An Avenue and Zheng Yi Street, and I raised my camera and snapped the scene. A cry of horror went up on the balcony. "Get out" shouted the Hong Kong businessman who had waved me in five minutes before. "I'm sorry, I'm sorry," I mumbled in shame . . . "I'm terribly . . ."

Since my third pedicab driver had abandoned me, I found myself walking slowly north on Wang Fu Jing toward the Palace Hotel. Despite the presence of troops, at each street corner citizens clustered to report news on the night's events, quiz each other, and offer ever-ready analysis. Not for years had Beijing people known such a sense of participation in news as it was made. The resulting feeling of citizenship did a little to mitigate the tragedy that engulfed Beijing.

A hubbub arose near the green-roofed Capital Hospital. Ambulances came and went, exhausted nurses and doctors mopped their brows as they moved along the verandas, and tense crowds pressed toward the hospital gates seeking news of family or friends. Near the Wang Fu Jing department store, fifty soldiers standing by two trucks stared at me. These dark skinned, round faced young men obviously were not from Beijing, and not northerners. Buses and trucks barricaded the Palace Hotel's doors. "It is for your protection," a flustered hotel manager said. "The trouble in the streets could overflow in here."

Just before 5 AM I fell into bed, 30-odd hours after leaving Boston, and on the pillow was a chocolate mint and a card from the Palace Hotel management with a quotation from Shakespeare's Macbeth: "Sleep that knits up the ravel'd sleeve of care, the death of each day's life, balm of hurt minds, great nature's second course. . ."

I awoke to the sound of gunfire and the sight of black smoke rising above parts of the city. On foot, reaching a lane by Capital Hospital on the way to Tiananmen, I came upon knots of people dissecting the night's bloody events with an openness that still made the foreigner welcome. I stopped by a wrecked minibus that smelled of burnt paint. "What about Wang, was he killed?" asked a man as beads of sweat stood out on his forehead.

"Have you heard anything about Chen?" a voice inquired from the knot of citizens. No one had. A shocked populace amidst the wreckage of street warfare was asking itself how and when China would recover from the night's trauma. An older man said an era was ending, and the Communist dynasty dating from 1949 had run its course.

My mind turned to Mao and I felt astonishment, not for the first time, at the durability of the dead leader's ideas. Decades earlier he had said, "Political power grows out of the barrel of a gun," and in Beijing in 1989, despite the sleek glass towers and the pollution and the trappings of cosmopolitanism, this horrible maxim still obtained. I could hardly believe that such an atavism could in 1989 dominate a great city.

Further south as the lane approached the hospital, an older woman shopkeeper said this was the lowest point in China since 1949. Worse than dark moments of the Cultural Revolution? She fixed me with large sad eyes. "In the Cultural Revolution there were no guns, and no shooting at Tiananmen Square, just sticks and stones."

The lobby of the Beijing Hotel resembled scenes of a civilization submerged by the flow of lava from a volcano. On the café tables, half eaten sandwiches, full ashtrays, and dishes of ice cream turned to liquid bespoke the rude intrusions of the night. Chairs were strewn or piled high, and the bar, restaurants and shops were dark. I went up to the seventh floor restaurant in the old wing of the hotel to view Tiananmen. "There will be no lunch," a waitress said with impeccable logic, "because there are no people."

From the restaurant balcony I saw a phalanx of tanks in the square, looking like even toothed, murky-green dragons, with a row of soldiers in front of them facing Chang An Avenue. Between Tiananmen and the Beijing Hotel, a further 15 tanks were arrayed on Chang An. A teenager beside me cut through the analyses of his elders, "We have no guns, that's the curse of it. If only the people had guns!"

In the hotel lobby I spoke with a thin man in his 20s, slumped on a couch in the gloom smoking one cigarette after another. He was a driver for a joint venture between a Chinese unit and a West German company who had taken refuge in the hotel during the night. "The center has gone crazy," he said of the Deng government through the smoke from his Marlboro, readily giving his views to a stranger. "This is absolutely 'it.' I'm going to Australia."

As people talked angrily in random groups, the Chinese words for "warlord" and "crazy" recurred. I asked a woman who said she had been in the vanguard of the crowd exactly what just happened in broad daylight. "People shouted insults at the soldiers," she replied, "and some threw rocks at them. The soldiers opened fire and shot at us, at first at our feet, and then higher up. Some people were killed."

As smoke curled into the sky on the afternoon of June 4, I left the Beijing Hotel, torn with emotions, and went to the Catholic cathedral, Nan Tang, southwest of Tiananmen Square. Mass was over, there were few people in and around the sanctuary, and the cathedral compound was a welcome place of retreat. I found a youth sitting in meditation within the gray stone walls of the compound.

Zhu Yasheng was a 16 year old middle school student who had marched with other Christians behind a banner that read, "THE LORD LOVES YOU, LONG LIVE DEMOCRACY." Zhu's father was a master chef for senior government leaders, his mother worked in the Communist Party secretariat of Beijing city, and no one else in the family only Yasheng was a Catholic. I asked why he had become a Catholic. He gave a smile that suggested both innocence and passion, and replied, "Because in China there is nothing you can believe in."

That afternoon, June 4, the last uncensored piece of reporting came from Radio Beijing. "Thousands of people . . . were killed by fully armed soldiers when they forced their way into Beijing. Among the dead are our colleagues at Radio Beijing." At the end of the account, the newsreader said, "Because of the abnormal situation here in Beijing, there is no other news we can bring you." Then Beethoven's Fifth Symphony was played, and that was the end of Beijing's season of press freedom.

The June 4 issue of People's Daily contained bitter gestures of rebellion by the staff. A trivial story about a problem of pesticides in a village carried the sensational headline, "HOW LONG CAN THE MASSES BE CHEATED?" Another on a handicapped person winning a sports medal was presented under the florid headline, "THE PEOPLE'S HEARTS WILL NEVER BE CONQUERED."[8]

"I wonder," I said to a trusted friend, "if Deng Xiaoping went through Beijing hospitals this evening and saw the results of last night, would he regret the decision to shoot?" Yuan (not his real name) replied, "If he went to the hospitals, he would not get past the door, he'd be killed stabbed, stoned."

256 Epilogue

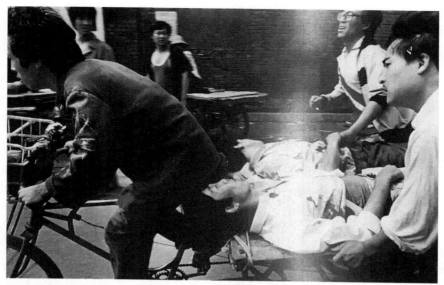

Figure E.4. A volunteer rushes two wounded youth to a hospital nearby Tiananmen, helped by onlookers, on the morning of June 4, 1989, as bullets sprayed last-ditch pro-democracy students. Charles L. and Lois Smith Collection on Contemporary China, Harvard-Yenching Library, Harvard University, courtesy Ma Xiaohe.

Yuan had never struck me as being interested in politics and his vehemence against Deng took me aback. "He's a serpent," Yuan went on. "We warmed him at our chest in 1979 [a reference to public support for Deng's climb to power over the top of the sinking Hua Guofeng], and now he bites us." Yuan and I kept in touch. "We can still talk," he said a week later, "but only in a swimming pool." In the water and the locker rooms of various sports facilities we found an oasis of anonymity.

A curfew was announced for our East District and we were supposed not to go out of the hotel after 9 pm. Loudspeakers late at night declared, "You should not be on the streets," and told people to "leave or accept the consequences." Peter Meade of WBZ radio station in Boston phoned to interview me, and his first question was about the situation in Tibet, but I could not even go to Tiananmen Square, let alone to Lhasa.

In the first week of June I saw anger was a powerful force; in the second week of June I learned fear was even more powerful. Deng finally appeared on TV on June 9, to bestow his congratulations on the military commanders who had crushed the "counter-revolution." The televised scene in the Huai-rentang Hall at Zhongnanhai recalled the parlor of a nursing home as Deng's old comrades gathered. "The storm was bound to happen," Deng croaked to the army men in remarks that blended militarism with nationalism. "For it to occur now is an advantage for us—while we still have a large group of old comrades who are living and healthy." He told the commanders, "Never forget how cruel our enemies are. We should have not an iota of forgiveness toward them."

The Palace Hotel dutifully put on the garments of political rectitude. "PROTECT THE LARGE PICTURE" said a banner draped near my window. "PROTECT STABILITY" urged its twin. Day by day, tongues ceased to move, the phone rang less, people found it safer to talk little with each other. Beijing became a city of silence.

Rumors flew, for the good reason that people were kept in the dark about many important matters by the government, and when the government did speak, few believed it. To exchange rumors was also a way of keeping alive some ray of hope; a "reality" could be invented that was an improvement on observed reality. "Li Peng has been shot . . ." "Deng has died of prostate cancer . . ." "The PLA is mounting a coup against Li Peng . . ." There even was talk that the Guomindang was on the way from Taiwan to retake the Mainland.

"Everything is back to normal," purred an official spokesman, yet my acquaintances in the government did not answer their phones, I had to pass by troops with fixed bayonets in order to keep appointments at offices and institutes, my car was often stopped at night and searched by soldiers, and my Chinese friends were leaving Beijing one by one. "How can the world believe the Li Peng government line?" I noted in my diary. "China itself does not believe it."

Beijing had seen three epochs within the span of three weeks: a festival of Jeffersonian freedom in late May; guns, Molotov cocktails, bleeding bodies, and the wail of ambulance sirens on June 3 and after; and now, Orwellian repression. From the authoritarianism of the Deng era China seemed to be back at the totalitarianism of the Mao era.

Helping a student search for a missing friend, I could feel her loss and anxiety. Walking in the street with a teacher who stiffened when he noticed we were being followed, I felt the newly-intrusive state. My Chinese friends' dismay, fear, and dashed hopes pulled me from my role as a "China watcher" and put me beside them as I had not felt before.

On June 5 there was a knock on my door at the Palace Hotel and there stood Lin Mu (not his real name), a friend recently graduated from Nankai University. "I saw a man die for the first time in my life," Lin said, as black smoke curled into the sky outside our window. "In Qian Men Street, near a bicycle shop. The left side of his face was blown away by a bullet. He was probably just a by-stander." I asked Lin if he threw rocks or Molotov cocktails. "Not exactly," he replied softly. "But I used a metal bar—the sort a cook uses to mix a large pot." I looked across at Lin's profile and his face had tensed. "I hit a soldier on the head with it." A silence stretched between us. "I was angry—the soldier had just shot that man."

Lin had not done any work for weeks although he went in periodically to his office in a government ministry. In the stillness of the hotel room he lit a cigarette. "These are our drugs," he said as smoke clouded his blue eyes, "like cocaine and marijuana for you in the West. Comfort for the spirit [*xinli anhui*]. "I have also taken up mahjong," Lin said. "I always thought of it as an old man's game, but now it's my game too. You see, mahjong is a good escape from reality. It has strict rules and everyone starts equal."

Lin felt discouraged about the role of educated young people after a decade of reform and its rude dénouement. "I didn't spend 18 years going to school in order to have guns pointed at me," he said. "There are only two ways out for people like us: go abroad or go into business."

Lin showed me a letter from his father, who years before had become an architect to transcend his "bad background" and had never trusted the Communists. "Please leave Beijing and don't have anything more to do with the democracy movement," the elder Lin wrote. "In China intellectuals are always getting out ahead of ordinary people. It makes trouble and it makes you young intellectuals vulnerable." The father felt talk about democracy for China was unrealistic.

"The crisis of 1989 was a small crisis, son, compared with the big crisis of the Cultural Revolution," the father wrote. "Just study, and try your best to scrape out a living [*huo ming*], for there are so many dangers."

Lin Mu, an only son, did not agree with his father. "Study, yes, but June 4 was not a 'small crisis,'" he said. "I am not content to live a life little different from the animals." He did not intend to leave the capital. "I want to see how history changes in Beijing." He gave three reflections on the crisis. "Never forget that China is a third world country, and it has a military to match," he said. "In China the military situation is the political situation." Lin's second point was, "Economic reform without political reform mainly benefits the bureaucrats." His third point, still sobering, claimed two kinds of reform, from above and from below. "In China, reform from below is difficult because of the horror of disorder that Chinese have," he said. "But now reform from above is also stalled."

One day Lin brought to the Palace Hotel a toy tank he had bought at a department store. "I am saving it to give to my first child when I have one," he said. "It will serve to remind him of something he must understand and should never forget." I asked Lin to buy me one. A week later Lin and his wife came in with the news toy tanks were sold out all over Beijing.

Tan Zhenzhou, the graduate student from Shenyang who had been a youthful soldier and a merchant marine, also was courageous enough to visit after the massacre. He said the PLA unit with which he and his classmates had reasoned for three days never got to Tiananmen. The students themselves brought these troops at the college gates the news of the massacre in central Beijing. Hearing it, the officer in charge of the unit which had been outside the college gates said to Tan: "Thank you for stopping us. Had we gone in toward Tiananmen Square, we would have participated in what happened."

Tan's background was rural and he had been among the more cautious of the student activists. In common with other graduate students, he felt the occupation of Tiananmen Square should have ended late in May. "Everyone knows the government was wrong to shoot," he said, "but we could have avoided it by leaving earlier. In South Korea it took 20 years of this activity to break down authoritarianism."

Of the student movement activists I knew, Tan was the most thoughtful about long-term goals. "You can't cry out, 'Down with the Communist Party,'" he reasoned, "because another party doesn't exist in China; we just have to move step by step." He took the view that "there are different views in the Communist Party, and we democrats should take advantage of this fact." Tan felt keenly the tragedy of the totally inadequate links between Zhao Ziyang's camp and the street politics of the student movement. Tan said he was afraid of the guns but not afraid of going to prison. "There is always something you can do in your cell," he said. "I won't be arrested now, but probably in two or three weeks."

Zhu Yasheng, the middle school student I met at the Catholic cathedral the day after the massacre, was not permitted by his family to have any contact with me at first, but late in June he phoned and we met at the Palace Hotel. Still bright-eyed but looking tired, he brought news that a close friend, a classmate who participated with him in the demonstrations, had just been arrested in Shijiazhuang after fleeing there from Beijing. "He attacked a soldier," Yasheng said of the 16-year-old, "and it turned out this action was recorded by a secret camera attached to a lamp post."

Not long afterwards, news reached me that Zhu had gone into the military. I went to the Zhu family house to seek light on this unexpected twist. Zhu's father, the master chef, could not have been nicer—although he could have been more candid. "Yasheng is fine," he said. "He is at an air force base south of Beijing. The discipline is good for him. You see, his grades were poor and his middle school thought the military would have a good effect on him." I was surprised, because Yasheng had told me his grades were excellent.

On June 16, Ted Koppel of ABC News boldly took me to Beijing University campus to film a "Nightline" special program. But at the gate our van with half a dozen people was refused entry. Koppel and I returned alone on foot and to the police at the gate I said in Chinese that we were professors visiting from Harvard. We were waved through ("That's the first time," said Koppel, "that I have heard anyone speak Chinese with an Australian accent"), but within half an hour Koppel, using his Video Eight camera, was detained by soldiers. He was released, but few students or teachers would talk to us.

I tried to phone a Beijing University friend, Professor Zhou Yiliang, a Harvard Ph. D, who had often talked with me about Deng's reforms. But on each occasion an operator said the line was "out of order," and by mid June the response was that the line was "cut off." I got into a taxi and drove to Zhou's spacious house.

"How did you get through the gate?" asked the son of Professor Zhou as he greeted me with a surprised look. He explained that his father was in New York attending a conference. "Hu Yaobang and Zhao Ziyang were the two arms of Deng Xiaoping in pursuing reform," the younger Zhou said in summing up the crisis. "Deng wants reform, but he has allowed the old revolutionary guard who want reform to fall short of political reform, to cut off his two arms, Hu in 1987 and Zhao in 1989."

A vast number of Chinese by late June accepted with equanimity the crushing of the democracy movement and the resurgence of leftist totalitarianism. One night I took a taxi from the Great Wall Hotel back to the Palace Hotel and the driver said just before I got out of his cab: "I supported the democracy movement, and now I support the government. The students were correct about corruption, but, you see, in China democracy is impossible."

It was time to leave China, but I wanted to revisit the Temple of Heaven first, not knowing when I would be in Beijing again. It took the taxi half an hour to go a few blocks from north of Chang An Avenue to the area south of it; the driver cursed the PLA for the obstruction. "Tanks around you, helicopters above, the only thing lacking is atomic bombs," he snarled. "If Mao were alive, this wouldn't happen."

At the Temple of Heaven, one feels the closeness of man and nature, one of Chinese culture's attractive traits. Under a cypress tree near the Hall of Prayer for Good Harvests, a young man was curled up on a park bench reading a book. The black cover with red endpapers looked familiar. It was the first Chinese edition of my Mao. I introduced myself and asked the reader to compare Mao and Deng. "Mao was far greater," he replied. "There were so many sides to Mao's talent and his interests. Only in one respect is Deng superior to Mao—economics."

Check in for my flight to Guangzhou (Canton) was in one building and the departure gate in another. Although I had a reserved seat, I was told the flight was full. Only when I marched across the luggage scales to the supervisor's office and shouted in very poor Chinese, "Are you an airline or a circus?" was I given a seat.

At Guangzhou airport for a connection to Hong Kong, I secreted photos and notes from the democracy movement in my shirt, trousers, jacket, and socks. I prayed there would be no body search at security. But the X-ray machine screeched. A stapler in my attaché case was the culprit. I was to be fingered to the last inch. The leaflets, notes and snapshots inside my garments, however, were almost the only items not hauled out.

The struggle inside the Communist Party influenced what happened in the streets. Basically it was about the succession to Deng, just as the turbulence of 1976, in streets and smoked-filled rooms was about the succession to Mao. If Zhao had made a challenge to colleagues blocking his policies, and won Deng's support, the democracy movement would have proved a key constituency for invigorated reform. Why, in the days of press freedom did Zhao not take his case directly to the nation in TV speeches? For the same reason Deng could not do this until Mao died in September 1976.

Tanks and guns may also have been forestalled if the student leadership had decided to beat a tactical retreat after ever-larger demonstrations and citizen-student rapport showed the weight of anti-government feeling. Substantial sections of the student ranks, and their senior advisers favored a retreat, but the emotion of street politics won the day.

If a move out of Tiananmen Square had come alongside a growing strength of Zhao at Deng's side, tactical retreat by the students would have been a heavy defeat for the leftist party elders. But without Zhao still fighting in the Politburo, and with Deng fearful and angry, student withdrawal from Tiananmen around May 19 might have been ambiguous and even worse.

"Tell the world our government has gone mad," the woman had cried near Tiananmen on June 4. But the government had not gone mad. It was preserving its power by the dictates of Leninism. The ideas of Marx and Mao had faded, but Deng needed the straitjacket of Leninism. The shooting was a calculated act of terror to make the point to all Chinese that Communist Party rule was a given and not to be questioned. Deng's CCP could be expected to put the maintenance of its own power ahead of all else at moments of crisis, tomorrow as well as yesterday.

To Chinese music lovers, one of the best-known PRC citizens is Cui Jian, a slight, diffident rock singer born in Beijing to a family of Korean background. His song, "Nothing to my Name" became an anthem for the democracy movement. "The important thing is to express my real feelings," the trail-blazer of Chinese rock music summed up the spirit of 1989 and his support for it.

After Tiananmen, Cui stayed in China and played a cat and mouse game with the authorities; able to give some concerts, but often censored. As Cui walked a fine line between conformity and dissent, Mongolian-origin singer Daiqing Tana of the Haya Band addressed him directly, "You are the backbone and gall of this land. Your music is the hope and despair of this country."

"Politics is physics," Cui Jian said as we sipped a drink in a shadowy Beijing nightspot. "Culture is chemistry—we need more of the chemical side." Cui, influenced by Western music as a boy, claimed music is the coinage of cosmopolitanism. He assailed Chinese fatalism after the collapse of the student movement. "One's mind is like a computer," he said with a half-smile. "When someone inserts software which says you are a dog, then you will live like a dog. I think Chinese youth should try to live with self-respect." Cui had sung a haunting song in the nightclub, "It's Not That I Don't Understand, It's That The World Is Changing Too Fast." As we talked, I saw the song's Delphic meaning: not that the world is changing too fast, but that China is not changing as fast as it should.

"Nationalism will give way to internationalism," Cui Jian said when I asked his vision of the future. "I don't want China to be thought of as a country that can offer Chinese food and nothing else. I'm interested in what Chinese culture can contribute to the world."

Born in 1961 and not remembering past bullying of China by the West and Japan, Cui's patriotism is not an automatic defense of the citadel. He sees a rich future for China based on self-realization of Chinese individuals. He transcends the post-Tiananmen cultural pessimism by an unselfconscious leap to cosmopolitanism. Cui and his audiences love China, but not quite in the old way of Deng. He thinks freedom of the individual is even more important than national loyalty.

Cui Jian thinks the Goddess of Democracy in Tiananmen Square did not threaten China's identity any more than Chinatowns in New York and San Francisco threaten America's identity. A free system, in a word, transcends much of the China-West gulf.

At the height of the anti-Deng demonstrations, a computer science student of rural background, seeking to explain why the April 27 rally did not raise slogans calling for the overthrow of the Communist Party, declared, "You may say that a mother acted wrongfully with good intentions, but you absolutely may not say that your mother is not your mother. Isn't this so?"[9] Next crisis, I doubt the Chinese majority will still accept dictators in the guise of parents.

Of course, trying to understand China is never completely objective. China is not a rock or a beetle, but a slice of humanity, as are Western observers of China. Between the phenomena of China and the analyst of China, events occur on both sides to affect perceptions. This book is my lens on the civilization, nation, and empire that is China. Each reader will have her own lens for assessing such a unique place.

"China obscures," French philosopher Blaise Pascale said a long time ago in his Pensées. Today Communist China obscures just as much. Yet Pascale's full remark suggests fascination as well as exasperation. "But China obscures, you say; and I reply, China does obscure, but there is light to be found. Look for it."[10]

Lin Mu, brilliant student and government employee, who struck a soldier's head with a cooking rod, said truly: "The trouble with many Chinese leaders is they think people must be given a truth. What we really need is to be taught to think, and then by ourselves, in freedom, we will find our way to the truth."

Perhaps Deng's regime was like a huge old man in a village, of whose death everyone is afraid because if he dies, he will topple over and crush the normal-sized folk around him. Deng went so far as to warn the world in 1989 that unless he is permitted to rule China his way with an iron fist, 100 million refugees from China will flood the world. Like the huge old man in the village, Deng was saying, "Be careful, because if I die, you will die too."

It is not reasonable to hope China will become more like ourselves, yet keep China confined within a magic box of the exotic. The student movement of 1989 did something to destroy the image of China as exotic, for the aspirations of the young in Tiananmen Square were recognizable (Thank you, Goddess of Democracy) to people all over the world.

China's exoticism is breaking down before the universals of the human condition, and the knowledge of China joins hands with the knowledge of ourselves; the bridge between us can be freedom and democracy. I do not think individualism and political pluralism will come to China from the West. The demand for them will burst out within China, not as a diktat from a father-figure from on high but as people express themselves politically, grabbed from below. In the bright light of freedom, the Chinese will discover an enduring solidarity with the West.

"When societies first come to birth, it is the leader who produces the institutions," said French philosopher Montesquieu. "Later it is the institutions which produce the leaders."[11] Later still, in a democratic era, a voting public sustains the institutions that, in turn, offer those leaders short-term authority to lead.

NOTES

1. Some passages in the Epilogue have been drawn, after adaptation, from the author's *China in Our Time*.

2. Michael Fathers and Andrew Higgins, *Tiananmen: The Rape of Peking,* London, *The Independent*, 1989, 31.

3. Mao, *Selected Works*, Volume 1, Beijing, Foreign Languages Press, 1965, 121.

4. Shen Tong, *Almost a Revolution,* Boston: Houghton Mifflin, 1990, 222.

5. Liu Binyan, *Tell The World,* New York: Pantheon, 1989, 25.

6. Han Minzhu, ed., *Cries for Democracy,* Princeton, 1990, 195.

7. An analysis of People's Daily's coverage from an insider's perspective, by Frank Tan, appears in *Pacific Affairs*, Summer 1990.

8. Che Muqi, *Beijing Turmoil*, Beijing, Foreign Languages Press, 1990, 29.

9. *Cries for Democracy*, 198.

10. Blaise Pascale, *Pensées de Pascale,* Paris: Dezobry et E. Magdeleine, 1852, Article XXIV, Number 46.

11. Cited in "Mao Now," *Wilson Quarterly*, Fall 2006.

Note on Sources

Publishing details of citations from books, journals and newspapers are given within the Notes. Among China specialists, diplomats, and journalists, many were known to the author (Edgar Snow, Helen Foster Snow, Theodore White, John Stewart Service, John Fairbank, Marshall Green, John Paton Davies, John Carter Vincent, David Bruce, Tillman Durdin). If not otherwise referenced, their words were communicated directly to the author. Interviews with American China diplomats (Marshall Green, Richard Solomon, Service) are from "Frontline Diplomacy: Foreign Affairs Oral History Collection of the Association for Diplomatic Studies and Training," Library of Congress, Washington D.C; abbreviated as ADST-LOC. Likewise, interviews with Australian diplomats (Hugh Dunn, Stephen Fitzgerald) are from Oral History of Australian Diplomacy, 1950–1990 at National Library of Australia, Canberra; abbreviated as OHAD NLA. Citations from the author's diary are not referenced in Notes; they are from an unpublished manuscript headed for publication under the title, *Man on the Balcony*. Letters to or from public figures are referenced in Notes (e.g. Governor Jerry Brown). Letters to and from friends or family members are not given exact dates or Notes. In some cases, I have changed a Chinese person's name, and said that. I first met Kissinger as his student 52 years ago and many times since. Our meetings have been conversations, not interviews. I think the book establishes the authenticity of our relationship. Deceased interviewees/conversationalists include: Pearl Buck, Richard Holbrooke, Henry Cabot Lodge, Dr. Li Zhisui. Gough Whitlam, Zhou Enlai.

FURTHER READING

Some facts, incidents, and opinions in the book are amplified in certain of the author's books, listed here. In addition, this Note includes some favorite works by other authors covering China in the period of the present volume, excluding titles mentioned in Notes.

By Author

The New Chinese Empire, Basic Books, New York (2003), paperback, 2004.
The Australians: The Way We Live Now, Random House, Sydney (2000).
China in Our Time, Simon & Schuster (1992), Touchstone paperback, 1993.
The White-Boned Demon: A Biography of Madame Mao Zedong, William Morrow (1984), Revised, Stanford University Press (1999).
Mao: A Biography, Harper & Row (1980). Revised and expanded, Stanford University Press (2000).
Flowers on an Iron Tree: Five Cities of China, Little Brown (1975).
800,000,000: The Real China, Little Brown (1972), Delta paperback, (1972), Laurel (1973).

Some Favorites

Bao Ruo-Wang [Jean Pasqualini] and Rudolph Chelminski. *Prisoner of Mao*. New York: Penguin, 1976.
Brady, Anne-Marie. *Marketing Dictatorship: Propaganda and Thought Work in China*. Buffalo: Rowman and Littlefield, 2007.
Buchheim, Hans. *Totalitarian Rule: Its Nature and Characteristics*. Middletown, CT: Wesleyan University Press, 1968.
Chen Dunde. *Mao Zedong yu Nikesong zai 1972*. Beijing: Kunlun chubanshe, 1988.
Chou, Eric. *A Man Must Choose*. New York: Knopf, 1963.
Davies, John Paton Jr. *Dragon by the Tail*. New York: Norton, 1972.
Fu Zhengyuan. *Autocratic Tradition and Politics*. Cambridge: Cambridge University Press, 1993.
De Jaegher, Raymond J. (and Irene Corbally Kuhn). *The Enemy Within*. Garden City, New York: Doubleday, 1952.
Guo, Sujian. *Post-Mao China: From Totalitarianism to Authoritarianism?* Westport, CT: Praeger, 2000.
Huang Hua, *Qin li yu jian wen: Huang Hua hui yi lu*. Beijing: Shi jie zhi shi chubanshe, 2007.
Khrushchev, Nikita. *Khrushchev Remembers*. New York: Bantam, 1976.
Masi, Edoarda. *China Winter*. New York: Dutton, 1982.
Patten, Chris. *East and West*. New York: Times Books, 1999.
Rittenberg. Sidney. *The Man who Stayed Behind*. New York: Simon & Schuster, 1993.
Shi Zhe. *Zai lishi juren shenbian*. Beijing: Zhongyang wenxian chubanshe, 1991.
Snow, Edgar. *Journey to the Beginning*. New York: Random House, 1958.

Index

About the Author

Ross Terrill, an Associate in Research at Harvard's Fairbank Center for East Asia, is the author of eleven books. He did history at the University of Melbourne and joined the Australian Army. He took a Ph.D. in political science at Harvard in 1970, where his thesis on the philosophy of R. H. Tawney was published by Harvard as *Socialism as Fellowship*. While associate professor at Harvard he taught political thought, Chinese politics, and international affairs, and wrote *800,000,000: The Real China*; *The Future of China after Mao*; *Flowers on an Iron Tree: Five Cities of China*, and the original edition of *Mao*. His other books include *White Boned Demon: A Biography of Madame Mao*; *The Australians*; *China in Our Time*, and *The New Chinese Empire*. Terrill was visiting professor at Shandong University in Jinan, University of Texas at Austin, and Monash University in Melbourne.